BLACK HISTORY:
"OLD SCHOOL" BLACK HISTORIANS AND THE HIP HOP GENERATION

Pero Gaglo Dagbovie

[handwritten inscription:] 10/12/2006 For Professor Williams; Thanks for your continued support... I appreciate your passion... — Pero

ISBN: 0-911557-27-X
Library of Congress Catalog Number: 2005922113

BEDFORD PUBLISHERS, INC.
4198 Carson Drive
TROY, MICHIGAN 48098-4402 USA

BLACK HISTORY: "OLD SCHOOL" BLACK HISTORIANS
AND THE HIP HOP GENERATION
by Pero Gaglo Dagbovie

Contributions to African American History, African American
Historiography, African American Intellectual Biographies,
American Historiography, Philosophy of History, African
American Studies
ISBN: 0-911557-27-X
Library of Congress Catalog Card Number: 2005922113
First Edition 2006

Bibliography: p.

        1. African American historians. 2. African Americans ----
----Historians. 3. Historians --- United States---Biography. 4.
Woodson, Carter G., 1875-1950. 5. Hip-Hop---History and
Criticism. 6. African American Intellectuals--History. 7. African
American History.

1.   Title

E 185.625 2006

First Edition 2006
Bedford Publishers, Inc.
4198 Carson Drive
Troy, Michigan 48098-4402, USA

Printed in the United States of America

10 9 8 7 6 5 4 3 2

For the upcoming group of hip-hop generation historians of the African American experience.
In memory of Adjinyo and the many deceased African American historians whose scholarship, philosophies, and sacrifices paved the way for me to be able to write this book.
And dedicated to three scholars who sparked within me a passion for Black history and taught me so much:
Professors Sharon Minor-King, Harry A. Reed, and Darlene Clark Hine.

Follow in the footsteps of your ancestors, for the mind is trained through knowledge. Behold, their words endure in books. Open and read them and follow their counsel. For one who is taught becomes skilled.

The Book of Kheti

Yes, the day your are fortunate is also the day you are the most unfortunate, for in good fortune you cannot imagine what suffering is.

Sundiata: An Epic of Old Mali

If a race has no history, it has not worth-while tradition, it becomes a negligible factor in the thought of the world, and it stands in the danger of being exterminated.

Carter G. Woodson
"Negro History Week"

History is the land-mark by which we are directed into the true course of life. The history of a movement, the history of a nation, the history of a race is the guide-post of that movement's destiny, that nation's destiny, that race's destiny. What you do to-day that is worthwhile inspires others to act at some future time.

Marcus Garvey
The Philosophy and Opinions of
Marcus Garvey

The Negro's growth will be great in the years to come. Yesterday, our ancestors endured the degradation of slavery, yet they retained their dignity...Tomorrow, a new Negro, unhindered by race taboos and shackles, will benefit from more than 330 years of ceaseless striving and struggle.

Mary McLeod Bethune
"My Last Will and Testament"

Of all our studies, history is best qualified to reward our research. And when you see that you've got problems, all you have to do is examine the historic method used all over the world by others who have problems similar to your. Once you see how they got theirs straight, then you know how you can get yours straight.

Malcolm X
"Message to the Grassroots"

Every generation has the opportunity to write its own history, and indeed it is obliged to do so. Only in that way can it provide its contemporaries with the materials vital to understanding the present and to planning strategies for coping with the future. Only in that way can it fulfill its obligation to pass on to posterity the accumulated knowledge and wisdom of the past, which after all, give substance and direction for the continuity of civilization.

John Hope Franklin
"On the Evolution of Scholarship
on Afro American History"

CONTENTS

PREFACE

The two different symbols on the cover of this book, *sankofa* (pronounced sang-ko-fah) and *nkyinkyin* (pronounced n-chin-chin), capture the essence of what this study seeks to do. These symbols belong to a larger group of the Akan people's adinkra symbols. According to W. Bruce Willis, author of *The Adinkra Dictionary: A Visual Primer on the Language of Adinkra* (Washington, D.C.: The Pyramid Complex, 1998), there are many theories concerning the origins and evolution of adinkra symbols. It seems to be widely accepted that they are at least several hundred years old and used to play vital roles in Akan people's funeral ceremonies. These symbols originally functioned as cultural signifiers in adinkra cloths often worn by the Akan peoples during funerals. The cloth was decorated with different adinkra symbols and "in a specific manner to convey a parting message to the deceased," Willis has noted. Though not as prevalent today as during pre-colonial times, adinkra symbols still function in their traditional capacity. They have been transformed, often reinterpreted, reconfigured, and incorporated into facets of Ghanaian, West African, and even African American popular culture. Throughout Ghana, Togo, Ivory Coast, and elsewhere in West Africa, adinkra symbols have been fused into textiles, clothing, buildings, drums, furniture, jewelry, and many other items. Many African Americans have shown appreciation for these symbols in similar ways. In major U.S. cities and over the internet, it is not difficult to purchase t-shirts, books, jewelry, and clothing incorporating adinkra symbolism. Many young black cultural nationalists and Afrocentric thinkers have also tattooed themselves with adinkra symbols.

Like the more than fifty adinkra symbols, *sankofa* and *nkyinkyin* have multiple meanings and have been and continue to be artistically rendered in many different ways. According to Willis's findings, *sankofa*, the heart-shaped symbol on the cover, means "go back to fetch it," "go back to the past in order to build for the future," and "we should not forget our past when moving ahead." In a popular version of this symbol, a bird with its head facing backward, often searching through its feathers, is used. The other symbol, *nkyinkyin*, in Willis's words, "refers to a person's ability to adapt and change in various circumstances" and "speaks to the resilience and adaptability of a person's character." This study embodies the philosophical meanings of the Akan's *sankofa* and *nkyinkyin* symbols.

These symbols should be embraced by members of the hip-hop generation. Black history and the strategies and philosophies of our ancestors should be a part of our daily lives, helping guide our actions, decisions, and thought in the present and future. In order to understand and contribute to the evolution of African American history and historiography, help facilitate natural transformations in the black historical profession, and address some of the dilemmas facing African Americans today, hip-hop generation historians, as well as those genuinely interested in Black history and the liberation of African Americans, must embrace *sankofa* and return to and reevaluate the African American experience as well as the scholarship and contributions of Black history's pioneers. Armed with this necessary historical knowledge and an intimate familiarity with the collective black experience, we can then move on into the future, embracing *nkyinkyin* and changing with the times as active rather than passive beings. At the same time, we need to be able to change and alter our predecessors' worldviews to suit the present conditions. Young blacks in academia and other mainstream institutions also need to play many roles, often simultaneously, without losing one's cultural identity, integrity, and commitment to the enduring black struggle.

This study revisits and reconsiders the concept of Black history, the ideologies and contributions of many "Old School" black historians, and the status of the hip-hop generation. I examine 1) how a wide array of black historians, as well as a few white historians, have responded to the inquiry "What is Black history?" since the dawning of the twentieth century; 2) Black history's relevance to the hip-hop generation; 3) the origins, development, and shortcomings of Black History Month, Kwanzaa, and Martin Luther King, Jr. Day; 4) the writings, philosophies, and activities of a wide range of "Old School" black historians from the antebellum era through the early twentieth century; and 5) the life, work, and contributions of Carter G. Woodson, "The Father of Black History." The essays in this book discuss the multidimensional value, versatility, importance, and overall use and misuse of Black history for more than one hundred years. If packaged correctly, Black history can continue to serve as a vital compass directing young blacks into the future. Hip-hop-generation historians cannot simply imitate the approaches, worldviews, and strategies of "Old School" black historians, but we can learn a great deal from their efforts, ideas, scholarship, and practical programs. A significant part of their platforms and philosophies can be fused into the new, refreshing initiatives that we must develop and employ.

This study meets what I consider a void in the current scholarship. Black history and Black Studies are far beyond their formative years. Both interrelated disciplines can be further cultivated, but they are advanced and are no longer largely ignored by the "white-stream" American academy. Easy-to-digest Black history textbooks, references books, juvenile literature, and informative Black history websites are common. Many mainstream and black grassroots presses are committed to publishing books in African American history. We now have more access than ever before to countless different types of illuminating sources for Black history, life, and culture. Whereas in the first half of the twentieth century students of black culture often faced great challenges in locating enough materials, at one level we currently face just the opposite dilemma, information overload. The present generation of historians-in-training must be extra critical in selecting sources. Type in any topic in African American history on any major internet search engine and one is likely to get hundreds to thousands of sources, many of which are nonscholarly and nonsense.

There are more than a few significant studies on black historians available and in print. Benjamin P. Bowser and Louis Kushnick have recently edited a volume, *Against the Odds: Scholars Who Challenged Racism in the Twentieth Century* (2003), which includes personal testimonies by half a dozen black scholars who were or acted as historians. At least one major scholarly biography on Carter G. Woodson, Jacqueline Goggin's *Carter G. Woodson: A Life in Black History* (1993), is still widely available in paperback and is suitable for university classroom use. In the 1990s, several books on "Old School" black historians were published, such as Robert Kenneth Janken's *Rayford W. Logan and the Dilemma of the African American Intellectual* (1993) and Arvarh Strickland's *Selling Black History for Carter G. Woodson: A Diary, 1930–1933, by Lorenzo Johnston Greene* (1996), a volume that supplemented his *Working with Carter G. Woodson, the Father of Black History: A Diary, 1928–1930, Lorenzo Johnston Greene* (1989). John Hope Franklin reached perhaps the peak of his notoriety in U.S. culture after former President Bill Clinton named him the head of his seven-member national advisory board on race in July 1997. More than a few mainstream newspapers and magazines have covered Franklin's career since the mid-1980s. And, in 2003, Beverly Jarrett edited a brief yet revealing collection of essays on Franklin entitled *Tributes to John Hope Franklin: Scholar, Mentor, Father, Friend*.

Despite such developments, scholarship on black historians and the philosophy of Black history is currently in need of rejuvenation. At one level, the large period between the 1930s and the 1980s produced some of the most wide-reaching essays and books on the black historical profession. These studies were written by the following historians, in chronological order: Vernon Loggins, Charles H. Wesley, L.D. Reddick, Wilhelmina E. Hamlin, Tomasina Talley, Helen Boardman, Carter G. Woodson, John Hope Franklin, Edward M. Coleman, Jessie P. Guzman, Earl E. Thorpe, Michael R. Winston, Janette H. Harris, Sister Anthony Scally, Linda O. McMurry, August Meier and

Elliott Rudwick, Darlene Clark Hine, Elinor Des Verney Sinette, and Arvarh E. Strickland. Among the most important of these works are Thorpe's *Negro Historians in the United States* (1958), later published as *Black Historians: A Critique* (1971), John Hope Franklin's *George Washington Williams: A Biography* (1985), Meier and Rudwick's *Black History and the Historical Profession, 1915–1980* (1986), and Hine's *The State of Afro-American History* (1986).

Currently there does not seem to be a general easy-to-read, yet challenging, study available and widely circulated that examines the philosophical underpinnings of Black history, Black History Month, the scholarship and contributions of "Old School" black historians, and the meanings of Black history to the hip-hop generation. Since the 1990s, more than fifty significant books on hip-hop have been published; however, none of these studies has extensively discussed the function and meaning of history to the hip-hop generation. Cultural critics and African American Studies scholars have taken the lead in analyzing and researching aspects of hip-hop. Historians have not been as actively engaged in this relevant and dynamic discourse.

Furthermore, black historians of my generation (those born during the late 1960s and the early 1970s) need to inject ourselves into the practical and theoretical discussions concerning the deeper meanings of Black history and the black historical profession. Based upon our unique experiences, we need to lay out original and creative interpretations of long-debated issues. In this manner, we leave our footprints in history, take the debates to another level, and inspire future generations of historians. This study provides straightforward entries into a range of important themes concerning Black history, African American historiography, and black historians. It is suitable for hip-hop generation historians, undergraduate university students, and first-year graduate students, as well as anyone interested in Black history, its past, present, and future. It also seeks to speak to the elder, seasoned generations of African American historians who have already helped shaped the evolution of the study of Black history. Intergenerational dialogues between black historians are important and should be encouraged.

I have admittedly drawn great inspiration from the "Old School" black historians featured in this book. I am open about my admiration of Woodson, his predecessors, co-workers, and disciples. *Black History, "Old School" Black Historians, and the Hip-Hop Generation* does not, however, simply revel in the past so-called glory days of Carter G. Woodson and other pioneering black historians. It critically explores multiple approaches to Black history as well as the lives, thoughts, and strategies of "Old School" black historians from a variety of historical contexts. I do not claim to have spoken the last or authoritative word on the issues explored in this book, but I do hope that I have raised some important, thought-provoking ideas. I humbly offer this book because I am deeply concerned with the future of black America, especially the younger generation, Black history, and the black historical profession. I actively mentor students interested in Black history and hope that they will be able to take the study and promotion of Black history to the next level. This book is part of this effort. Any faults that still remain in the text are my responsibility.

NOTE ON TERM USAGE

Throughout the text, I use several different terms to describe African descendants born and raised in the United States. The terms of reference by which African Americans have identified themselves have changed significantly over time. I use *black*, *black American*, and *African American* interchangeably. When referring to Black history as a scholarly discipline, I capitalize the letter *b* in black. The term *Negro*, which is no longer an acceptable term, also appears throughout this study. The term was commonly used by whites as well as blacks from the antebellum era through the Civil Rights Movement. When I use the term, it is either part of a book title, article, or movement (i.e., Carter G. Woodson's *The Negro in Our History*, L.D. Reddick's article "A New Interpretation for Negro History," and the annual celebration formerly known as Negro History Week). The term *Negro* also appears in direct citations from people writing when the term was widely used and acceptable to blacks. The terms *hip-hop generation* and *"Old School" black historians* are central to this study and are defined in detail in the introduction. This book does not contain a standard bibliography. The notes, many of which are detailed and explanatory in nature, contain all of the sources used in this study and should be consulted if the reader is interested in any of the subjects raised herein.

P.G.D.

INTRODUCTION

When the dead leaves fall,
they go back to the roots.
                    —Togolese proverb

Just as a tree without roots is dead,
a people without history or cultural roots
becomes a dead people.
                    —Malcolm X

This book is designed to provide a brief, straightforward discussion of many important facets of Black history as a philosophy and concept, an academic field of study, a popular cultural symbol, and as an actual and potential vehicle for social reform, black self-empowerment, and collective liberation. A handful of questions helps us frame the variety of issues with which I am primarily concerned. What is Black history? What are the origins of Black history as a field of study? How did "Old School," pioneering black historians use Black history as what historian Earl E. Thorpe called a "weapon" in the enduring struggle for black equal rights, freedom, consciousness, and self-definition? What were the vital contributions of Carter G. Woodson and other "Old School" black writers of history to the early Black history movement, the current advanced state of African American historiography, and to today's popular expressions of Black history such as Black History Month? How has the study of Black history and the black historical enterprise evolved from the era of slavery until the present? What does history mean to the hip-hop generation and how can hip-hop generation historians and others employ Black history in practical ways? What are the challenges

1

that hip-hop generation historians presently face and will en-
counter in the near future, and how can they learn from our "Old
School" foreparents?

Chapter 1 is concerned with defining Black history as a
field of study, a philosophy, and as a specific part of America's
complex past. Many students of history take for granted that the
history of anything as we know it is the direct product of historians who are themselves the products of specific historical envi-
ronments that molded their worldviews. Further elaborating on
this aspect of history, I draw primarily from the scholarship of
Carl Becker and Edward Hallett Carr. Though they did not support the Black history movement, nor were they concerned with
Black history, their broader philosophical ideas regarding history
are useful points of departure. While Black history is currently a
well-established field of scholarly inquiry, not many historians
have philosophized extensively about Black history. Over the
last century, however, there have been important ideas offered
that are worthy of reconsideration. Building upon the ideas of
black historians—and a few white historians—who have set
forth definitions of Black history from the publication of Du
Bois's *The Souls of Black Folk* (1903) until the present, I provide
a brief, introductory discussion of the multiple meanings of
Black history. Unsurprisingly, it becomes clear that there are
many ways to define and interpret Black history. This chapter
provides a comprehensive definition of Black history by examin-
ing a century of black historical discourse. It also provides a
periodization and thematic breakdown of the African American
historical experience in a way that historicizes blacks' present
status.

Chapter 2 concerns the relationship between the hip-hop
generation and Black history. It is guided by Earl E. Thorpe's
and John Hope Franklin's sentiments that each generation of
black historians must leave its distinct marks on the profession,
the production of scholarship, and the debates surrounding Black
history's function. My discussion is guided by the premise that
hip-hop culture is the single most widespread preoccupation of

today's black American and African diasporan youth, and has the potential to play an important role in rejuvenating the modern Black history movement and raising the hip-hop generation's cultural and historical consciousness. I argue that black historians, especially those of the hip-hop generation, could help advance approaches to teaching and popularizing Black history by using elements of hip-hop culture while helping the hip-hop generation better understand its peculiar position within the broader scope of Black history.

Chapter 3 critically examines the history of what we now recognize as Black History Month, the annual celebration which, in Dick Gregory's words, occurs during "the month of February with all them days missing." I argue that the contemporary Black History Month celebrations, proclamations, and celebrations are indebted to the Negro History Weeks of Carter G. Woodson's time (1926 until 1950) and have drifted far from the Woodsonian mission of Negro History Week as a practical, hands-on ritual. Black History Month, very much like Kwanzaa and Martin Luther King, Jr. Day, has become watered-down, commercialized, and in many respects nonpragmatic. I compare the commodification processes of Kwanzaa and Martin Luther King, Jr. Day with the commercialization of Black History Month. The similarities are striking. For nearly three decades, countless large U.S. corporations have used these black cultural celebrations to market their products to African American communities, especially to members of the black middle-class. This discussion should resound well with the hip-hop generation, given the hypercommercialization of hip-hop music and culture over the last several years. The commodification and "white-streaming" of hip-hop culture has produced results similar to those of the commercialization of Black History Month, Kwanzaa, and Martin Luther King, Jr. Day. My detailed overview of the Negro History Weeks during Woodson's times reveals how his celebration has been transformed for the worse over the last several decades and demonstrates the value of re-embracing the Woodsonian approach and philosophy. Black History Month is still important and useful, but needs to be reconfigured.

Chapter 4 explores the history of black historians, as well as the variety of meanings of history to black Americans, before Carter G. Woodson came on the scene and revolutionized the study and promotion of Black history in the early twentieth century. Many historians have acknowledged Woodson's pivotal role in the evolution of Black history as a discipline. Fewer have explored the contributions of the diverse range of historians active before Woodson. Particular attention is paid to the role of history in traditional, pre-colonial, Sub-Saharan African societies, antebellum era historians, George Washington Williams, W.E.B. Du Bois, and a dynamic group of self-taught and self-proclaimed black women historians. These historians paved the way for Woodson who admitted that he drew great inspiration from many among their ranks.

Chapter 5 explores the life, work, contributions, and legacy of Carter G. Woodson, "The Father of Black History." I discuss his early years, his scholarship, how he popularized Black history, his attitudes towards African American intellectuals, the role of black women in his movement, and his legacy. Woodson, like all human beings, was inevitably flawed. He was also arguably not the best black historian to ever live, if such a thing can be determined. Since his death in 1950, generations of historians have revised and expanded upon much of his historical scholarship. Though not nearly as concerned with popularizing Black history as Woodson, and not as close to him as Charles H. Wesley, Rayford W. Logan, and Lorenzo Johnston Greene, John Hope Franklin, dubbed by many as "the historian of the century," in many respects replaced Woodson as the leading authority on Black history from 1950 through the 1980s and 1990s and even the dawning of the new millennium.

Still, it cannot be forgotten that much of Woodson's scholarship was truly pathbreaking, that he literally sacrificed his life for the promotion of Black history in a manner unmatched by anyone before or since, and that his life was nothing short of remarkable. His life mirrored the African American experience as a whole and the lives of today's young blacks' icons. Like many of the hip-hop generation's heroes and symbols—Tupac, Notorious B.I.G., Allen Iverson, Mike Tyson, Mary J. Blige, Venus and Serena Williams, P. Diddy, "King James," Jay-Z, and countless other entertainers and athletes—Woodson overcame seemingly insurmountable obstacles in order to attain his once celebrity-like status within the black community. Many of his ideas, especially his preoccupation with converting Black history into a tool of racial uplift and advancement, were modern and are still relevant to the black struggle for identity and survival. If repackaged correctly, many of Woodson's strategies would blend smoothly in with hip-hop culture. Revisiting his life and work is therefore timely.

In the Conclusion, I expand further upon the importance of the study and promotion of Black history to the hip-hop generation and how it can be taught and presented to best meet its needs. As we enter a new millennium, African Americans continue to face a multitude of life-threatening problems. Of course, the study of Black history could not on its own fully liberate black America, especially the youth. Nothing short of a true revolution could accomplish this. Nonetheless, if correctly reconceptualized, Black history could function in a practical way. The hip-hop generation, feasting on an at-times unhealthy diet of popular hip-hop magazines, internet sources, materialism, narcissism, and watered-down and "commercial" rap, is arguably one of the most anti-historical and historically alienated generations of black youth in history. As Malcolm X proclaimed in a speech in Harlem in the early 1960s, "You have to have a knowledge of history no matter what you are going to do; anything that you undertake you have to have a knowledge of history in order to be successful in it."[1]

Revisiting and Conceptualizing
"Old School" Black Historians

In February 1966, on the eve of the Black Power era's beginnings, John Hope Franklin wrote a brief yet important article
in *Negro Digest* in which he chronicled the contributions of
black historians from James W.C. Pennington's 1841 *A Text
Book of the Origins and History of Colored People* until the
early works of W.E.B. Du Bois and Carter G. Woodson. In an
uncharacteristically emotional manner, Franklin concluded his
essay, "Pioneer Negro Historians," by declaring:

> One of the most cruel things that one could do today
> would be to forget or ignore pioneers such as these
> early Negro historians. One of the most praiseworthy
> things one could do would be to recognize the enor-
> mous importance of their keeping the light of truth
> flickering until it could be kindled by greater resources
> and many more hands.[2]

Nearly four decades after Franklin made his plea, I share his sentiments in believing that there is a great deal of value in critically
revisiting the lives, works, and contributions of pioneering African American historians.

This study focuses on the ideologies and contributions of
what I have termed "Old School" black historians: those black
historians, professionally trained and self-taught, who published
historical writings and promoted and popularized the study of
Black history during the vast period of time from the antebellum
period until Woodson's death in 1950. I highlight Woodson's
contributions as well as those of many of his well-known and
lesser acknowledged predecessors, those many black historians,
professionally trained and self-taught, active before Woodson
founded the Association for the Study of Negro Life and History
in 1915.

A handful of historians have already chronicled and analyzed the lives and scholarship of black historians and have cate-

gorized black historians based upon the time periods in which they were active, their level of training, their scholarly foci, the quality of their scholarship, and their overall influence. In the late 1930s, L.D. Reddick subdivided black historians into two major periods: *"before* Woodson and *after* Woodson." In *Black Historians: A Critique* (1971), originally published as *Negro Historians in the United States* in 1958, Earl E. Thorpe examined black historians in the following major groups and time periods: "The Beginning School" (1800–1896), "The Middle Group" (1896–1930), "The Modern Laymen" (1896–late 1960s), and "The New School" (about 1930 to 1960). In a 1986 essay entitled "On the Evolution of Scholarship in Afro-American History," John Hope Franklin, dealing with both black and white historians, located four generations of scholarship in Black history: 1882–1909, 1915–1935, 1935 until the late 1960s, and 1970 until the mid-1980s. In their exhaustive study *Black History and the Historical Profession, 1915–1980* (1986), August Meier and Elliot Rudwick, also dealing with black and white historians, divided the history of African American historiography into five major periods: 1915 into the 1930s, the New Deal through World War II, post-World War II until the early 1960s, "the brief half-dozen years marked by the apogee of the direct-action phase of the black protest movement," and 1967–1980. Most recently, W.D. Wright in *Black History and Black Identity: A Call for a New Historiography* (2002) has posited that black historians can be best subdivided into four major groups: early, "precursor" black historians (before Du Bois); "First-Wave" black historians (professional historians from Du Bois to Woodson's disciples who earned Ph.D.s from the 1920s through the 1940s); "Second-Wave" black historians (active mainly since the 1960s); and "Third-Wave" black historians who embraced "historical sociology."[3]

These studies are insightful; however, they are not widely accessible and understandably were not written with the hip-hop generation in mind. This study speaks primarily to various subgroups of the hip-hop generation and also represents a hip-hop-generation historian's interpretation of various themes, old and new, in Black history. This study addresses a host of issues, personalities, and thoughts from various time periods.

I deal with "Old School" black historians differently than the previously mentioned scholars. The "Old School" black historians of this study can be subdivided into many different groups and generations. They were active during the following general time periods: 1836 until the outbreak of the Civil War, 1863–1876, 1882 until the early 1890s, 1895–1915, and the long period from 1915 until 1950. These specific periods were not mutually exclusive: overlapping occurred. A few of these historians were active in more than one period, most notably William Wells Brown and W.E.B. Du Bois. The earlier scholars also influenced the later ones in varying degrees. "Old School" black historians can also can be broken down into about four main subgroups: 1) antebellum-era writers of black history, 2) professionally trained historians, 3) self-taught and self-proclaimed historians, and 4) black women historians. Each subgroup of "Old School" black historians was impacted by different sets of historical conditions, responded accordingly, and created historical narratives that reflected their specific historical circumstances.

Towards a Woodsonian Paradigm: Recognizing Black History's Potential

While this study examines the lives and contributions of many black historians, it is openly Woodson-centric. I compare and contrast the ideas and strategies of black historians from different generations, but I focus on Woodson' life, work, and contributions and often examine other historians in relation to Woodson. I am a hip-hop-generation Woodsonian historian. I wholeheartedly believe that Black history can be used to help inspire young African Americans to overcome obstacles, promote a greater understanding between blacks and whites, help white Americans better understand African Americans' present status, and perhaps help us introduce and justify public policies and legislation that more concretely address the massive, lingering disparity between blacks and whites. We could still learn a lot from how Woodson envisioned Black history in the struggle for universal black liberation. Of course his strategies would need to be adjusted to suit the present times. Several historians have chronicled Woodson's life and work, yet "The Father of Black History" still remains an obscure figure in African American popular culture and a largely unknown icon to members of the hip-hop generation. His message and mission of popularizing, resurrecting, and ritualizing Black history could be especially useful for the hip-hop generation that actively samples from past musicians, fashions, and cultural icons while, unfortunately, often largely ignoring the deeper meanings of African American history.

This book constitutes a sound prerequisite for African American history and Black Studies majors, Black history enthusiasts, or those simply interested in the study, popularization, and future development of Black history. Given the overall hyperadvanced state of technology, the widespread appeal of hip-hop music and culture, and the hip-hop generation's willingness to selectively sample from the past, now perhaps more than ever Black history could return to its function as an empowering, regenerative, educational force. Black history could not in and of itself solve the major escalating economic, social, and political problems facing African American communities across the nation. It could, however, very easily help inspire young blacks to achieve great feats as their ancestors did, alter and adjust their worldviews in positive ways, better understand where they fit within the broader scope of the more than 200-year African American struggle for equality, and recognize the collective debt they owe to the countless generations of their elders, deceased and still living, who paved the way for us to be here today. The best way we can give thanks to our ancestors and mentors is by helping make the future better for the upcoming generations. At the same time, Black history can also be used in the battle

against racial prejudice and cultural ignorance. Though it would
be naïve to believe that Black history could abolish racism,
knowledge of it could help attack and decrease anti-black stereotypes and, more important, could help whites better comprehend
the concrete historical antecedents of African Americans' current
problems.[4] As it has in varying degrees for more than one hundred years, Black history in the 21st century has the potential to
humanize American culture and significantly expand our interpretations of U.S. history.

Notes

Introduction

[1] Benjamin Goodman, ed., *The End of White World Supremacy: Four Speeches By Malcolm X* (New York: Merlin House, 1971), 26.

[2] John Hope Franklin, "Pioneer Negro Historians," *Negro Digest* 15 (February 1966): 8–9.

[3] L.D. Reddick, "A New Interpretation for Negro History," *The Journal of Negro History* 22 (January 1937): 17, 19, 21, 27; Earl E. Thorpe, *Black Historians: A Critique* (New York: William Morrow, 1971), v–vi; John Hope Franklin, "On the Evolution of Scholarship on Afro-American History," in *The State of Afro-American History: Past, Present, and Future*, ed. Darlene Clark Hine (Baton Rouge: Louisiana State University Press, 1986), 13; August Meier and Elliott Rudwick, *Black History and the Historical Profession, 1915–1980* (Urbana: University of Illinois Press, 1986), 73; W.D. Wright, *Black History and Black Identity: A Call for a New Historiography* (Westport: Praeger, 2002).

[4] As Philip Rubio recently argued in *A History of Affirmative Action 1619–2000* (2001) and as several authors elaborate on in *Should America Pay?: Slavery and the Raging Debate on Reparations* (2003), most white Americans are opposed to, ignorant about, and/or disinterested in affirmative action and reparations because, for one, they do not recognize how the clear history of racial inequality and black oppression in the United States has directly impacted the present repressive conditions endured by many blacks today. Both of these studies are crucial in helping us understand the history behind affirmative action and reparations, respectively. They also help explain why there is such a widespread backlash among white Americans against affirmative action and reparations. Part of Rubio's study assesses why "the mere mention of...modest compensatory civil rights enforcement programs known as affirmative action drive[s] so many white people crazy." In *Should America Pay?*, several whites, namely Tim Wise and Molly Secours, help explain why many whites are so reluctant to discuss reparations. See Philip F. Rubio, *A History of Affirmative Action, 1619–2000* (Jackson: University Press of Mississippi, 2001); Raymond A. Winbush, ed., *Should America Pay?: Slavery and the Raging Debate on Reparations* (New York: HarperCollins, 2003).

CHAPTER 1

What Is Black History?

What is Black history? For non-historians, the answers to this question may seem simple, straightforward, or unimportant. There are indeed many ways to address this loaded question, as evidenced by roughly one hundred years of historical scholarship. I attempt to respond to the inquiry "What is Black history?" in four main ways: 1) by identifying and elaborating on some key elements and features of history in general terms; 2) by chronologically exploring how a variety of twentieth century black historians, as well as a few white historians, have conceptualized the purpose, meaning, and function of Black history as a philosophy, concept, and scholarly field of study; 3) by synthesizing these scholars' ideas, making them relevant to the hip-hop generation; and 4) by breaking down the African American experience into major periods and subthemes.

Reconsidering Carl Becker's and Edward Hallett Carr's Conceptualizations of History

In defining Black history, it is logical to start by defining history in general terms. Historians from all over the world have struggled with this demanding intellectual task for hundreds of years, publishing a variety of books and articles on this topic. Debates surrounding the general question "What is history?" are ongoing and will continue to be. *The New Oxford American Dictionary* (2001) defines history as being "the study of past events, particularly in human affairs;" "a continuous, typically chrono-

13

logical, record of important or public events or of a particular trend or institution." Similarly, *Webster's Universal College Dictionary* (2001) describes history as constituting "the branch of knowledge dealing with past events;" "a continuous, systematic narrative of past events as relating to a particular people, country, period, person, etc., usually written as a chronological account;" "acts, ideas, or events that will or can shape the future;" "the aggregate of past events." Such definitions may satisfy some, but they do not capture the deeper issues surrounding the inquiry "What is history?" Though they did not consider African Americans as subject matter in their scholarship or directly speculate how their theories could have related to Black history, historians Carl Becker (1873–1945) and Edward Hallett Carr (1892–1982) have offered some elementary yet deep insight into the multilayered meanings of history that can help our general understanding of any type of history. I use some of their ideas as fruitful starting points for defining Black history beyond the surface level because they have thought hard about the role, function, and significance of history.

In his 1932 essay "Everyman His Own Historian," Carl Becker defined history in the ideal, "ultimate sense" as being "a series of events" that "actually" occurred "throughout all past time." He admitted that our knowledge of the *actual* history of anything was uncertain. In other words, we can never know for certain what really went down in history. Becker's theory of history exposes the challenges and limitations that historians inevitably face as they attempt to write history. He commented:

> Much of the great part [of historical events] we can know nothing about, not even that they occurred; many of them we can know only imperfectly; and even the few events that we think we know for sure we can never be absolutely certain of, since we can never revive them, never observe them directly.

Becker stressed that most historians base their interpretations of the past on written documents, what he deemed merely "traces of vanished events." Becker surmised:

> Let us then admit that there are two histories: the actual series of events that once occurred; and the ideal series that we affirm and hold in memory. The first is absolute and unchanged—it was what it was whatever we say about it; the second is relative, always changing in response to the increase or refinement of knowledge...the actual series of events exists only for us in terms of the ideal series which we affirm and hold in memory...history is...what we know it to be.[1]

Becker's ideas can be helpful to our definitions of Black history. In fact, he could have used Black history as an ideal example to further argue some of his points. It is often extremely difficult to discern the *actual* realities of Black history. Despite the fact that African Americans had been chronicling their history since the antebellum era (more rigorously and "scientifically" after Du Bois and Woodson came onto the scene), the history of African Americans, as well as other African peoples, was systematically misconstrued, ignored, or downplayed for centuries by U.S. academic and popular culture. It was not until the 1960s, the 1970s, and in some cases the 1980s that Black history began to become acknowledged as an important field of scholarly inquiry in the mainstream U.S. academy. In order to justify the oppression of African Americans, for centuries it was maintained by many of those in positions of power that African Americans had no actual history, at least not one worthy of serious academic consideration. Though some historically black colleges and universities began offering courses in Black history during the era of the Harlem Renaissance and the 1940s, the first academic courses in African American history were not offered in major predominantly white colleges and universities until the late 1960s and 1970s as a result of the Black Studies movement.[2]

At another level, when dealing with the masses of blacks, whether it be during the days of slavery, Reconstruction, the "nadir", the Great Depression, or any other major historical period through the modern Civil Rights Movement, it is often quite challenging, though possible, to discover what really went down among the black masses themselves, from their perspectives. Sources in Black history are by no means lacking. Various nontraditional sources can be used such as oral tradition, folktales, spirituals, music, cultural artifacts, and material from popular culture. Black history is a quintessential rendition of the "history from below" genre. Nonetheless, it is still challenging to decipher the actual historical experiences of many African Americans. Since the 1960s and 1970s, slave culture and community historians have been especially creative and resourceful in reconstructing the realities of slave life. While their interpretations revised the scholarship of U.B. Phillips, Kenneth Stampp, Stanley Elkins, and Fogel and Engerman, they often created an "ideal series" of historical behavior that was influenced by more historical knowledge, the Civil Rights and Black Power movements, as well as new generational worldviews. Slave culture and community historians such as Sterling Stuckey, John W. Blassingame, George Rawick, Peter Woods, Leslie Owens, Lawrence Levine, Herbert Gutman, Eugene Genovese, Albert Raboteau, Thomas Webber, and others sought to empower enslaved blacks with agency. They depicted slaves with the power to resist, maintain a vibrant culture, and determine their own destinies.[3]

What was it really like to be a slave? There is no single way to answer this question. As Peter J. Parish highlighted in *Slavery: History and Historians* (1989), there is no one way to approach U.S. slavery because it was "a growing, changing, mobile, flexible, and variable institution…Slavery was a system of many systems, with numerous exceptions to every rule."[4] No matter how many WPA narratives, slaveholders' diaries, court records, and slave narratives that we read, or former plantations that we visit, it is still very difficult for us, in the 21st century, to truly comprehend the realities of slavery. Though many of today's slavery historians have produced very insightful scholarship, our inability to discover in totality the *actual* daily lives of enslaved blacks is one of the biggest challenges facing historians of the African American experience. This challenge increases the further we move on into the future. How does one best explain the realities of antebellum slavery in the 21st century? It is not only difficult to understand the realities faced by blacks in the more distant past, but it is equally difficult to translate these realities into a language understandable to those of us in the present, especially to the hip-hop generation. "Brother Future" (1991), directed by Roy Campanella, and Haile Gerima's "Sankofa" (1992) have successfully and creatively translated the history of slavery to those of us who came of age in the 1980s, the 1990s, and later. Because media and popular culture is playing an increasingly more central role in youths' acquisition of information and knowledge, more films of this genre are needed.

Though like Carl Becker he was not interested in Black history, Edward Hallett Carr also raised some issues that are relevant to theorizing Black history. After being a professional historian for more than four decades, at seventy years of age Carr published *What is History?* (1962). He embraced the task of defining history from various vantage points. His most profound discussion concerned historical facts, the role of the historian in selecting which facts to showcase, and the intricate relationship between the past and the present. Arguing against the archaic 19th century "belief in a hard core of historical facts existing objectively and independently of the interpretation of the historian," Carr stressed that so-called historical facts "never come to us pure," that they are preselected for us, and that, before becoming widely accepted, facts undergo a sometimes elaborate validation process. "The facts of history cannot be purely objective, since they become facts of history only in virtue of the significance attached to them by the historian." He added that historical facts—essentially uncertainties in his mind—were "raw materials of the historian rather than history itself."[5]

Implicit in Carr's discussion of history is the necessity of acknowledging that history as we read it in scholarly texts—or in the case of many of today's high school and college students, on the internet—is the product of professional historians or those acting or posing as historians. Carr thus instructed students of history to "study the historian before you begin to study the facts." Young students of history hope or often assume that what we read in historical scholarship is accurate, objective, and based upon a rigorous examination of a variety of primary and secondary sources. We must, however, remember that history is interpretation and that the historian doing the interpreting for us, however well trained he or she may be, is or was the product of a particular sociohistorical environment and personal background that significantly shaped his or her overall worldview. All historians' interpretations of the past are or were largely influenced by the once present state in which they wrote their scholarship. Echoing Becker, Carr's preliminary definition of history is that it constitutes "a continuous process of interaction between the historian and his facts, an unending dialogue between the present and the past."[6] Carr did not consider African Americans in his philosophical inquiry. Nevertheless, at several points in his discussion, Black history could have served as an instructive case study.

Carr's insistence that we begin with the historian and the sociohistorical context that molded his or her perceptions is especially important when dealing with Black history. When one picks up a text in Black history, one should pay close attention to the author and the publication date. Many of the texts published before the classic Civil Rights Movement—if they were not published by Du Bois, Woodson, Woodson's disciples, co-workers, and colleagues and a select group of "liberal" white historians—sought to justify the oppression of African Americans, belittled black culture, and/or oversimplified the black experience. At the same time, while many classic studies may have been produced in the 1960s and 1970s, as John Hope Franklin and others have argued much of the historical scholarship on black America during this pivotal time capitalized on Black history as a "fad-field." Like all histories, writings in Black history were greatly impacted by the major changes in African Americans' enduring struggle for basic civil rights. As Robert L. Harris, Jr. has suggested, there is ample evidence to argue that the largest transformation in African American historiography took place during and after the 1960s.[7] But, a similar argument could be made about other periods when placed in their proper historical contexts. Du Bois's historical scholarship from his 1895 dissertation until *The Negro* (1915), for instance, could be interpreted as marking one of the most drastic changes in African American historiography when one compares his early work to the scholarship of antebellum era historians and even to George Washington Williams and other black writers of history active during the "nadir." Likewise, the large quantity of quality books published during the 1980s and 1990s will perhaps lead future generations of historians to identify these decades as being especially crucial in the evolution of black historiography.

Carr's notion that an effective historian must have an "imaginative understanding of the minds of the people with whom he is dealing" and can only be successful if he can come into contact with his subjects is also very applicable to Black history.[8] This is a crucial concept for historians of the Black past. Black history challenges its students to imagine, understand, and translate how African Americans survived and persevered during crazy oppressive times. While countless groups of people throughout the world have endured and overcome massive obstacles, Black history is especially amazing. It is characterized by a people being required to face and for the most part overcome oppression of various sorts. How did Africans survive the middle passage and the enslavement processes? How did enslaved blacks make it from sunup to sundown, day to day, year to year? How did blacks survive the openly anti-black years of the "nadir"? How did blacks cope with lynching? How did blacks live under a system of government-sanctioned Jim Crow segregation for more than fifty years? How did the recently de-

ceased Mamie Till-Mobley maintain her composure in the national media spotlight after the brutal murder of her son, Emmett
Till?

Responding to such questions beyond the surface level is a
great challenge for students of Black history and requires that
students develop rigorous, imaginative methodologies for revisiting African Americans' past experiences. Attempting to place
oneself in the shoes of blacks at various points before the classic
Civil Rights Movement is hard to say the least. Even more recent
historical tragedies in Black history pose similar challenges.
What was black life like in the Miami black neighborhoods of
Liberty City and Overtown in 1980 after five days of rioting following the death of Arthur McDuffie at the hands of the Miami
police? How did blacks in New York City deal with the attack on
three black men in Howard Beach in 1989 that lead to the death
of an innocent black man? How did blacks in L.A. cope with the
beating of Rodney King? How did blacks in Jasper, Texas cope
with the brutal lynching of James Byrd in June 1998? How did
blacks deal with the killing of Amadou Diallo by the NYPD's
Street Crime Unit in 1999 and the eventual acquittal of the four
officers involved a year later? Such tragedies are not uncommon
in the African American experience and challenge us to probe
into the minds of those blacks directly and indirectly impacted
by these events.

This process of imagining what life was like for African
Americans in the seemingly distant and the not-so-distant past
could be one effective strategy that the hip-hop generation could
employ to help motivate themselves to persevere and contribute
to the ongoing black struggle for equal rights. Whenever a young
African American thinks that he/she is having it bad and that the
cards are stacked against him/her, he/she should just take a quick
visit to the trials and tribulations of his/her foreparents. This is
said not to oversimplify the complexities of Black history or to
claim that a quick reading or recounting of Black history can
solve the major crises facing young blacks today. This process of
revisiting African American history should not be done as a way

to excuse the reality of young blacks' hard times or to romanti-cize the black past. It should, on the other hand, help one put things in perspective, remain humble, and gain inspiration. In this manner, history becomes practical and relevant to young blacks' everyday life.

A last key issue Carr raises that is relevant to Black history is his conceptualization of history's purpose and function. For him, the function of history was to "master and understand it as the key to the understanding of the present." The best type of history, Carr reasoned, was that which was "written precisely when the historian's vision of the past is illuminated by the in-sights into the problems of the present...The function of history is to promote a profounder understanding of both the past and the present through the interaction between them."[9]

This is precisely why critically studying Black history is so vital. Today, blacks face seemingly countless problems, most of which have concrete historical roots and antecedents in the long history of anti-black culture in the United States. Today's endur-ing variations of racial prejudice and institutional racism can not really be understood without placing them in the long history of racism in the United States, going back to the founding of the nation. Henry Wienek's recent revisionist study on George Washington, *An Imperfect God: George Washington, His Slaves, and the Creation of America* (2003), highlights the nation's first President's openly anti-black behaviors. His study also helps us better understand President Bush's, and other U.S. Presidents', attitudes towards race and African Americans. Many Americans suffer from historical amnesia, especially when dealing with sen-sitive, controversial, or so-called "racial" issues. Those who de-cide to acknowledge America's complete history will recognize that the long history of black oppression in the United States—concretely from about 1789 until 1965, and consequently more than 80% of the total black experience in America—has directly impacted the vast majority of blacks' present status. The more one understands the oppression endured and overcome by black Americans during a vast period of the African American experi-

ence as a whole, the better one understands the monumental
problems facing blacks today and the potential solutions to these
mounting dilemmas.

100 Years of Defining Black History

In an unpublished essay written in the late 1970s, recently
deceased iconoclast Harold Cruse praised John Hope Franklin's
contributions to U.S. and African American history, but asserted
that "the student looking for the 'seminal ideas,' the challenge of
unique 'interpretations,' or anything resembling the unorthodox
in the philosophy of history would be hard put to find such intellectual qualities in Franklin's body of work."[10] Although I dis-
agree with Cruse's assessment of Franklin, who published several thought-provoking essays addressing the deeper issues of
Black history and history in general from the 1940s on, Cruse
still raises an important point. It appears that prominent black
historians such as Franklin did not devote extensive energies towards directly philosophizing about Black history. On the other
hand, many white American and European historians seem to
have pondered the theoretical and philosophical meanings of
history.

There are seemingly countless books, anthologies, and articles defining history in general; but it seems that historians have
not extensively philosophized the deeper meanings of Black history. Even Earl E. Thorpe, the first historian to produce a monograph-length study on black historians, spent more time discussing the philosophy of history from Eurocentric vantage points
than he did discussing the deeper meanings of Black history.
Black historians have not devoted complete books to defining
and theorizing Black history. However, in the prefaces, introduc-
tions, and conclusions of their monographs as well as in important essays and articles, many have conceptualized African
American history in provocative manners. During the twentieth
century, a handful of professionally and nonprofessionally

trained black historians as well as a few white historians have offered some intriguing definitions of Black history.

Though more than a few blacks wrote history before him, in the 1890s and early 1900s W.E.B. Du Bois posited some of the earliest concrete definitions of Black history. From the immediate aftermath of World War I through the 1950s, Woodson, his protégés, and his co-workers then dominated the scene in conceptualizing Black history. From the founding of *The Journal of Negro History* in 1916 until the early 1960s and beyond, many black historians, and at least one white historian, articulated their definitions of Black history. During the 1960s and 1970s, some of Woodson's disciples, by this time seasoned historians, continued to theorize Black history. A new school of black cultural nationalist historians also emerged, linking Black history to Black Power. Since the 1980s, a pivotal decade in defining Black history at one level symbolized by Lerone Bennett, Jr.'s ideas, there have been a few key studies that have creatively defined Black history. By the 1990s, definitions of Black Women's history gained more prominence, adding further complexity to our notions of Black history.

The overall lack of scholarship that directly responds to the question "What is Black history?" is not hard to explain. Black historians, especially before the 1960s, were preoccupied with recording events and analyzing personalities in Black history, establishing a scholarly tradition, and creating a discipline that for so long had been ignored and denied entry into the U.S. academy. Since the 1960s and 1970s, when Black history supposedly became mainstreamed in many historians' estimation, it seems as if black historians assumed that they all agreed upon what Black history meant or that philosophically defining Black history was unimportant. The lack of philosophical treatises on Black history also suggests that black historians have been preoccupied with researching historical events, leaders, periods, groups, and themes. Others, especially during the Black Power era, were perhaps more concerned with engaging in more practical endeavors. Whatever the case may be, discussions of Black history in basic and abstract philosophical terms are long over-due.

Recognized in many circles as the father of modern black intelligentsia, W.E.B. Du Bois (1868–1963) was the first profes-sionally trained black historian. He theorized Black history in a variety of manners that both further refined antebellum era histo-rians' ideas and influenced black historians who came of age after him. In his famous *The Souls of Black Folk* (1903), Du Bois laid out his widely cited "double-consciousness" theory. This idea, which he revised and developed throughout his long schol-arly career, must be the single most frequently cited intellectual theory in African American scholarly discourses. Indeed, one hundred years ago Du Bois eloquently captured what would be-come a significant subtheme in African American history and culture. He reasoned that as an African American, one possessed a sense of "two-ness—an American, a Negro; two souls, two thoughts, two unreconciled strivings; two warring ideals in one dark body, whose dogged strength alone keeps it from being torn asunder." In defining Black history, Du Bois stressed this sense of black America's cultural duality. "The history of the Ameri-can Negro," he noted, "is the history of this strife,—this longing to attain self-conscious manhood, to merge his double self into a better and truer self. In this merging he wishes neither of the older selves to be lost..."[11]

Du Bois was among the first to highlight that African American history was a combination of African and African American cultural elements and experiences, and that blacks' Africanity was a central component of American life and history. He told his white readers that it was around black people that "the history of this land has centered for thrice a hundred years."

Du Bois empowered ordinary blacks, nameless and faceless to historians, with historical agency and he did not hesitate to identify with early black makers of history. Abandoning the ob-jectivity exhibited in *The Suppression of the African Slave-Trade to the United States of America, 1638–1870* (1896), *The Phila-delphia Negro* (1899), and his early Atlanta University studies, in *The Souls of Black Folk*, Du Bois celebrated the contributions of blacks to U.S. history:

> Actively we have woven ourselves with the very warp and woof of this nation,—we fought their battles, shared their sorrow, mingled our blood with theirs, and generation after generation have pleaded with a head-strong, careless people to despise not Justice, Mercy, and Truth, lest the nation be smitten with a curse. Our song, our toil, our cheer, and warning have been given to this nation in blood-brotherhood. Are not these gifts worth giving? Is not this work and striving? *Would America have been America without her Negro people?*[12]

At the dawning of the twentieth century when Du Bois wrote "Of Our Spiritual Strivings," he was clearly a cultural pluralist who envisioned an American society in which blacks would be "co-workers in the kingdom of culture." He envisioned Black history as representing a struggle for human rights, American citizenship, cultural recognition, and integration. Like the ideas of all the historians addressed in this book, Du Bois's conception of history was shaped by the context in which he formulated his ideas. When *The Souls of Black Folk* was published, the vast majority of African Americans had been "free" for only thirty-eight years. Despite emancipation, Reconstruction, and the 13th, 14th, and 15th Amendments, the period from 1865 until 1903 was characterized by open anti-black behavior. Black history for Du Bois in 1903 was dominated by slavery, a denial of basic civil rights, and overall struggle. Despite his overarching idealism, he did not hesitate to highlight the struggles characterizing Black history. He shared with his readers (mainly white intellectuals and black leaders) his view of the tragic side of Black history.[13] "Throughout history," he noted, "the powers of single black men flash here and there like falling stars, and die sometimes before the world has rightly gauged their brightness."[14]

Du Bois's view of Black history in *The Souls of Black Folk* is multilayered: he acknowledged the beauty, perseverance, and influence of black culture; revealed the openly anti-black nature of U.S. culture; and discussed Black history as being a combination of African and African American experiences. Most black historians active since *The Souls of Black Folk* have shared and/or elaborated upon aspects of Du Bois's fundamental beliefs concerning African American history.

Carter G. Woodson (1875–1950), "The Father of Black History," wrote many books, articles, and book reviews and delivered countless lectures, addresses, and speeches that elaborated upon the function of Black history in detail. He did not, however, devote a great deal of his scholarship to defining Black history in poignant, abstract, and philosophical terms. He was too pragmatic for such an approach and perceived his primary function as creating the fundamental bases for Black history and stimulating widespread interest in it among a black population that possessed intellectual skills, but not the leisure time and skills to grapple with scholars' complex ideologies and theories. Woodson's ideas of Black history's meaning and function were influenced by the Progressive era, the Harlem Renaissance, the Great Depression, World War II, and the Cold War era, all of which constituted important dimensions of the proto civil rights movement. While discussing what history entailed, Woodson often preferred to cite well-versed scholars. In a 1928 pamphlet on Negro History Week, he expanded upon many conventional ideas of history and briefly defined history as "clarified experience...the depository of great actions, the witness of what is past, the examples and the instructor of the present, and the monitor to the future." Woodson argued that "there was no such thing as Negro History in the sense of isolated contributions." He proposed that all peoples in the United States contributed significantly to the nation's development. "History, then, is a record of the progress of mankind rather than of racial or national achievement," Woodson noted.[15] He was opposed to history as "the record of the successes and disappointments of those who engage in contentions for power" and as a "register of the crimes and misfortunes of mankind."[16] As a result, while he shared many of Du Bois's sentiments, Woodson did not classify Black history in the manner that Du Bois did in *The Souls of Black Folk*. Woodson's view of history was fundamentally pragmatic and directly connected to the present.

Woodson stressed that history was a necessary ingredient to a people's self-knowledge and collective identity. One of his most famous sayings, shared by Marcus Garvey and appreciated by many Black Power activists, was: "If a race has no history, if it has no worthwhile tradition, it becomes a negligible factor in the thought of the world, and it stands in the danger of being exterminated."[17] Woodson perceived Black history as being an essential part of American history. In a 1927 Negro History Week circular, he asserted:

> We should emphasize not Negro History, but the Negro in history. What we need is not a history of selected races or nations, but the history of the world void of national bias, race hate, and religious prejudice. There should be no indulgence in undue eulogy of the Negro. The case of the Negro is well taken care of when it is shown how he has influenced the development of civilization.[18]

Woodson routinely stressed that the purpose of Black history was not to focus on how blacks had been victimized, but instead was to demonstrate how blacks influenced U.S. and world history. Woodson opted for this approach because during the openly racist era of Jim Crow segregation, he attempted to integrate Black history within mainstream American educational institutions. This could not have been accomplished by indicting white America for its historical mistreatment of black Americans. Woodson, in many ways, shared black, white American, and European nineteenth century historians' "fetishism of facts."[19] An important part of history for Woodson was knowing the "facts." In promoting Black history, Woodson argued that "the aim has been to emphasize important facts in the belief that facts properly set forth will speak for themselves."[20] As it was for Du Bois, Black history for Woodson was American history: the two were inseparable. This idea has been long-lasting, gaining prominence in the 1980s with historians such as Nathan Huggins who advocated "a new synthesis, a new American history." Huggins believed that U.S. history "cannot be told as a story of black history and white history." He noted:

> It must be told as one. While that idea is simple enough—a truism indeed—too few of us accept the radical implications of it. We do not put it into our thinking, our writing, our courses. That idea, nevertheless, is key to any new, successful narrative of American history.[21]

Multicultural U.S. historians such as Ronald Takaki have sought to expand Huggins's plea to include all major U.S. ethnic groups.

Throughout the pages of *The Negro History Bulletin* during the late 1930s and the 1940s, Woodson articulated his vision of how history could serve mankind. Woodson never really altered his fundamental belief that history entailed the objective laying down of the "facts." While he certainly did emphasize black achievements and at times employed history as some form of propaganda, he insisted to *Bulletin* readers that "real history requires the elimination of self...Facts properly set forth will tell their own story."[22] Woodson also wanted history to be a major part of black people's everyday life. He often called upon blacks to act and change the course of history. For the Association founder, the status of black people was a "life-and-death struggle." In an essay appearing in the February 1940 issue of the *Bulletin*, Woodson challenged his readers to do great things based upon the deeds of their ancestors. History was for Woodson a tool of inspiration.

To you, then, comes the challenge as to what you will do in building upon the foundation which they have laid. These people whose civilization was marked by the kerosene lamp, the wash tub, the hoe, and the ox-cart disappointed the prophets who said they would be exterminated; and on the contrary they enrolled themselves among the great.

Woodson continued his plea, "*What will you do in the day of the moving picture, the radio, and the aeroplane? If we do not take hold where they left off and advance further in the service of truth and justice, we are unworthy to claim descent from such a noble people.*"[23] Pleas such as this were resurrected decades later by Lerone Bennett, Jr., long-time historian for *Ebony* and self-proclaimed Woodson disciple.

During Woodson's times, a few of his protégés and co-workers offered philosophical inquiries into what Black history constituted. In the widely read *The New Negro* (1925), pioneering black bibliophile Arthur A. Schomburg (1874–1938) shared Woodson's sentiments and defined Black history as being functional to black peoples' struggle to recover from the dehabilitating effects of slavery. "The American Negro must remake his past in order to make his future," Schomburg asserted, "History must restore what slavery took away, for it is the social damage of slavery that the present generations must repair and offset." Schomburg argued that Black history was revisionist in nature, a record that challenged Americans to rewrite "many important paragraphs of our common American history."[24] Many "New Negro" intellectuals shared Schomburg's beliefs. Schomburg also influenced historians of the next generation, such as John Henrik Clarke.

During the peak of the Great Depression, in a 1935 essay entitled "The Reconstruction of History," Charles Wesley (1891–1987)—one of Woodson's disciples and co-workers and the third African American to earn a Ph.D. in history from Harvard in 1925—explored conceptualizations of history from the writings of Herodotus through the early 1900s. Wesley defined history as "the study of the development of men and things throughout the ages." In a Woodsonian fashion, he stressed that history needed to be all-encompassing, acknowledging the contributions of all people throughout the world.

> History is not the study of men and women of one race or color and the neglect and omission of the men and women of another race or color. It is neither the glorification of white people nor black people, but it is the story of the people irrespective of race or color. It should deal with people in all times and places and should present the contributions of all the people to civilization.

Wesley concluded, "When a past of a people has been neglected or given subordinate places, history in order to be truthful must be reconstructed."[25] At the same time, he called for the writing of history to be reconstructed to place Africa at the center and to give African Americans a central place in world history as agents of their own destiny.

Several years after Wesley's article appeared, L.D. Reddick (1910–1995), a lesser-known Woodson disciple, published an essay that called for a reevaluation and refashioning of Black history. He defined Black history as having a distinct "purpose which is built upon a faith." Reddick argued that "all history has been written with an 'other' purpose," that the writing of history was not objective. He agreed with Croce that history was "contemporary thought about the past." Reddick defined the purpose of Black history as being three-fold: "to discover and record the role of African peoples," to educate "a majority population," and to instill within blacks race pride. Reddick divided black historiography into "two divisions, *before* Woodson and *after* Woodson." He also called for the writing of Black history to be all inclusive. In his view, it needed to be viewed along with the histories of other Americans and needed to highlight "the feelings and thought of the common folk."[26] Reddick's article was significant in that he explicitly called upon black historians to create new historiographies. Interestingly, he argued that black historians were preoccupied with slavery studies. He wanted his colleagues to spend more time cultivating other subfields of study. Reddick claimed that slavery historiography was exhausted perhaps because he feared that slavery was too much characterizing Black history and even perhaps becoming synonymous with it. Reddick may also have wanted to move beyond the stigma of slavery. Before the 1960s and 1970s, much of slavery historiography highlighted the victimization of enslaved blacks.

In the early 1940s, novelist Richard Wright (1908–1960) offered his ideas of what constituted Black history. In his *12 Million Voices*, Wright—not formally trained in history—defined Black history by comparing it to whites' historical experiences, and by highlighting the elements of struggle in the African American past. Wright proclaimed:

> The many historical phases which whites have traversed voluntarily and gradually during the course of Western civilization we black folk have traversed through swift compulsion...Brutal, bloody, crowded with suffering and abrupt transitions, the lives of us black folk represent the most magical and meaningful picture of human experience in the Western world...We black folk, our history and our present being, are a mirror of all manifold experiences of America...If America has forgotten her past, then let her look into the mirror of our consciousness, for our memoirs go back...[27]

Though Wright's heartfelt discussion of Black history overgeneralized U.S. history and was not very sophisticated, the tone of his study and his overarching view of Black history was ahead of its time in terms of its underlying message. His study resembled many black cultural nationalists' writings during the Black Power era. Unbound by the at times restricting mores, standards, and quest for objectivity of the U.S. historical profession,

Wright's take on Black history was very emotional, African American centered, and even radical in tone when compared to John Hope Franklin's notion of Black history as expressed years later in his 1947 classic *From Slavery to Freedom: A History of Negro Americans*. Several years before publishing this landmark study, however, Franklin (b. 1915) did publish a highly emotional essay in *Phylon*, "History—Weapon of War and Peace" (1944), in which he sought to answer the long-debated inquiry "What *is* the field and function of history?"

In the midst of World War II, Franklin (who followed in Du Bois's, Woodson's, and Wesley's footsteps by earning his Ph.D. in history from Harvard in 1941) argued that the time was ripe "to find some specific function for the historical process in the shaping of human destiny." Franklin was disturbed by the fact that history had been used as a "weapon in waging war" and in the promotion of nationalism and notions of racial superiority. He offered his own ideal notion of how history should function. He called upon students of history to use the field as a "constructive" force. "As a social discipline, the historical process should," Franklin reflected, "be forged into a mighty weapon for the preservation of peace." He believed that "the study of history demands the use of our best developed faculties of fairness and impartiality," that history should be ideally written with "dispassion, impartiality, and cautious judgment," that it needed to be "the truth, the whole truth," and that in post-World War II America, history could be used as an essential tool of social reform, as "a means of guiding man towards a better life."[28] In this essay, Franklin promoted a philosophy of history that would remain consistent during the remainder of this career: objective, at times hyperobjective, history. Unlike antebellum era historians, Du Bois, and Woodson, Franklin wrote his major historical essays and books in a manner that did not reveal his black pride or his common experiences and worldviews with his historical subjects. Yet, at the same time, in a few instances he argued that history should be used to help reform American thought and behavior. He did not mention Black history by name in his 1944

Phylon essay, but his conception of history could have very easily been substituted with Black history. Franklin avoided doing so because he probably did not want to be dubbed and dismissed as being a *black* historian or a protest writer who was politicizing history.

Like Woodson, Franklin defined Black history by paying close attention to its symbiotic relationship with U.S. history in general. For Franklin, it was above all else necessary to be objective and scientific in treating Black history. As he revealed in *From Slavery to Freedom*, he believed that Black history needed to acknowledge the "discreet balance between recognizing the deeds of outstanding persons and depicting the fortunes of the great mass of Negroes." Franklin added that "the history of the Negro in America is essentially the story of the strivings of the nameless millions who have sought adjustment in a new and sometimes hostile world." Because he was seeking to introduce Black history into mainstream U.S. historical discourse, Franklin did not dwell upon the tragedies of Black history, but instead highlighted African Americans' efforts to "accommodate...to the dominant culture." [29]

In the dawning of the 1950s, the recently deceased Herbert Aptheker (1915–2003) published *A Documentary History of the Negro People in the United States* in two volumes, one of the most important collections of primary sources of Black history for its time. This study was one of many studies that he produced in the field of Black history from the 1930s through the 1990s. Aptheker, who joined the Communist Party in 1939, began studying Black history as an M.A. student at Columbia University. His 1937 thesis celebrated the largest slave rebellion in U.S. history, Nat Turner's revolt. Influenced by his outspoken Communist leanings, in the late 1930s and early 1940s Aptheker published several pamphlets on Black history addressing slave revolts, black abolitionists, and blacks in the Civil War. He celebrated blacks' "deeds of unsurpassed heroism and titanic efforts." In his pamphlet on slave revolts, which laid the foundation for his 1943 classic, *American Negro Slave Revolts*, Aptheker maintained that the history of slavery could be used to help inspire black self-pride and black-white unity. He did not hesitate to make sweeping connections between the past and the present. He molded, and at times mythicized, Black history to suit his goal of uniting blacks and whites:

> American slavery was a barbarous tyranny...Its history, however, is not merely one of impoverishment, deprivation, and oppression. For imbedded in the record of American slavery is the inspiring story of the persistent and courageous efforts of the Negroes (aided, not infrequently, by poor whites) to regain their heritage of liberty and equality, to regain their right to the elemental demands of human beings...An awareness of its history should give the modern Negro added confidence and courage in his heroic present-day battle for complete and perfect equality with all other American citizens. And it should make those other Americans eager and proud to grasp the hand of the Negro and march forward with him against their common oppressor—against those industrial and financial overlords and the plantation oligarchs who today stand in the way of liberty, equality, and prosperity.
>
> That unity between whites and Negro masses was necessary to overthrow nineteenth-century slavery. That same unity is necessary to defeat twentieth-century slavery—to defeat fascism.[30]

In the late 1940s, Aptheker reiterated his belief in the need to use Black history as a tool of liberation. In an article entitled "Negro History: Arsenal for Liberation," a Negro History Week tribute in *New Masses*, Aptheker declared that Black history was an essential ingredient of U.S. history and that it could "serve as a weapon of incalculable power in our present critical period when each man must stand up and be counted."[31] Aptheker was certainly not the first white historian to examine Black history in a sympathetic manner. He was, however, the first and one of the few white historians to radicalize Black history in hopes of challenging American capitalism and influencing whites to re-think their status.

In introducing the first volume of *A Documentary History of the Negro People in the United States*, Aptheker characterized Black history as being a history of oppressed yet resilient people. Aptheker asserted:

> Black history demonstrates that no matter what the despoilers of humanity may do—enslave, segregate, torture, lynch—they cannot destroy the peoples' will to freedom, their urge towards equality, justice and dignity...To work in their history, to see the defiance of slaves, the courage of martyrs, the resistance of the plain people, and to study the great human documents they left behind is a most rewarding experience.

Aptheker viewed Black history as being the history of how the masses lived. Despite Harold Cruse's openly harsh indictment of his motivations, Aptheker was relatively unique in that he was among the very few white historians who embraced a black nationalist-like interpretation of Black history. Harry Washington Greene certainly thought that Aptheker possessed a black perspective in writing history. He apparently thought that he was an African American and included him in his study *Holders of Doctorates Among American Negroes: An Educational Study of Negroes Who Have Earned Doctoral Degrees in Course, 1876–1943* (1948).[32] Similarly, Robin D.G. Kelley, who himself discovered that Aptheker was not black more than several years after first reading *American Negro Slave Revolts* as a high school student, asserted that Aptheker was an honorary "black historian" based upon his commitment to understanding and overturning racial and economic oppression.[33]

A decade after first publishing *From Slavery to Freedom*, John Hope Franklin expanded upon his conceptualization of Black history in "The New Negro History" (1957). Echoing Carl Becker, Franklin argued:

In discussing the history of a people one must distin-
guish between what has *actually* happened and what
those who have written the history have *said* has happened. So far as the *actual* history of the American
Negro is concerned, there is nothing particularly new
about it. It is an exciting story, a remarkable history. It
is the story of slavery and freedom, humanity and in-
humanity, democracy and its denial. It is tragedy and
triumph, suffering and compassion, sadness and joy.[34]

Though he has maintained an objective approach throughout his
remarkably long career, in this article Franklin acknowledged the
element of struggle characterizing Black history more explicitly.
Brown v. Board of Education, Topeka, Kansas, the Montgomery
Bus Boycott, and the lynching of Emmett Till certainly altered
Franklin's vision of and approach to Black history when he
wrote "The New Negro History." Franklin suggested that the
interpretation of what actually occurred in Black history must be
explored side by side with what actually happened, since the ac-
tualities of Black history had been so much distorted in order to
justify the subordination of African Americans. The overall tone
of Franklin's article is optimistic. Writing during the classic
Civil Rights era, Franklin was hopeful about the state of Black
history, commenting that there was a "striking resemblance" between what historians wrote about Black history and the history
that "actually happened."[35]
    A year later, in 1958, Earl E. Thorpe (1924–1989), histo-
rian, educator, ordained minister, and longtime faculty member
at North Carolina Central University, published the first major
study on the black historical enterprise, *Negro Historians in the
United States* (1958). Thorpe briefly defined Black history as
"not simply a biography of great men and the chronicling of noble achievements," but as "a record, viewed in the light of condi-
tioning circumstances, of the race's achievements and failures,
dreams and lack of dreams." Thorpe added that "Negro history is
largely social history. And running throughout the dark gloomy
picture which it usually depicts is a small note of optimism, of

faith in a coming new day."[36] By labeling Black history social history, like Aptheker and Reddick, he meant that it was largely the history of the black masses. Social history, "history from below," "history from way, way below," or the history of everyday people is arguably the most appropriate genre of history for any group of people.[37] The histories of great men and women, presidential politics, and wars are informative, but often tell us little about the historical experiences of the actual people who create history on a daily basis. Given the history of slavery, second-class citizenship, and overall oppression in the African American experience, Thorpe's contention that Black history is social history is important and deserves to be further unpacked. It is interesting to note that Thorpe did not analyze the philosophy of Black history in greater depth during the mid to late 1950s. In 1956 and 1957, Thorpe published four articles in *The Quarterly Review of Higher Education Among Negroes*, all of which focused on Western philosophers' notions of history.

Some of the more profound definitions of Black history surfaced during and after the peak of the modern Civil Rights Movement. In the early 1960s, political scientist Samuel Du Bois Cook, a professor at Atlanta University at the time and later the first African American to hold a regular faculty appointment at a predominantly white university in the South, contended that Black history, its "grim and grinding realities," could be best understood within a "framework of tragedy." Cook refined his view of Black history by arguing that "the tragic conception of Negro history" is "an interpretation which seeks to grasp the full dimension and naked depths of the systematic, persistent, and institutionalized negation of the Negro's meanings and values on grounds of ethical desirability and necessity." Cook claimed that blacks, especially during the era of slavery, were creatures and objects "of action," not participants, that they were excluded from the "historical process." In making such claims, he downplayed and even ignored black agency and implied that Black history was characterized by victimhood and victimization. When viewed in the context of how most blacks characterized

Black history, Cook's approach was refreshing. Perhaps Cook highlighted the "tragic dimension" of Black history because so many of his predecessors had portrayed a much more optimistic, less harsh version of Black history in hopes of integrating blacks into white America. He argued that the "tragic conception of Negro history" had three main virtues: it helped blacks better understand their contemporary struggles; it helped them appreciate the achievements of blacks in the past; and it could help blacks better understand their status in U.S. history.[38]

During the Black Power era, black historians shifted towards more directly defining Black history in relation to the black struggle for liberation. They were influenced by the black cultural rejuvenation of the time. Perhaps more than any other scholarly discipline, history became an important tool for young blacks during the 1960s and 1970s. It served as a source of pride and inspiration and also helped so-called "militant" blacks hold white America accountable for past crimes against African Americans. In more explicit manners than in previous periods, blacks during the Black Power era drew heavily upon the collective history of their people to shape their consciousness and help them attain their "revolution of the mind." In this process of self-enlightenment, many young blacks were shocked, angered, and amazed by what they discovered in the reservoirs of their people's past. Young blacks translated this mixed bag of emotions into a viable tool of liberation, inspiration, energy, and hope. Black history became vital knowledge that helped young blacks make the necessary psychological and cultural transformations.

Black Power movement historian William Van Deburg has suggested that black intellectuals coming of age between 1965 and 1975, especially poets, playwrights, musicians, and novelists, used Black history as a "wellspring of group strength and staying power," which could help them create "the black nation" in the future. Malcolm X, "archetype, reference point, and spiritual advisor in absentia" for Black Power activists, believed adamantly that Black history was central to the black struggle.[39] Malcolm X first discovered the power of history while imprisoned in the Norfolk Prison Colony in Massachusetts. Black history was an essential ingredient to his transformation from a convicted criminal to a conscious critical thinker. While in prison he studied history "intensively," reading the historical scholarship of Du Bois, Woodson, and J.A. Rogers, among others. He was especially intrigued by the history of slavery,[40] one of his favorite lecture topics as a member of the Nation of Islam.

After he was released from prison in 1952, Malcolm incorporated history into his ideology and program. While he was the Minister of the very popular and important Nation of Islam Temple Number 7 in Harlem, New York (also known as the Muhammad Temple of Islam and Muhammad's Mosque No. 7), Malcolm routinely lectured to his followers about the importance of Black history. In a speech from the early 1960s, "Black Man's History," he envisioned history as being an important factor in black liberation. His definition of Black history was directly related to uplifting African Americans.

> The honorable Elijah Muhammad teaches us that of all the things that the black man, or any man for that matter, can study, history is best qualified to reward all research. You have to have a knowledge of history no matter what you are going to do; anything that you undertake you have to have a knowledge of history in order to be successful in it. The thing that has made the so-called Negro in America fail, more than any other thing, is your, my, lack of knowledge concerning history. We know less about history than anything else...We have experts in every field, but seldom can you find one among us who is an expert on the history of the black man. And because of his lack of knowledge concerning the history of the black man, no matter how much he excels in other sciences, he's always confined, he's always neglected to the low rung of the ladder that the dumbest of our people are relegated to. And all this stems from his lack of knowledge concerning history.[41]

As a follower and mouthpiece of Elijah Muhammad, Malcolm
believed that a knowledge of history would be very liberating for
African Americans. Malcolm maintained this respect for and
faith in Black history after his 1963–1964 split with Elijah Muhammad and the Nation of Islam. In a speech to members of the
Organization of Afro-American Unity in January 1965, Malcolm
argued that blacks lacked a knowledge of their history, which
contributed directly to their oppression. He defined Black history
in direct relation to the present.

> When you deal with the past, you're dealing with his-
> tory, you're dealing actually with the origin of a thing.
> When you know the origin, you know the cause. If you
> don't know the origin, you don't know the reason,
> you're just cut off, you're left standing in mid-air.

Malcolm continued to break down history in laymen's terms to
his followers, "It is so important for you and me to spend time
today learning something about the past so that we can better
understand the present, analyze it, and then do something about
it."[42] For Malcolm, ever since he had been a member of the Nation of Islam, Black history had to be, above all else practical,
and help in the fundamental, psychological black struggle for
liberation. Perhaps more than any other leader, after his death
Malcolm shaped the worldviews of black activists during the
Black Power era. He became "a Black Power paradigm," "the
embodiment of a timeless black rage."[43]

Malcolm's tone was echoed by many black historians during the Black Power era. Seasoned, professional black historians
such as Benjamin Quarles and John Hope Franklin, who had established themselves as objective historians, published essays in
which they adopted a more emotional, popular tone. Black nationalist scholars John Henrik Clarke and Harold Cruse continued to advocate a philosophy of Black history closely linked
with a desire to liberate black Americans and aid in the struggle
of nation-building. The younger generation of budding black
historians during the late 1960s and early 1970s, such as Vincent

Harding and Sterling Stuckey, articulated Malcolm's ideas in more scholarly terms. *Negro Digest*, published from 1942 until 1950, from 1962 until 1969, and then from 1970 until 1976 as *Black World*, served as an important outlet for black historians to share their philosophies of Black history. Beginning in the 1960s, *Negro Digest* routinely published an "Annual History Issue." The magazine's motto, "Knowledge is the Key to a Better Tomorrow," reflected the pragmatic vision of Black history articulated by Woodson and his Black Power era protégés.

In February 1966, John Hope Franklin offered some philosophical thoughts on the meaning of history to *Negro Digest* readers. He noted that history was not static and unchanging, that each generation wrote history. He believed that how a people approached their past reflected "the way it will approach the future." Franklin suggested that Black history was the product of historians who were molded by various historical experiences. "The changes that each generation experiences provide new ways of looking at the past," Franklin said, cognizant of the pivotal social transformations ushered in during the 1960s, "Nothing better illustrates the way that experience guides the writing of history than the manner in which the history of the Negro has been viewed and written."[44]

Among those black scholars who validated Franklin's assessment of how historical contexts impacted the writing of history, who connected with Malcolm, and who defined Black history as a philosophy quite extensively, were Harold Cruse, Vincent Harding, and John Henrik Clarke. One of the main subarguments in Harold Cruse's controversial *The Crisis of the Negro Intellectual* (1967) was that black activists, creative artists, and intellectuals of the Civil Rights and Black Power era failed to critically study the thoughts, actions, successes, and failures of their early twentieth-century predecessors, especially those active during the "nadir" and the Harlem Renaissance, in order to construct new ideologies and programs. Throughout his work, Cruse (1916–2005), a freelance journalist, labor activist, television film editor, theatrical stage manager, drama producer, creative writer, and African American Studies pioneer, repeatedly chastised blacks coming of age in the 1960s as being "anti-historical," for failing to "see the historical connections." He defined Black history in several instances. At one point, Cruse commented that "American Negro history is basically a history of the conflict between integrationist and nationalist forces in politics, economics, and culture, no matter what leaders are involved and what slogans are used."[45] Though this definition is problematic because it seems to exclude the black masses by focusing on black leadership trends and implies that there are two main lines of black social thought, Cruse expanded upon an idea first raised by Du Bois in *The Souls of Black Folk* and then by Ralph Bunche in his research for Myrdal's *An American Dilemma* (1944).[46] At one level, Black history is characterized by African Americans' struggle to find their proper and acceptable status in American society, often between the extremes of autonomy and separation and full integration. In reality, neither of these ends was/is usually achieved.

In another instance, Cruse told his readers coming of age during the Black Power era that history was the most important component of their lives. In Woodsonian fashion, he proclaimed:

> The farther the Negro gets from his historical antecedents in time, the more tenuous becomes his conceptual ties, the emptier his social conception, the more superficial his visions. His one great and present hope is to know and understand his Afro-American history in the U.S. more profoundly. Failing that, and failing to create a new synthesis and a social theory of action, he will suffer the historical fate described by the philosopher who warned that "Those who cannot remember the past are condemned to repeat it.[47]

Cruse's conception of Black history is best understood as operating at several levels. One, he viewed it as being a struggle between nationalist and integrationist tendencies. Two, he maintained that an intimate knowledge of Black history was central to young black Americans' abilities to survive in the U.S. and to leave their mark on civilization. Cruse's observations are relevant to the hip-hop generation.

Vincent Harding's most noted publication is *There Is a River: The Black Struggle for Freedom in America* (1981). But a decade before this work appeared, he published an essay in *Negro Digest* and a brief pamphlet in which he laid out his philosophy of Black history. Harding, the first director of the Martin Luther King, Jr. Memorial Center in Atlanta and former director and chairperson of Institute of the Black World, opened *Negro Digest's* 1968 Black history issue with an article entitled "The Uses of the Afro-American Past." He adamantly supported the Woodsonian philosophy that "American history that ignores the central role of black people as actors is a falsified and misleading history." He believed that blacks' knowledge of history was "absolutely indispensable" in helping them place their lives in perspective. In an unapologetic tone, Harding proclaimed:

> The Afro-American past must remind black people that we are children of the humiliated and the oppressed, that our fathers were colonized and exploited subjects, and that the ghettos we have recently left are still too often filled with the stench of poverty and despair.

Harding called upon blacks to use their history as a force to help them push on and persevere. He declared that blacks should routinely remember their ancestors and create a future based upon how they in their times sacrificed for future generations. Like Woodson, he told blacks that if they forgot and/or did not live up to the contributions of their ancestors, they would "deserve nothing but the scorn of men and the judgments of the gods."[48]

In his pamphlet *Beyond Chaos: Black History and the Search for the New Land* (1970), Harding proclaimed that Black history sought to recognize blacks' contributions to American culture in an objective manner, yet with emotion, "writing history through tears." Harding did not share the optimism of many of his predecessors. Like Samuel Du Bois Cook, he stressed the more tragic component of Black history. Yet, unlike Cook, he argued that his ancestors' past could be used to help redefine American history. Rejecting notions of "great man" history, Harding declared that Black history focused on "exposure, disclosure, on reinterpretation of the entire American past." Black history in Harding's view was an ideal counter-narrative that could deconstruct American history, suggesting that "the American past upon which so much hope has been built never really existed, and probably never will." Harding believed that Black history needed to expose the suffering of black people accurately without glossing over the harsh realities. Harding reasoned that it was time to abandon the goal of integrating into American society, as John Hope Franklin had argued about a decade earlier. "Black history...is...the hard and unromantic reading of the experiences of black people in America. It is the groans, the tears, the chains, the songs, the prayers, the institutions." "It is," Harding professed, "a recording of the hope, even if we no longer participate in them. It is seeing not only what we have done, but what has been done to us."[49] Harding the pragmatist argued that Black history be used to instruct blacks as to the realities that they have faced and would face in America.

One of Harding's colleagues, Pan-African educator, poet, editor, Africana Studies pioneer, scholar-activist, and historian John Henrik Clarke (1915–1998) was a regular contributor to *Negro Digest* and *Black World*. His main concern was African history, but he occasionally delved into African American history. In "The Meaning of Black History," Clarke, a student of Arthur Schomburg, viewed African American history as being a key factor in helping blacks rebuild the black community and in instilling black people with pride, a psychological necessity for survival, he reasoned. "To some extent, Black history is a restoration project," Clarke asserted,

> The role of history and the history teacher in this restoration project is to give Black people a sense of pride in their past and memories that they can love and respect. The fulfillment will be in the total restoration of

the manhood and nationhood of Black people, wherever they live on earth.

Echoing Malcolm X, with whom he worked in Harlem, Clarke argued that Black history told blacks "where they have been where they are and what they still want to be." Black history in Clarke's view was synonymous with black identity. He called upon "scholar-activists" like himself to research Black history and "weld it into an instrument of our liberation." Like much of the black cultural nationalist rhetoric of the 1960s, Clarke did not detail how Black history could be used to liberate blacks. Nevertheless, he did certainly practice what he preached while teaching the history of African peoples at the grassroots level.[50]

Sterling Stuckey, who earned his Ph.D. in history from Northwestern University in 1971, authored one of the most critical analyses to date of the role of black historians. He also provided an intriguing definition of Black history. During the middle of the Black Power era, Stuckey echoed iconoclasts Carter G. Woodson and Harold Cruse in attacking professionally trained black historians and scholars for not producing innovative scholarship, which in his mind adequately challenged racist historiography while embracing an African American-centered approach. As he argued in his classic essay "Through the Prism of Folklore," Stuckey believed that folklore was an essential source for reconstructing the history of slavery from the perspective of the slaves themselves. He chastised "most black historians," "reflecting their training in white institutions of higher learning," for ignoring "the realities as projected" in slave folklore. Stuckey believed that the failure of black and white historians to seriously address slave folklore reflected their inability to make Black history what it really was in his mind, the "values and life styles of the supposedly inarticulate" black masses.[51]

Beyond serving as a window into the consciousness of enslaved blacks and the black masses, Stuckey maintained that Black history needed to serve as "a research light flashing over the terrain of the American night, illumining hidden, horrible truths." For Stuckey, a self-proclaimed ideological disciple of Du

Bois, Black history was to be used to better understand the "white institutional and personality development" that perpetuated racism and black oppression. In order to attack and dismantle American racism, Stuckey reasoned that it was necessary to carefully revisit and genuinely understand its deep historical roots. Stuckey was open about Black history's function as a political tool. He shared Du Bois's vision that "Art and Propaganda be one." "Black history recognizes the indivisibility of history and politics: As history has been used in the West to degrade people of color, black history must seek dignity for mankind," Stuckey noted. He was openly pessimistic about his contemporaries' abilities to embrace his approach to Black history. Based upon the middle-class black intellectual community's overall treatment of Du Bois and Paul Robeson while they were being prosecuted for their Communist leanings, Stuckey deromanticized Black historiography and called out his colleagues: "We cannot with absolute certitude state that this generation of black historians will have the integrity to tell the full story."[52]

Around the same time that Harding, Clarke, and Stuckey laid out their visions and interpretations of Black history, Earl E. Thorpe revised his *Negro Historians in the United States* (1958) by publishing *Black Historians: A Critique* (1971). Thorpe elaborated on his earlier study and stressed the aspect of struggle in the black experience. This shift in approach was most likely dictated by the Black Power era. "Black history is American history with the accent and emphasis on the point of view, attitude, and spirit of Afro-Americans, as well as on the events in which they have been either the actors or the objects of action." Thorpe added:

> Black history is that American history which, until the
> 1960s, was viewed by white America with contempt
> and disdain or ignored altogether, just as black people
> themselves were viewed and treated. Men tend either
> to deny or force out of consciousness the evil that they
> do. Much of black history, then, is the story of the cru-

elties and inhumanities which a powerful white majority has inflicted on a defenseless black minority.[53]

Thorpe posited that the "central theme of black history is the
quest of Afro-Americans for freedom, equality, and manhood."[54]

In the immediate aftermath of the Black Power era, discussions concerning the question "What is Black history?" continued to be of some concern among black scholars and historians.
A look at two very different views highlights the diversity of
opinion that persisted. In the closing of the 1970s, poet and longtime activist Haki R. Madhubuti captured many of the sentiments
of black nationalists' interpretations of Black history's meaning
and function. In an essay in *Enemies: The Clash of Races* (1978),
Madhubuti echoed Stuckey and argued that whites had historically used history as an "effective weapon" of war to conquer
African Americans. He envisioned Black history, "the sum total"
of black people, as being "a fighting history—a war history
documenting our struggle against white domination." Like others
before him, Madhubuti maintained that Black history was dominated by the lives of the black masses. "History is produced from
the gut of the people...the history of a people is the survival and
development record of that people. It tells of their accomplishments and defeats, of their ups and downs," Madhubuti added,
"One of the greatest accomplishments of a people is to produce
their own history."[55] This cultural nationalist chastised blacks for
not taking control of their history and, in turn, allowing whites to
control a significant part of their identity. Black history for Madhubuti was, in essence, the key to self-knowledge.

In the immediate post-Black Power era, Benjamin Quarles
(1904–1996)[56], a longtime professor of history at Morgan State
University, offered a much different view of what Black history
meant. As a well-known and respected historian, he published
"Black History's Diversified Clientele," in which he explored
how Black history functioned and was being used and defined in
distinctly different ways by four groups of people: the black
masses, "black revolutionary nationalists," professional black
scholars, and whites in general. Black history for "the black rank

and file," Quarles claimed, was fundamentally a therapeutic version of the African American experience, a hero-worshipping
rendition of history aimed at creating "a sense of racial pride and
personal worth." On the other hand, black nationalists in
Quarles's view used history "as grievance collecting, a looking
back in anger...Black nationalist history is essentially the story
of a powerful white majority inspiring its will upon a defenseless
black minority."[57] This approach also sought to explicitly use
Black history in the struggle for liberation and nation-building.
Sterling Stuckey, John Henrik Clarke, Vincent Harding, Malcolm X, and others would all fit into this category.

Quarles's third group, "black academicians," is similar to
the first two groups in their use of Black history as a repository
of pride. At the same time, implicit in Quarles's view of an African American academician's view of Black history is objectivity,
something that he himself embraced. He asserted that this group
ideally avoided "passionate and deeply emotional language."
Quarles was very straightforward in how Black history should be
viewed by white Americans. "The aim of black history for white
readers is twofold: first to eliminate the myth that our country's
past was rosy and romantic...and second, to illustrate the centrality of the black American in our national experience." Quarles
identified Black history for whites as being one of America's
"tragic components."[58] Though Quarles admitted that his article
was a "short excursion" into various viewpoints on the function
and meaning of Black history, the brevity of his essay leaves
many important issues unexplored and glossed over.

Quarles's description of each of his four "publics" lacks
detail and oversimplified how certain people have viewed Black
history. His "black academicians" could have been broken down
into many different subgroups. Professionally trained black historians could have been subdivided based upon their scholarly
approaches, strategies, generational affiliations, and foci. He
seemed to homogenize black historians. Quarles also seemed to
have subtly dismissed the approach of the black revolutionary
nationalistic interpretation of Black history as not being as rigor-

ous or relevant as that of objective, professionally trained historians. Although Quarles did not really directly propose his own authentic philosophy of Black history—he appeared to identify himself with the "black academicians'" approach—his essay is of value in that he acknowledged that Black history meant multiple things to a range of people. This, after all, is the fundamental theme of this chapter. Black history has indeed meant different things to different people during different time periods. It will continue to be defined in a range of different manners by various individuals and schools of thought based upon inevitable changing circumstances.

During the 1980s, many key definitions about Black history were put forth, corresponding with the substantial growth in African American historiography and the black historical profession. There seems to be a consensus among historians that Black history was mainstreamed and legitimized in the U.S. academy during the 1960s and 1970s and that this era produced some of the most pathbreaking historical scholarship in the field. Major transformations in African American history and historiography occurred during every major period in twentieth century U.S. history. For hip-hop generation historians, the 1980s was a very important decade. Historical scholarship from this decade as well as the 1990s was crucial in molding hip-hop generation historians' perspectives. Many genres of Black history developed and matured during the 1980s. Several important books on Black history as a discipline and profession were published in the 1980s, namely *The State of Afro-American History: Past, Present, and Future* (1986) edited by Darlene Clark Hine and August Meier's and Elliott Rudwick's *Black History and the Historical Profession, 1915–1980* (1986). Black history as an important source and vehicle of pride, self-definition, and liberation continued through the 1980s in part in response to racial oppression prevalent during the anti-civil rights Reagan years. In his popular book *There Is a River: The Black Struggle for Freedom in America* (1981), Vincent Harding eloquently likened Black history to a river. He asserted:

We may sense that the river of black struggle is people,
but it is also the hope, the movement, the transforma-
tive power that humans create and that create them, us,
and makes them, us, new persons. So we black people
are the river; the river is us. The river is in us, created
by us, flowing out of us, surrounding us, re-creating us
and this entire nation. I refer to the American nation
without hesitation, for the black river in the United
States has always taken on more than blackness. The
dynamics and justice of its movement have continually
gathered others to itself, have persistently filled other
men and women with the force of its vision, its indomi-
table hope. And at its best the river of our struggle has
moved consistently toward the ocean of humankind's
most courageous hopes for freedom in integrity, for-
ever seeking...the right to develop our whole being.[59]

In 1983 in *The Journal of American History*, August
Meier—arguably the leading white historian of black America
from the early 1960s until the early 1980s—critiqued Harding,
Mary Frances Berry, and John W. Blassingame, for the so-called
"pessimistic air" of their scholarship. Meier contended that the
"militant" and "radical" tone of these black historians abandoned
the idealistic "hopefulness and optimism" stressed by John Hope
Franklin and Benjamin Quarles.[60] It appears that Meier was unprepared to deal with younger black historians active in the post-
Civil Rights era who, unlike Franklin and Quarles, disregarded
hyperobjectivity and wrote with a great deal of emotion and anger. While their scholarship did evolve over time, both Franklin
and Quarles remained committed to objective, nonemotional,
integrationist history throughout their long and impressive careers. William H. Harris agreed with Harding that Black history
needed to focus on the multiple forms of oppression overcome
by black people. In defense of Berry, Blassingame, and Harding,
Harris believed that the pessimism expressed by his colleagues is
"easily understood when one does perceive our time from the
perspective of the black experience. It is a pessimism that I share

as a historian and a sentiment that I share as a historian."[61] Franklin and Quarles probably shared much of the pessimism of their progeny; however, they could not as easily express it during the periods in which they came of age.

By the early 1980s, Lerone Bennett, Jr. (b. 1928) had clearly established himself as a seasoned, leading African American historian, one who had popularized Black history in a manner very similar to Woodson. In 1954, a year after becoming associate editor for *Jet*, Bennett became the associate editor for *Ebony*. Several years later, he became the magazine's first senior editor. By 1987, he was named executive editor of *Ebony*. Bennett almost single-handedly popularized Black history among the many *Ebony* and *Jet* readers. *Ebony*, founded in 1945, routinely featured a history section in the contents of its issues, mainly from the 1960s through the 1970s and 1980s. Beginning in the 1970s, Bennett published more than a few articles under the heading "Great Moments in Black History." From the 1960s through the present, Bennett published countless passionate, relevant, wide-reaching, and at times sophisticated historical articles in *Ebony*. He has also published many books, his most famous being *Before the Mayflower* (first published in 1962). Perhaps inspired by the growth and mainstreaming of Black history as a discipline and field of study in the 1960s and 1970s, between 1981 and 1985 Bennett published three major articles in *Ebony* that creatively probed into the deeper meanings of Black history.[62]

In a provocative essay, "Listen to the Blood: The Meaning of Black History," a speech that he originally delivered at the annual Association for the Study of Afro-American Life and History meeting in 1980, Bennett laid out and discussed several different ways that blacks have interpreted, and should view in the future, the meaning of Black history. Many blacks, Bennett posited, interpreted Black history as being dictated by God in "mysterious ways" and believed that history "moved at the behest of other forces—charms, curses, and so forth." In this sense, he suggested that blacks have often viewed history, as he routinely seems to, as a spiritual concept bound to blacks' daily lives, to their daily actions and beliefs. Bennett also suggested that during the modern Civil Rights Movement, especially during the 1960s, the "God-controlled" notion of Black history gained popularity. As a scholarly field of study, Bennett believed that Black history needed to be viewed within the broader scope of world history and that it was "a history of the insider outsiders. And it must be interpreted...both in terms of its particularity and its universality." In other words, he believed that Black history shared certain commonalities with others' histories throughout the world, but at the same time was distinctly different and unique.[63]

Bennett stressed that Black history was "real," something much deeper than "a story in a book or a career or a monograph in a scholarly journal." He noted that Black history was relevant to the daily lives of African Americans. He told black people:

> You *are* that history. And there is nothing you can do
> in history that will free you of the historical responsi-
> bility of being born at a certain time, in a certain place,
> with a certain skin color. You cannot, no matter what
> you do, escape the meaning history gave you and that
> history demands of you.

Bennett believed that African Americans living in the present owed a great debt to those who laid the foundations for their existence. His message is especially relevant to the hip-hop generation. "We are responsible," Bennett proclaimed, "totally responsible, not only for ourselves but for the whole of the Black experience. For it is only through us that the dreams of the past can be fulfilled. It is only through us that the first slave can reach the finish line."[64] Bennett's ideal conception of Black history would have required the blacks of his times to sacrifice. Unfortunately, today it is harder to convince members of the hip-hop generation that this approach to Black history is necessary. They are being socialized in one of the most individualistic, anti-historical periods ever in American history and culture.

In another article, "Why Black History is Important to You," Bennett defined history in an all encompassing manner:

> History is everything; it is everywhere. It is an all-pervading atmosphere, an ambiance, a milieu. History to us is what water is to fish...History is knowledge, identity, and power. History is knowledge because it is a practical perspective and a practical orientation. It orders and organizes our world and valorizes our projects.

Bennett sought to convince *Ebony* readers that history was much more important than most probably thought that it was. He acknowledged that Black history had multiple expressions, appearing as an ideology, a scholarly discipline, and a source of pride and energy. Bennett argued that Black history needed to be functional in its meaning. Blacks, in his opinion, needed to "base their vision of the future on the Black past and...must justify their calls by a historical analysis of the Black experience." Bennett went a step further declaring that "no one interested in mobilizing Black people can escape the necessity of thinking historically." Bennett's argument should not be overlooked by members of the hip-hop generation. Bennett lamented that many viewed Black history as "an intellectual ghetto" and "a minor-league pastime" and pointed out how it was an essential part of U.S. history. Echoing Vincent Harding's ideas from the Black Power era, he suggested that Black history constituted a "total critique" of what most Americans, whites, perceived as being standard U.S. history. Black history, he noted, challenged the uncritical vision of America as being the "land of the free." Bennett also believed that there was a revealing universality to Black history, that it was similar to the histories of many people throughout the world and was "the history of man taken to the nth degree."[65]

Bennett's observation is quite interesting and relates to the present state of hip-hop culture. There is a certain humanity in African American history that many people, especially oppressed people, seem to be able to relate to and become captivated by. The popularity of hip-hop music and culture, which draws directly and indirectly from the black historical experience, demonstrates the relevancy and currency of Bennett's comments. Hip-hop music, hands down, is the most popular form of music throughout the world. The majority of consumers of hip-hop music are white youths. Beyond being attracted to the flash, flair, and image of hip-hop culture, as Tricia Rose has suggested in *Black Noise: Rap Music and Black Culture in Contemporary America* (1994), and as Bakari Kitwana has updated in *Why White Kids Love Hip Hop* (2005), many non-black hip-hop fans listen to rap music in order to enter a black world that the popular dominant white culture frowns upon and misrepresents. At the same time, more than a few white hip-hop fans also relate to many of the messages of struggle implicit in hip-hip music. In his recently released documentary "Tupac: Resurrection" (2003), a must-see for all hip-hop fans, Tupac offered some thoughts concerning the appeal of his music among whites. He welcomed his white listeners and explained that many of his white fans related to the universally human aspects of his message. Such is the case with African American history, a history that is, arguably more than any other people's history, characterized by a struggle for the most fundamental human rights.

One of the last major articles that Bennett seems to have published in *Ebony* that directly delves into the deeper meanings of Black history appeared in 1985. In "Voices of the Past Speak to the Present," which appeared in issues of *Ebony* in the 1990s upon several occasions, Bennett summarized his strong belief that Black history needed to be functional, pragmatic, and this-worldly in orientation. Black history, he eloquently maintained,

> is a challenge and a call...To understand Black history today is to understand that something or somebody in that history is calling your name. For in and through Black history, the voices of the past speak to us personally, calling us by name, asking us what we are doing and what we are prepared to do to ensure that the

slaves and activists and martyrs did not dream and die
in vain...Black history is a perpetual conversation in
which men and women speak to one another, echoing
one another, blending together into a mighty chorus
which contrasts and combines different themes.

Bennett called Black history a "living history," a series of ongoing interactions between various generations of blacks, living
and deceased. He stressed that African Americans must approach
Black history "actively and not passively." He ascertained:

We must become, as we read and celebrate, slaves and
sharecroppers, victims and martyrs...and rebels. We
must relate these images to the challenges and opportunities of our own lives, or we shall learn nothing and
remember nothing.[66]

Bennett's belief that blacks need to "actively" get involved
in history is reminiscent of Woodson and Carr. Central to
Woodson's philosophy was that black children reenact scenes
from Black history in plays and pageants. He also instructed
young blacks to interact with their elders in order to secure first-
hand accounts of the past. Carr, though unconcerned with Black
history, encouraged historians to use their imaginations in reconstructing history. If one were to embrace Bennett's approach to
Black history, one would certainly need to have a productive
imagination. Becoming a slave or a sharecropper would have
been a great challenge to many blacks in the mid-1980s. Now,
we would have to take more extreme measures to realize Bennett's approach. Hands-on African American museums, such as
the state-of-the-art project at the Charles Wright Museum of African American History in Detroit, Michigan are steps in the
right direction.
    Bennett's passion, which he still possesses today, is refresh-
ing. He adamantly maintains that African Americans need to
know their history. In the late 1980s, after supplying *Ebony*
readers with a 20-question multiple choice quiz on Black history,

Bennett chastised those blacks not well-versed in the history of their people. "If you scored less than a 70, you are, according to Black history partisans, culturally deprived and should run to the nearest library and check out a book on Black history."[67] In the 2003 February issue of *Ebony*, Bennett posed a similar challenge to his readers. Bennett's intensity is appreciated and still much needed, but *Ebony*, as well as other popular African American magazines, needs to initiate new strategies to reach the hip-hop generation. A Black history quiz or a group of biographies on black "firsts" is not going to cut it.

In the mid-1980s, V.P. Franklin, the prolific editor of *The Journal of African American History*, provided a definition of Black history that focused on blacks' "predominant cultural values." He argued that slavery, more than any other collective experience in Black history, shaped blacks' post-emancipation worldview and history: "that it was the common experience of slavery that served as the foundation for the 'cultural value system' that was handed down from the African to their American-born offspring, the Afro-American." Franklin maintained that "since more than one generation of Afro-Americans was victimized by enslavement in the United States, certain values remained relevant for one generation to the next and indeed became 'core values' of the Afro-American experience." Franklin identified the main "core values" of Black history as being striving towards freedom, resistance, a quest for education, and self-determination.[68] Such a thematic approach is useful and must be adjusted to suit the specific time periods under investigation.

In the 1980s and 1990s, Robert L. Harris, Jr. presented some intriguing definitions of Black history. In an article entitled "Coming of Age: The Transformation of Afro-American Historiography," Harris not only noted that Black history needed to be interpreted "within the context of American history," but added that it needed to be analyzed within the context of Afro-diasporan history. Simply put, "events on the African continent and in the African Diaspora have profoundly affected Afro-American thought and action."[69] Indeed, the African American experience is better understood when viewed within the context of Africans' experiences throughout the Diaspora. Many important connections can be made. In a brief, informative pamphlet first published in 1985 and then re-released in 1992, Harris defined African American history as "the study of the thought and actions of people of African ancestry in the United States over time and place." He explained that we studied African American history in order "to understand the positions that black people have occupied in American society, their efforts to cope with their status, and their successes and failures in pursuing full equality.[70] While Harris's definitions are straightforward, he did not really provide a philosophical discussion of the deeper meanings of Black history, something that was needed during the 1990s.

One of the most recent and extensive assessments of the deeper philosophical meanings of Black history, which critiques Harris's ideas as well as those of many others, belongs to W.D. Wright, Professor Emeritus of History at Southern Connecticut State University. In 2002, he published two studies that critically explore African American history and historiography, *Critical Reflections on Black History* and *Black History and Black Identity: A Call for a New Historiography*. Wright offers several definitions of Black history in these think-pieces. Wright surmised:

> As a philosophical, perceptual, and historio-graphical understanding, Black history should be understood as Black history that focuses on Black people, their identity, their culture, their social life, their psychology, and the way they have used their ethnic, group, and personal attributes to make history in America and to contribute to histories, countries, and peoples elsewhere on the globe.[71]

In another instance, Wright, echoing Du Bois's "double-consciousness" theory, stresses that Black history has "two dimensions: a Black dimension and an American dimension." For

him, both "tracks" must be acknowledged because they both impacted "the functioning, development, and reality of the
other...Black history, as a history, has never been an either-or
history, where Black people did this but not that."[72] Wright's
idea that Black history must be approached as a part of American
history is important, especially since the Black Power era university courses in Black history have all too often been taught sepa-
rately, as being distinctly different from so-called standard,
mainstream U.S. history. Isolating the African American experience gives it the attention that it deserves, yet at the same time
allows for professors of U.S. history—the vast majority of whom
are white—to inject aspects of Black history, usually in the form
of token leaders or select incidents here and there, without really
highlighting the centrality of African Americans to U.S. life, history, and culture. While it would be very easy to defend placing
black America at the center of U.S. history, very few U.S. historians teach U.S. history from such a revealing vantage point.
Like Robert L. Harris, Wright also points out that Black history
"in a whole and deeper manner" needs to be linked to African
history as well.

In one of the most recent general surveys of the African
American experience, *Fire from the Soul: A History of the African American Struggle* (2003), Donald Spivey defines Black
history as being directly related to the present. Black history for
Spivey is an essential key for understanding the present battle
against racism. "How can appropriate programs be implemented
to combat racism if the roots of the dilemma are not understood?
They cannot." Spivey ascertains: "Solutions flow from understanding history. The past is our source of enlightenment and
wisdom...What we know for sure is that failure to embrace the
past will yield a problematic outcome in the present and future."[73] Without really providing a philosophical inquiry into the
deeper meaning of Black history, Spivey advocates an openly
pragmatic vision of Black history. His pragmatism echoes the
sentiments of many black historians from the Black Power era.
He also shares their pessimistic critique of the future. He re-

marked that "the historical barometer is a stern warning of peril-
ous waters ahead."[74] Spivey's message is relevant to the hip-hop
generation, most of whom appear to think that the present cur-
rents of time are yielding smooth sailing.

Philosophies of Black Women's History

Thus far, the conceptualization of Black history that I have
addressed has been offered by male historians, all black with the
exception of Herbert Aptheker, whom Robin Kelley dubbed a
"black historian" based upon his ideologies. As I explore in
Chapter 4, black women, though operating in nonprofessional
capacities until the 1940s, acted as historians since the late
1800s. About a decade before Du Bois's *The Souls of Black Folk*
(1903) appeared, Gertrude E.H. Bustill Mossell published *The
Work of the Afro-American Woman* (1894) in which she asserted
that "the intellectual history of a people or nation constitutes to a
greater degree the very heart of its life" and "is always of value
in determining the past and future of it."[75] Other black women
writers of history during the era of Jim Crow segregation shared
similar ideologies. Nonetheless, professional black women historians began to define history in greater depth with the emergence
of Black Women's history as a subfield of historical inquiry.

During the 1970s, 1980s, and 1990s, historians, especially
black women, began to offer definitions of Black history that
acknowledged that the history of black women was distinctly
different than that of black men. Prior to the 1970s and 1980s,
black men dominated scholarly discussions of what constituted
Black history. This has something to do with the fact that black
women were largely excluded from the historical profession. It
was not until 1940 that a black woman, Marion Thompson
Wright, earned a Ph.D. in history in the United States. During
the remainder of the 1940s and 1950s, about half a dozen black
women earned doctorates in history. The next group of black
women to earn Ph.D.s in history did so in the Black Power and
immediate post-Black Power era.

Several publications in the early 1970s sparked scholars' active interest in Black Women's history and studies.[76] In 1970, *The Black Woman: An Anthology* was published and its editor, Toni Cade, opened the volume by candidly discussing the problems faced when turning to traditional fields of academic study for the ultimate goal of black women's liberation. Her assessment of history was critical and was laced with the pessimism popular during the Black Power era.

> History, of course, offers us much data...and much more difficulty. For the very movements that could provide us with insights are those movements that are traditionally taught in the schools or made available without glamorized distortions by show business...But even our skimpy knowledge of these phenomena shows us something: the need for unified effort and the value of a vision of a society substantially better than the existing one.[77]

Cade's notion of history for black women suggested that it should be practical, helping black women construct a better future. It is surprising that none of the more than thirty contributors to *The Black Woman* focused on Black Women's history.

In 1971, *The Black Scholar* devoted an entire issue to black women. Angela Davis's "Reflections on the Black Woman's Role in the Community of Slaves"—which she wrote while in jail with limited resources—was the volume's main historical essay and represents an early attempt at exploring issues in Black Women's history. An outspoken civil and human rights activist, Davis broke new scholarly ground, addressing some of the issues that Deborah Gray White would address more than a decade later in her classic study on enslaved black women in the antebellum South. In concluding her essay, Davis called upon her contemporaries to study Black Women's history and she defined it by linking it to the struggles faced by black women during the Black Power era. "The black woman in her true historical contours must be resurrected. We, the black women of today, must accept the full weight of a legacy wrought in blood by our mothers in chains." Drawing connections between the past and the present, she concluded:

> Our fight, while identical in spirit, reflects different conditions and thus implies different paths of struggle. But, as heirs to a tradition of supreme perseverance and heroic resistance, we must hasten to take our place whenever our people are forging on towards freedom.[78]

One of the first major scholarly texts on Black Women's history was a volume of primary sources by Gerda Lerner, *Black Women in White America: A Documentary History* (1972). Lerner, co-founder of the first Women's History Master's degree program in the U.S. in 1972, argued that Black history was essential for countering "racial indoctrination," creating a "truly democratic nonracist society," and for "arousing" within blacks a sense of racial pride and self-respect. Lerner avowed that black and white historians should play a key role in writing Black history. Lerner argued that Black history, which she perceived as being historians' interpretations of blacks' past, should be debated by black and white historians because of their different backgrounds and approaches. The results, she believed, would be fruitful. "In the clash of opinions, in debate, in the juxtaposition of different interpretations, a richer and fuller and more solidly based history will emerge."[79] In addressing the need for conventional U.S. historians to address blacks and women in history, Lerner remarked that "no white historian can ever approach his work without recognizing that there were black people in the American past whose contributions and whose impacts must be considered. Similarly, I believe it is necessary to recognize that there is a female aspect to all history." Black women, Lerner observed, had been rendered "doubly invisible" by most U.S. historians.[80]

Six years after Lerner's path-breaking volume appeared, Sharon Harley and Rosalyn Terborg-Penn, two important members of the second wave of black women historians, edited the

first major anthology of essays devoted to components of Black
Women's history. Harley and Terborg-Penn outlined the significance of Black Women's history in a succinct and straightforward manner:

> The history of the Afro-American woman and her role
> in the making of America has been neglected by histo-
> rians, just as the history of women in the United States
> has been neglected. Much of the history has been of the
> black woman's struggle for equality in America. The
> struggle has been against sexism, which all women
> have experienced. It has been also against racism,
> which both black men and black women have experi-
> enced. This struggle has been compounded because at
> times white women created barriers to achieving the
> goal of equality for black women. Other times black
> men stood as obstacles to the development of their own
> women. For the most part, racism has been the greatest
> obstacle to the black woman's struggle.[81]

Expanding upon Lerner's notion of black women as being "doubly invisible," Harley and Terborg-Penn highlighted that racial
and sexual discrimination and oppression constituted "the historical plight of Afro-American women throughout the history of
the United States."[82]

Another important study that addressed Black Women's
history was also published in 1978. In *Black Macho and the
Myth of the Superwoman*, self-proclaimed black feminist Michele Wallace envisioned Black history as being important in terms
of shedding light on the "misunderstanding between the black
man and the black woman, a misunderstanding as old as slavery." Wallace incorporated the scholarship of slavery historians
into her polemic and acknowledged the significance of Black
Women's history. At the same time, she also challenged the
strategy of using Black history as a source of pride. Instead, she
called upon black women to create their own legacy and not get
caught up in past successes or failures.

> Yes, it is very important that we never forget the trag-
> edy of our history or how racist white people have
> been or how the black man has let us down. But all of
> that must be set in its proper perspective. It belongs to
> the past and we must belong to the future. The future is
> something we can control.

Wallace pleaded to her fellow black women, "The imperative is clear: Either we will make history or remain the victims of it."[83] Wallace's declaration that black women needed to "make history" was her response to the fact that the popular press and mainstream historians ignored the historical and contemporary realities of black women. She believed that historical scholarship was important, but maintained that actions spoke louder than words ever could. At bottom, she wanted black women to become proactive agents of the historical process. She found little value in celebrating or dwelling upon black women's past accomplishments.

In 1972, Gerda Lerner had claimed that it was "too early to attempt the writing of a social history of black women." In many regards, her opinion held up. The first major, scholarly, interpretive historical monograph on black women by a professional black woman scholar was editor, journalist, and social historian Paula Giddings's *When and Where I Enter: The Impact of Black Women on Race and Sex in America* (1984). For Giddings, Black Women's history was "at once a personal and objective understanding. It is personal because the women whose blood runs through my veins breathe amidst statistics." Giddings still considered her work to be "an objective enterprise, because one must put such experiences into historical context, find in them a rational meaning so that the forms that shape our own lives may be understood." As many black historians from the Black Power era argued, Giddings advocated that Black history—in this case Black Women's history—should not apologize for being from an emotional, insider vantage point and must be made relevant to the present. Giddings lamented that black women were largely marginalized and tokenized by black men and white feminist thinkers. "Black women have a history of their own," Giddings asserted, "one which reflects their distinct concerns, values, and the role they have played as both Afro-Americans and women. And the unique status has had an impact on both racial and feminist values."[84]

A year after Giddings's path-breaking study appeared, Deborah Gray White, at the time an associate professor of history and Africana Studies at Rutgers University, noted that Black Women's history must be envisioned in a manner distinctly different from male-centered Black history.

> Few scholars who study black women fail to note that black women suffer a double oppression: that shared by all African-Americans and that shared by most women. Every economic and political index demonstrates the black woman's virtual powerlessness in American society at large. A consequence of the double jeopardy and powerlessness is the black woman's invisibility.[85]

In writing her pioneering study on enslaved black women, White lamented that the history of black women, especially during the antebellum era, had been ignored by white America and black men. White was creative in her reconstruction of Black Women's history, relying largely upon the WPA interviews with former slaves, anthropological theories, and other scholarly vantage points of analysis. White and others were in the process of creating interpretations for "the yet unwritten history of the American black woman."[86] This point needs to be highlighted. The actual history of African American women of course dates back to the origins of the African American presence. The sustained, systematically chronicled, interpreted history of African American women written by professionally trained scholars is remarkably young, no more than several decades old. When viewed within this sociohistorical context, scholarship in Black Women's history is quite fascinating, representing one of the most revisionist, revolutionary subfields within the study of Black history.

By the late 1980s and the 1990s, many black women historians as well as a handful of white women historians contributed to the evolution of Black Women's history, including Darlene Clark Hine, Dorothy Sterling, Beverly Guy-Sheftall, Jacqueline Jones, Jacqueline Rouse, Cynthia Neverdon-Morton, Elsa Barkley Brown, Evelyn Brooks Higginbotham, Bettye Collier-Thomas, Nell Irvin Painter, Wilma King, Linda Reed, Rosalyn Terborg-Penn, Deborah Gray White, Elizabeth Clark-Lewis, Stephanie Shaw, Francille Rusan-Wilson, Tera Hunter, Wanda Hendricks, and Chana Kai Lee.[87]

Darlene Clark Hine, who made her most significant contributions to Black Women's history while a John A. Hannah Professor of History at Michigan State University, has been largely responsible for helping institutionalize Black Women's history during the last several decades. She has defined Black Women's history upon several occasions. In the "Editor's Preface" of *Black Women in America: An Historical Encyclopedia* (1993), Hine defined Black Women's history as a discipline which needed to be directly related to the contemporary conditions facing black women. "We cannot accurately comprehend either our hidden potential or the full range of problems that besiege us until we know about the successful struggles that generations of foremothers waged against virtually insurmountable obstacles." She continued, "We can, and will, chart a coherent future and win essential opportunities with a clear understanding of the past in all its pain and glory."[88]

Echoing generations of black historians before her, Hine openly linked the past to the present in defining Black Women's history.

> History has its own power and Black women more than ever before need its truths to challenge hateful assumptions, negative stereotypes, myths, lies, and distortions about our role in the progress of time. Black women need to know the contradistinctions and ironies that our

unique state presents...Yet it is not enough only to
know about the injustices and exploitation Black
women have endured...As we garner inspiration contained in past and present Black women's lives, we acquire the power to take history further and the will to
use the power of history to construct a better future.[89]

Hine's statement resonates with the clear influence of Woodson
who advocated that Black history be used to combat racism
while inspiring blacks. In another instance, Hine observed that
Black Women's history was instructive in helping us piece together the various processes of history-making. Hine remarked:

Black women's history compels the individual to come
to grips more completely with all of the components of
identity. Through the study of Black women it becomes increasingly obvious how historians shape,
make, or construct history, and why we omit, ignore,
and sometimes distort the lives of people on the mar-
gins.[90]

Towards a Comprehensive Definition
of Black History

My examination of how Black history has been defined,
theorized, and envisioned clearly demonstrates that there is a
range of ways to conceptualize Black history. I have examined
the ideas of those whom I consider to be the most important and
insightful scholars in terms of philosophizing the deeper meanings of Black history. I have not covered all historians', scholars', and intellectuals' definitions of Black history. I have given
attention to many of the key thinkers. Black historians, as well as
a few white historians, have defined the purpose, meaning, and
function of Black history as a philosophy, concept, and field of
study in a variety of manners. Their definitions have been shaped
by many factors, especially by the sociohistorical contexts in

which they existed. All of the historians surveyed in this chapter have offered some useful definitions of Black history which, taken together, help us better understand what Black history is and means.

As a field of study, Black history is the interpretation, application, and rigorous study of the Black past with all its complexity. Though a vital part of American history, it is different than conventional, "white-stream" U.S. history. The black experience is an experience dominated by struggle. Black history is, in essence, a history of struggle and survival. It is a bittersweet history. It is a history of great hopes, great despair, great achievements, and great failures. It is a rollercoaster ride of optimism and pessimism. It is one of the most challenging subjects to teach. The teacher of Black history must be able to maintain a delicate balance between themes of victimization and perseverance. In order to really appreciate Black history, the harsh oppression that generations of African Americans have experienced from the era of the slave trade through the "nadir" and beyond must be acknowledged. This is often an unpopular topic. It makes many people feel uncomfortable, guilty, dumbfounded, angry, and confused. In the mid 1990s, several black scholars argued that a significant part of the African and African American experience needed to be viewed within the context of genocide and holocaust. In *Yurugu: An African-Centered Critique of European Cultural Thought and Behavior* (1994), Marimba Ani introduced the term *Maafa* to describe "over five hundred years of warfare and genocide experienced by African people under enslavement and colonialism and their continued impact on African people throughout the world."[91] Other scholars, like S.E. Anderson, author of *The Black Holocaust for Beginners* (1995), have used the politically loaded term "holocaust" to describe the impact of the slave trade and the middle passage on blacks. Black holocaust or *Maafa* studies are unpopular, but necessary. Such approaches challenge us to acknowledge the seemingly insurmountable obstacles that blacks overcame. Delving into the mad levels of oppression endured by generations of blacks helps us better understand blacks' historical achievements.

When one looks back at all that blacks have overcome, it is truly amazing. Afrocentric psychiatrist Na'im Akbar has captured this in addressing slavery.

> The survival of the fundamental human initiative among African-Americans, despite over 300 years of the most inhuman conditions ever experienced by any people in the current historical epoch, is indicative of human resilience. Despite the lingering vestiges ... recovery has been substantial.

Akbar continued in *Chains and Images of Psychological Slavery*: "The triumphs of America's former slaves far exceed the deficits attributed to us. African-American people exist more as a monument of human accomplishment than the remains of human destruction."[92] Joseph L. White and James H. Cones, III have expanded upon Akbar's ideas in identifying five major characteristics of African American psychology, one of the most important components they address being resilience, "the capacity to rebound from a major setback or tragedy. In the Black experience, this means more than stoicism or a return to the status quo; it involves going beyond healing and recovery."[93] So much of the African American experience has been marked by overcoming and rebounding from many different types of tragedies and setbacks.

Black history is, of course, not just one experience. Like the histories of other groups, it is comprised of many diverse experiences. When analyzing the history of African Americans, we must acknowledge that blacks' day-to-day lives in many different time periods depended upon a host of factors including region, religious orientations, intraracial dynamics, gender and sex, class, legal and extra-legal forms of oppression, broader social, political, economic, and cultural transformations, change over time, and other components. When envisioned as such, Black history becomes what all histories are: unstatic, dynamic, and complex.

Black history is the total experience of black people in the United States. At the same time, Africa and the diaspora can not be taken out of the picture. African Americans are an African people, African descendants. Many scholars have convincingly argued that African Americans are culturally an African people and have, in turn, Africanized American culture. Throughout history, many landmark events in Africa and the Diaspora, especially the Caribbean, have impacted black Americans in meaningful ways. The Haitian Revolution, the abolition of slavery throughout the Caribbean, Paul Bogle's rebellion, the construction of the Panama Canal, the colonial conquest, colonization, decolonization of Africa, and even the explosion of Reggae and Dancehall music have all influenced black life in the United States in varying degrees.

The African American experience, African Americans' lives in the formal United States, has lasted from 1789 until the present. This experience of 216 years can be broken down into three major broad periods: (1) 1789–1865, 76 years, 35.2% of the total experience, (2) 1865–1965, 100 years, 46.3% of the total experience, and (3) 1965–2005, 40 years, 18.5% of the total experience.

In 1789 the U.S. Constitution was ratified and supported the oppression of African Americans with three specific articles. Article I, Section 3 contained the famous 3/5 clause; Article I, Section 9. 1. allowed for the slave trade to take place in the United States until 1808; and Article IV, Section 2. 3. basically made it unconstitutional for a slave to run away. In 1865, the 13th Amendment was ratified and abolished slavery. Between these two turning points in U.S. history, the vast majority of African Americans were slaves. The first federal census of 1790 indicated that there were 697,897 enslaved blacks and 59,557 free blacks. In 1820, there were 1,538,125 enslaved blacks and 233,504 free blacks. And in 1860, there were 3,953,160 enslaved blacks and about 488,000 free blacks.[94] It must also be recognized that oftentimes free blacks in the North and South were no more free than slaves. They were, in John Hope Franklin's terms, "quasi free." Leonard Curry's research has demonstrated that free blacks in the urban North were oppressed in many ways. They were: politically disenfranchised, forced into low-paying, insecure jobs, segregated, often the victims of racial violence, educationally disadvantaged, and were victims of high mortality rates. Speaking about free blacks in the antebellum South, Ira Berlin commented:

> Once free, blacks generally remained at the bottom of the social order, despised by whites, burdened with increasingly oppressive racial proscriptions, and subjected to verbal and physical abuse. Free Negroes stood outside the direct government of a master, but in the eyes of many whites their place in society had not been significantly altered. They were slaves without masters.[95]

Of course, some free blacks in the North and South were able to transcend such limitations. But they were exceptions.

The years from 1865 until 1965 were marked by African Americans' struggles for basic civil and human rights. Beginning with the abolition of slavery in 1865 and ending with the passage of the Voting Rights Act in 1965, which abolished literacy tests and poll taxes as requirements to vote, this 100-year period included Reconstruction (1865–1877); the "nadir" (the low point of black life from 1877 through the early 1920s); World Wars I and II and the Korean War; the Great Depression; the era of Jim Crow segregation from the Plessy v. Ferguson case in 1896 until Brown v. Board of Education, Topeka, Kansas (1954); the Cold War; and the modern or classic Civil Rights Movement (roughly 1954–1966). Despite the continuing oppression of African Americans and the permanence of institutional racism, it is safe to say that from 1965 until the present African Americans have enjoyed most, by no means all, of their fundamental civil rights. Of course, many would argue the accuracy of such a conclusion.

But, for the sake of argument, I will say that for about 40 years, less than 20% of blacks' total experience in the U.S., African Americans have had most of their basic civil rights.

By looking at Black history within the broad timeline provided here, it becomes clear that the vast majority of the African American experience in the United States, about 82% of the total experience, has been spent in some form of overt and obvious struggle for basic equal rights and justice. And the struggle still continues. When one looks at the African American experience in this manner, it becomes clear that African Americans' pre-Civil Rights era history has significantly shaped the present status of blacks. Those of us hip-hop generationers who have not directly lived through these more challenging times may face a form of "new jack slavery," but we still owe a great debt to those who paved the way for us to do everything that we have been able to do and are doing. Many members of the hip-hop generation are enjoying rights that past generations of blacks only dreamed about.

A Critical Assessment of the Mainstreaming of Black History

Writings in Black history date back to the antebellum era and can be subdivided into many periods and subgroups. Yet, what several scholars have referred to as the mainstreaming of Black history is a very recent phenomenon in the U.S. For the most part, African American history is recognized today as a legitimate field of study in the American academy. Over the last century or so, Black history's and African historians' enduring battle for recognition in the academic mainstream has undergone various transformations signaled by key turning points.

During the antebellum era, Black history was essentially written and researched by a small group of free black intellectuals, journalists, and abolitionists. Their main purpose in writing Black history was to inspire literate blacks, challenge racist scholarship, and defend their people. These writers were not formally trained historians, but they were dedicated to vindicating the race. This approach continued after emancipation until well into the 20th century. John Hope Franklin has argued that George Washington Williams's *History of the Negro Race in America 1619 to 1880* (1882) was the first major Black history text and marked a key shift in the study and writing of Black history. Nonetheless, one of the first major shifts in the study of Black history more appropriately came when W.E.B. Du Bois became the first black to earn a Ph.D. in history from Harvard University in 1895. Du Bois, who researched Black history throughout his long life, added a sense of scholarly legitimacy to African American history. He almost singlehandedly represented African Americans in the professional U.S. historical enterprise during its formative years.

Between 1915 and 1950, Carter G. Woodson (Ph.D., Harvard, 1912) worked hard at legitimizing black history and integrating it into mainstream U.S. history. He published dozens of historical studies and founded the Association for the Study of Negro Life and History, *The Journal of Negro History*, Negro History Week, and *The Negro History Bulletin*. More than a few of Woodson's disciples and co-workers joined him in gaining Black history a place in the "ivory towers" of the U.S. academy. As August Meier and Elliott Rudwick detailed in *Black History and the Historical Profession, 1915–1980*, during Woodson's times a handful of white historians began to recognize and produce scholarship in Black history. After Woodson's death in 1950, the modern Civil Rights Movement helped transform blacks' status and race relations in U.S. society, thus paving the way for the mainstreaming of Black history.

Writing during the anti-civil rights Reagan years, more than a few optimistic historians posited that Black history was accepted by the general American historical profession somewhere during the Black Power era. Meier and Rudwick posited that by the late 1960s "Afro-American history had become fashionable, a 'hot' subject finally legitimated as a scholarly specialty." Black history, in their estimation, had "achieved a central place in the

writing and study of the American past" because many historians, especially their liberal white colleagues inspired by the Civil
Rights Movement, published key monographs within the field,
while many predominantly white university history departments
began offering courses in Black history. Robert L. Harris argued
that African American history "came of age" during the 1960s
and 1970s. "The civil rights struggle, urban uprisings, and the
Black consciousness movement," Harris noted, "forced a reas-
sessment of the Black experience in America." For another Harris, William H. Harris, "the formal acceptance by the general
historical profession of Afro-American history as a legitimate
and respected field" arrived when Meier delivered a paper on
African-American historiography at an annual American Historical Association meeting in 1974.[96]

Meier, Rudwick, Harris, and Harris were accurate in highlighting the importance of the Civil Rights and Black Power
movements in transforming the study of Black history in mainstream American academic circles. Still, it may have been
somewhat optimistic for them to argue that African American
history was truly legitimized and welcomed by the mainstream
American academia at this juncture. The teaching of Black history at many predominantly white universities, with few exceptions, began during the 1960s and 1970s. The optimistic theory
of Black history's becoming mainstreamed and legitimized in the
U.S. academy raises several issues. As countless Black Studies
pioneers have testified, many of the early courses in Black history were created in haste, directly responding to the immediate
demands posed to predominantly white colleges and universities
by black students. Much of the scholarship followed this trend.
Writing at the same time as Meier, Rudwick, Harris, and Harris,
John Hope Franklin praised the meticulousness of the "fourth
generation" of scholarship of African American history that began in 1970. At the same time, he noted that during Black history's so-called legitimization process many 'instant' professors...rushed into the field to make a quick reputation as well as
a quick buck." Franklin added that many monographs, especially

anthologies, were "literally thrown together, without any thought being given to arrangement or organization and without any introduction, interpretation, or connective tissue."[97] A casual reading of Meier's, Rudwick's, Harris's, and Harris's assessment may even lead one to think that the struggle for Black history to gain acceptance peaked or ended in the 1970s, that the Civil Rights Movement somehow solved black America's major problems. Black historians and Black history still face serious issues of academic legitimization and recognition.

The struggles to validate and promote Black history and the challenges facing black historians and historians of the black experience are by no means finished. Today, the challenges arise in a variety of oftentimes subtle forms, especially for those whose historical frames of reference are limited. Today's struggles for Black history and black historians manifest themselves in different forms than those of Woodson's times, the reform-spirited 1960s and 1970s, or the 1980s and 1990s. A major issue facing the black historical profession today, one which Woodson and his disciples grappled with, is the significant integration of African American history into the standard, mainstream teaching of U.S. history. Black history courses are mainly offered as electives in colleges and universities. In other words, Black history courses are optional. They are there for those who want to explore the African American experience. It is rare that standard, conventional university U.S. history survey courses place African American history at the center of the American experience or even adequately integrate the African American experience into the overall American historical landscape. African American history, as is the case with U.S. history for many high schools and universities, should be a requirement. The widespread study of Black history could potentially help improve U.S. race relations.

Three decades removed from the early Black Studies movement, black historians and scholars stand at an interesting crossroads. Nell Irvin Painter recently highlighted the gains and struggles for black professors in the pages of *The Chronicle of*

Higher Education. "After 30 years," she said, "fresh black Ph.D.'s face too many of the some old difficulties," from being stereotyped, to enduring forms of harassment.[98] Hip-hop generation historians must play an important role in placing African American history at the center of U.S. history. While revisiting "Old School" practitioners' approaches, we must also contribute in our own distinct ways to the black historical enterprise and Black Studies. One way that we can begin is by injecting our own definitions of Black history into the dialogue. As Earl E. Thorpe observed more than forty years ago:

> Each generation, depending on its problems and needs, must select and arrange the specific facts which form the best system for its own inspiration and guidance. It is because the past is a guide with roads pointing in many directions that each generation and epoch must make its own studies of history.[99]

Notes

Chapter 1

What is Black History?

[1] Carl L. Becker, "Everyman His Own Historian," *American Historical Review* 37 (January 1932): 221–236.

[2] For a variety of discussions pertaining to the Black Studies movement, see Nathaniel Norment, Jr., ed., *The African American Studies Reader* (North Carolina: Carolina Academic Press, 2001).

[3] For an interesting discussion of the evolution of scholarship in slavery, see "The Historiography of Slavery: An Inquiry into Paradigm-Making and Scholarly Interaction," in Meier and Rudwick, *Black History and the Historical Profession, 1915–1980*, 239–276; Peter J. Parish, *Slavery: History and Historians* (New York: Harper and Row, 1989).

[4] Parish, *Slavery*, 5.

[5] Edward Hallett Carr, *What is History?* (New York: Alfred A. Knopf, 1963), 10, 35, 24, 159, 8.

[6] Ibid., 35.

[7] For such discussions, see Franklin, "On the Evolution of Scholarship in Afro-American Scholarship," 13–22; Robert L. Harris, Jr., "Coming of Age: The Transformation of Afro-American Historiography," *The Journal of Negro History* [hereafter *JNH*] 67 (Summer 1982): 107–121.

[8] Carr, *What is History?*, 26–27.

[9] Ibid., 29, 44, 86.

[10] William Jelani Cobb, ed., *The Essential Harold Cruse: A Reader* (New York: Palgrave, 2002), 209.

[11] W.E.B. Du Bois, *The Souls of Black Folk* (New York: Dover, 1995), 2–3.

[12] Ibid., 163.

[13] Ibid., 2–3.

[14] Ibid.

[15] Carter G. Woodson, "Negro History Week," *JNH* 13 (April 1928): 121–125.

[16] Carter G. Woodson, "Negro History Week," *JNH* 11 (April 1926): 238–239.

[17] Ibid., 239.

[18] Carter G. Woodson, "The Celebration of Negro History Week, 1927," *JNH* 12 (April 1927): 105.

[19] Carr, *What is History?*, 15.

[20] Carter G. Woodson, "The Annual Report of the Director," *JNH* 12 (October 1927): 573.

[21] Earl E. Thorpe, *Black Historians*, 4, 18; Nathan I. Huggins, "Integrating Afro-American History into American History," in *The State of Afro-American History*, ed. Hine, 166–167.

[22] Carter G. Woodson, "Timely Suggestions for Negro History Week," *The Negro History Bulletin* [hereafter *NHB*] 1 (February 1938): 11.

[23] Carter G. Woodson, "The Heritage of the Negro," *NHB* 3 (February 1940): 79 [italics mine].

[24] Arthur Schomburg, "The Negro Digs Up His Past," in *The New Negro*, ed. Alain Leroy Locke (New York: Atheneum, 1969), 231–232.

[25] Charles H. Wesley, "The Reconstruction of History," *JNH* 20 (October 1935): 411, 421–422.

[26] L.D. Reddick, "A New Interpretation for Negro History," *JNH* 22 (January 1937): 17, 19, 21, 27.

[27] Ellen Wright and Michael Fabre, eds., *Richard Wright Reader* (New York: Harper and Row, 1978), 240.

[28] John Hope Franklin, "History—Weapon of War and Peace," *Phylon* 5 (1944): 249–250, 255–257, 259.

[29] John Hope Franklin, *From Slavery to Freedom: A History of Negro Americans* (New York: Vintage Books, 1969), xii.

[30] Herbert Aptheker, *Negro Slave Revolts in the United States*, 1526–1860 (New York: International Publishing Company, 1939), 69–70.

[31] Herbert Aptheker, "Negro History: Arsenal for Liberation," *New Masses*, 11 February 1947, 12.

[32] Herbert Aptheker, *A Documentary History of the Negro People in the United States, Volume I* (New York: Citadel Press, 1968), "Introduction." For Cruse's critique of Aptheker, see Harold Cruse, *The Crisis of the Negro Intellectual* (New York: Quill, 1984), 471–472, 505–508, 511–517. For Greene's description of Aptheker, see Harry Washington Greene, *Holders of Doctorates Among American Negroes: An Educational Study of Negroes Who Have Earned Doctoral Degrees in Course, 1876–1943* (Boston: Meador Publishing Company, 1948).

[33] Robin D.G. Kelley, "Afterword," *The Journal of American History* June 2000
<http://www.historycooperative.org/journals/jah/87.1/afterword.html>. For more information about Herbert Aptheker, see Herbert Shapiro, ed., *African American History and Radical Historiography: Essays in Honor of Herbert Aptheker* (Minneapolis: MEP Publications, 1998); Christopher Lehman-Haupt, "Herbert Aptheker, 87, Dies; Prolific Marxist Historian," *The New York Times*, March 20, 2003, p. B8(L); Robin D.G. Kelley, "Interview of Herbert Aptheker," *The Journal of American History* June 2000
<http://www.history   cooperative   .org/journals/jah/87.1/interview.html>

[34] John Hope Franklin, "The New Negro History," *JNH* 42 (April 1957): 89–97.

[35] Ibid., 95.

[36] Earl E. Thorpe, *Negro Historians in the United States* (Baton Rouge: Fraternal Press, 1958), 9, 151.

[37] For a provocative discussion of Black social history and for one of the first major examinations of Black "history from below," see Robin D.G. Kelley, *Race Rebels: Culture, Politics, and the Black Working Class* (New York: The Free Press, 1994), 1–13. Kelley dubbed Black "history from below" as being "Black history from way, way below."

[38] Samuel Du Bois Cook, "A Tragic Conception of Negro History," *JNH* 45 (October 1960): 219–240.

[39] William Van Deburg, *New Day in Babylon: The Black Power Movement and American Culture, 1965–1975* (Chicago: University of Chicago Press, 1992), 280, 2–10.

[40] Malcolm X, *The Autobiography of Malcolm X* (New York: Ballantine, 1965), 175, 180.

[41] Goodman, ed., *The End of White World Supremacy*, 26–27.

[42] Malcolm X, *Malcolm X on Afro-American History* (New York: Pathfinder, 1988), 4–5.

[43] Van Deburg, *New Day in Babylon*, 2, 8.

[44] Franklin, "Pioneer Negro Historians," 4.

[45] Cruse, *The Crisis of the Negro Intellectual*, 533, 564.

[46] For Bunche's assessment of black leadership, see Ralph Bunche, "Conceptions and Ideologies of the Negro Problem," in *Contributions in Black Studies* (1990–1992): 70–114. For a recent discussion of Bunche, see Jonathan Scott Holloway, *Confronting the Veil: Abram Harris, Jr., E. Franklin Frazier, and Ralph Bunche, 1919–1941* (Chapel Hill: University of North Carolina Press, 2002).

[47] Cruse, *The Crisis of the Negro Intellectual*, 565.

[48] Vincent Harding, "The Uses of the Afro-American Past," *Negro Digest* 17 (February 1968): 5–6, 81.

[49] Vincent Harding, *Beyond Chaos: Black History and the Search for the New Land* (Atlanta: Institute of the Black World, 1970), 7, 16, 26–27.

[50] John Henrik Clarke, "The Meaning of Black History," *Black World* 20 (February 1971): 27, 34, 36.

[51] Sterling Stuckey, "Twilight of Our Past: Reflections on the Origins of Black History," in *Amistad 2*, ed. John A. Williams and Charles F. Harris (New York: Vintage, 1971), 270–272.

[52] Ibid., 290, 293; Meyer Weinberg, ed., *W.E.B. Du Bois: A Reader* (New York: Harper Torch, 1970), 239.

[53] Thorpe, *Black Historians*, 3–4.

[54] Ibid., 4.

[55] Haki Madhubuti, *Enemies: Clash of Races* (Chicago: Third World Press, 1978), 14, 17.

[56] August Meier wrote an essay on Quarles' historical scholarship in the late 1980s, but Wilson Jeremiah Moses has presented the most intriguing assessment of Quarles to date. In his view, Quarles blended two major themes in his analyses of Black history—"contributionism

and messianism." He also dubbed Quarles a "progressive historian" in that he possessed an optimistic view of history and believed that scholarship could help reform American society. See Wilson Jeremiah Moses, "African American Historiography and the Works of Benjamin Quarles," *The History Teacher* 32 (November 1998): 77–88.

[57] Benjamin Quarles, *Black Mosaic: Essays in Afro-American History and Historiography* (Amherst: The University of Massachusetts Press, 1988), 204–205.

[58] Ibid., 208–209.

[59] Vincent Harding, *There Is a River: The Black Struggle for Freedom in America* (New York: Vintage Books, 1983), xix.

[60] August Meier, "Whither the Black Perspective in Afro-American Historiography?," *The Journal of American History* 70 (June 1983): 101–105.

[61] William H. Harris, "Trends and Needs in Afro-American Historiography," in *The State of Afro-American History*, ed. Hine, 153.

[62] After a survey of *Ebony* magazines from the late 1950s through the 1990s, I located three major articles in which Bennett directly attempted to define Black history as an ideology, a philosophy, a spiritual concept, and/or field of study. He has published countless articles on many different aspects of Black history in *Ebony*. Among some of his other articles that address the meaning of Black history are: "Reading, 'Riting and Racism," *Ebony* 22 (March 1967): 130–138; "Guardian of the Truth of Black History," *Ebony* 35 (February 1980): 94–98; "The Ten Biggest Myths about Black History," *Ebony* 39 (February 1984): 25–32.

[63] Lerone Bennett, Jr., "Listen to the Blood: The Meaning of Black History," *Ebony* 36 (February 1981): 35–36.

[64] Ibid., 36, 38, 42.

[65] Lerone Bennett, Jr., "Why Black History is Important to You," *Ebony* 37 (February 1982): 61, 62, 66.

[66] Lerone Bennett, Jr., "Voices of the Past Speak to the Present," *Ebony* 40 (February 1985): 27–28.

[67] Lerone Bennett, Jr., "What is Your Black History IQ?," *Ebony* 44 (February 1989): 173.

[68] V.P. Franklin, *Black Self-Determination: A Cultural History of the Faith of the Fathers* (Westport: Lawrence Hill and Company, 1984), 4. This book was later republished in 1992 as *Black Self-Determination: A Cultural History of African American Resistance.*

[69] Harris, "Coming of Age," 116.

[70] Robert L. Harris, Jr., *Teaching African American History* (Washington, D.C.: American Historical Association, 1992), ix.

[71] W.D. Wright, *Critical Reflections on Black History* (Westport: Praeger, 2002), 19.

[72] Wright, *Black History and Black Identity*, 55.

[73] Donald Spivey, *Fire from the Soul: A History of African American Struggle* (North Carolina: Carolina Academic Press, 2003), xiv.

[74] Ibid., x.

[75] N.F. Mossell, *The Work of the Afro-American Woman* (New York: Oxford University Press, 1988), 48–49.

[76] For a brief review of the 1970s historiography in Black Women's history, see Rosalyn Terborg-Penn, "Teaching the History of Black Women: A Bibliographical Essay," *The History Teacher* 13 (February 1980): 245–250.

[77] Toni Cade, ed., *The Black Woman: An Anthology* (New York: A Mentor Book, 1970), 9.

[78] Angela Davis, "Reflections on the Black Woman's Role in the Community of Slaves," *The Black Scholar* 3 (December 1971): 15.

[79] Gerda Lerner, *Black Women in White America: A Documentary History* (New York: Vintage, 1972), xix–xx.

[80] Ibid., xix, xvii.

[81] Sharon Harley and Rosalyn Terborg-Penn, eds., *The Afro-American Woman: Struggles and Images* (New York: Kennikat, 1978), ix.

[82] Ibid.

[83] Michele Wallace, *Black Macho and the Myth of the Super-woman* (New York: Warner, 1978), 25, 248, 250.

[84] Paula Giddings, *When and Where I Enter: The Impact of Black Women on Race and Sex in America* (New York: Bantam, 1984), 6.

[85] Deborah Gray White, *Ar'n't I A Woman?: Female Slaves in the Plantation South* (New York: W.W. Norton, 1985), 23.

[86] Ibid., 25.

[87] During the late 1980s and the 1990s, there were many black women who produced important historical scholarship. I have not listed all of them here. The roll call would include many more than those names I have mentioned here. I included the names of many, not all, black women historians who published important monographs during the late 1980s and 1990s.

[88] Darlene Clark Hine, "Editor's Preface," in *Black Women in America: An Historical Encyclopedia*, ed. Hine, Elsa Barkley Brown, and Rosalyn Terborg-Penn (Bloomington: Indiana University Press, 1993), xix.

[89] Ibid.

[90] Darlene Clark Hine, *Hinesight: Black Women and the Reconstruction of American History* (New York: Carlson, 1994), xxi.

[91] Marimba Ani quoted in Molefi Kete Asante, "The African American Warrant for Reparations: The Crime of European Enslavement of Africans and Its Consequences," in *Should America Pay?*, ed. Winbush, 9.

[92] Na'im Akbar, *Chains and Images of Psychological Slavery* (New Jersey: New Mind Productions, 1984), 34.

[93] Joseph L. White and James H. Cones, III, *Black Man Emerging: Facing the Past and Seizing the Future in America* (New York: Routledge, 1999), 49.

[94] For figures and statistics such as these, see Darlene Clark Hine, William C. Hine, and Stanley Harrold, *The African-American Odyssey* Combined Second Edition (New Jersey: Prentice Hall, 2003).

[95] John Hope Franklin, *The Free Negro in North Carolina, 1790– 1860* (Chapel Hill: University of North Carolina Press, 1943); Leonard Curry, *The Free Black in Urban America, 1800–1850: The Shadow of the Dream* (Chicago: The University of Chicago Press, 1981); Ira Berlin, *Slaves Without Masters: The Free Negro in the Antebellum South* (New York: Oxford University Press, 1974), xiii.

[96] Meier and Rudwick, *Black History and the Historical Profession*, 161, 177–178; Harris, "Coming of Age," 107; Harris, "Trends and

Needs in Afro-American Historiography," 139. It should be noted that Meier's paper was not the first paper presented at an AHA conference pertaining to black history. In 1969, John Blassingame delivered a paper that critically assessed the role of Black Studies and black historians. Blassingame's paper could have easily been overlooked by the profession at the time because of the marginal status occupied by black historians in academia. At this time there were at most a dozen black Ph.D. holders in history. Meier, an established historian, was in a position of power within the American historical profession when he called for the serious study of Black history. It is similar to the so-called legitimization of certain brands of Afrocentric thought. When Martin Bernal published the first volume of *Black Athena* in 1987, an international community of Egyptologists began to revisit the African origins of Western civilizations. Yet, scores of African and African American scholars, such as Frederick Douglass, Du Bois, Woodson, George G.M. James, Ivan Van Sertima, and Cheikh Anta Diop had been discussing these same themes raised by Bernal decades before he decided to enter the debate. It seems that Bernal's status as a white scholar added legitimacy, in the eyes of the white academy, to the Afrocentric movement's argument.

[97] Franklin, "On the Evolution of Scholarship in Afro-American History," 20.

[98] Nell Irvin Painter, "Black Studies, Black Professors, and the Struggles of Perception," *The Chronicle of Higher Education*, 15 December 2000, p. B9.

[99] Earl E. Thorpe, "Philosophy of History: Sources, Truths, and Limitations," *The Quarterly Review of Higher Education Among Negroes* 25 (July 1957): 183.

CHAPTER 2

"Of all our studies, history is best qualified to reward our research"[1]: Black History's Relevance to the Hip-Hop Generation

> History inspires. History teaches. History also guides ...We, as a Hiphop people, must come out of the past and into our present. We, as a Hiphop people, must re-create ourselves. True freedom for us Hiphoppas is to create and live a lifestyle that uniquely empowers us...True freedom is self-creation...We Hiphoppas will be busy at work creating a history that simply works better for our children.
>
> KRS-One, 2003[2]

The meaning, purpose, and function of Black history as a field of academic inquiry, a philosophy, and "as a weapon in the fight for racial equality" has undergone a host of significant transformations and stages since the antebellum era and the professionalization of the black historical enterprise during the early 20th century.[3] Building upon the institutions and paradigms created by Woodson and other contributors to the early Black history movement, black and white historians and scores of black activists during the Black Power era significantly transformed the scientific study and day-to-day application of Black history. Black Power era historian William Van Deburg has pointed out the ways in which the masses of young blacks from about 1965 until 1975 collectively drew upon Black history as "a wellspring of group strength and staying power."[4] Likewise, in their exhaustive study on the black historical enterprise, August Meier and Elliott Rudwick argued that by the late 1960s "Afro-American history had become fashionable, a 'hot' subject finally legitimated as a scholarly specialty."[5]

Challenging the widely accepted thesis of Black history's unprecedented growth, centrality, and legitimization during the Black Power era, in his 1967 classic *The Crisis of the Negro Intellectual*, iconoclast Harold Cruse indicted young black intellectuals for being tragically "uninterested in history." On the last page of his mammoth study, Cruse concluded:

> The farther the Negro gets from his historical antecedents in time, the more tenuous become his conceptual ties, the emptier his social conceptions, the more superficial his visions. His one great and present hope is to know and understand his Afro-American history in the United States more profoundly. Failing that, and failing to create a new synthesis and social theory of action, he will suffer the historical fate described by the philosopher who warned that 'Those who cannot remember the past are condemned to repeat it.'[6]

In the "Foreword" to a 1984 edition of Cruse's opus, Bazel E. Allen and Ernest J. Wilson pronounced that "the message of this book remains painfully apt today."[7] Cruse's observations are still relevant and especially applicable to the hip-hop generation, a group existing during African American history's and the black historical profession's most advanced state, yet a group whose references to and expressions of Black history are often shallow and ineffective, manifested in symbolic materialistic items such as throwback jerseys, hardwood classic oversized baseball hats, red-black-and-green wristbands, and other surface level commodities.

This chapter concerns the relationship between the hip-hop generation and Black history and is guided by the premise that each generation of black historians must leave its distinct marks on the profession, the production of scholarship, and the debates surrounding Black history's function. My discussion is guided by the premise that hip-hop culture is the single most widespread preoccupation among today's black American and African diasporan youth and has the potential to play an important role in rejuvenating the modern Black history movement and raising the hip-hop generation's cultural and historical consciousness. Black historians, especially those of the hip-hop generation, could help advance approaches to teaching and popularizing Black history by using elements of hip-hop culture while helping the hip-hop generation better understand its peculiar position within the broader scope of Black history. Articulating the ideas of more than a few hip-hop scholars, in an important 2004 issue of *Black Issues in Higher Education*, Scott Heath astutely remarked that hip-hop is

> an area where we might see theory and practice coming together inside African American intellectualism, where we might see an attempt to develop innovative approaches to using hip-hop as a method for organizing African American youth around issues that are important to their survival.[8]

Many broad, interconnected questions help frame my analysis. How do we best conceptualize, subdivide, and historicize the hip-hop generation? How has Black history been interpreted by popular, "commercial" hip-hop culture within the last several years? Generally speaking, how do some of today's most popular mainstream hip-hop magazines and emcees present Black history to today's black youth? How do these popular representations of Black history compare to those of the Black Power era, a period that is often romanticized by, and compared to, the hip-hop generation? How can hip-hop generation black historians historicize their generation's experiences and worldviews while explaining and reintroducing Black history to black youth culture?

Theoretically, this essay is openly Woodson-centric in maintaining that Black history can still help foster healthy black youth identity and contribute to American social and educational reform. Black history can help hip-hop generationers develop a better appreciation of the once more common values of sacrifice, service, unity, and historical consciousness. Woodson's mission of popularizing and ritualizing Black history could be especially useful for the hip-hop generation that actively samples from past musicians, fashions, cultural icons, and other phenomena from "back in the day" and the "Old School." Historical dialogues of some sort are common even in today's most "commercial" rap music. A central component of hip-hop culture and rap music involves hip-hop artists who routinely recount their own personal histories of resilience that mirror the overall theme of persever-ance over oppression characterizing African American history. With the exception of Robin D.G. Kelley and perhaps a few oth-ers, black historians have not played a leading role in analyzing hip-hop or critically tapping into hip-hop culture as a viable dis-cursive space for the black historical experience.[9] Given the tra-dition of "historical revivalism" in rap's heyday, black histori-ans' underrepresentation in hip-hop scholarship is surprising.

Conceptualizing the Hip-Hop Generation

Within the last decade, scholarly works on rap music and hip-hop culture have skyrocketed. Several dozen books were published on facets of hip-hop during the 1980s and 1990s.[10] As Kendra Hamilton has noted, 1994 represented a landmark year in the legitimization process of hip-hop scholarship with the publi-cation of Tricia Rose's *Black Noise: Rap Music and Black Cul-ture in Contemporary America* and Robin D.G. Kelley's *Race Rebels: Culture, Politics, and the Working-Class.*[11] Adhering to rigorous scholarly standards, these works historicized and theo-rized dimensions of hip-hop culture in a discourse that would

probably seem foreign to most of the emcees whose art Rose and
Kelley analyzed. In 2000, the Brooklyn Museum of Art presented a first of its kind multimedia exhibition on hip-hop. "Hip-
Hop Nation: Roots, Rhymes, and Rage," in one reviewer's
words, portrayed hip-hop "as a cultural wealth of America to be
appreciated by a larger crowd than the hip-hop fans." Other critics believed that the museum's liberalism crept in too much at
the expense of watering down hip-hop's "political message" and
radicalism.[12] In 2002, one scholar published a dictionary on hip-
hop terminology, and during the dawning of the 21st century
many scholarly studies on hip-hop were published by mainstream presses.[13] Hip-hop studies, perhaps soon to be called "Hiphopology," is one of the newest fad-fields in academia. Major
universities have been offering courses in hip-hop for more than
a few years. The courses are popular and have been legitimized
in the mainstream academy by established black scholars, such
as Todd Boyd, Michael Eric Dyson, Mark Anthony Neal, and
Tricia Rose, who was recently dubbed the "Ph.D. Diva" by *The
New York Times*.[14] Nonetheless, as one scholar noted in 2002,
while a significant "rap and hip-hop canon" exists, there is room
for expanding this discourse.[15] Inquiries into hip-hop as representing a generation deserve to be elaborated upon.

In *The Hip Hop Generation: Young Blacks and the Crisis in
African American Culture* (2002), journalist and cultural critic
Bakari Kitwana provides a provocative definition of the hip-hop
generation that expands upon what scholars have called, in
Robin Kelley's terms, "a lot of things: the post-soul generation,
the post civil rights generation, the postindustrial generation,"
and even "soul babies."[16] Kitwana uses the hip-hop generation
"interchangeably with black youth culture." He designates the
hip-hop generation as including those blacks born between
roughly 1965 and 1984 who share a common worldview concerning "family, relationships, child rearing, career, racial identity, race relations, and politics." Shaped by the rise of corpora-
tism, globalization, neo-segregation, racialist public policy, the
media, and an overall poor life quality for blacks, members of

the hip-hop generation are linked mainly by the fact that we were born after the major struggles of the Civil Rights and Black Power movements and have collectively inherited a great deal from the battles waged by our elders.[17] Echoing others, Kitwana notes that the hip-hop generation seems cut off from the activist tradition prior to the Civil Rights and Black Power movements. I agree with Kitwana's critiques in this instance.

In his benchmark study, *The Origins of the Civil Rights Movement*, Aldon Morris argued that civil rights activists recognized that they were part of a "rich tradition of protest." Many members of the hip-hop generation seem alienated from the important influences of previous generations, those—in Morris' terms—traditionally "transmitted across generations by older relatives, black educational institutions, churches, and protest organizations."[18] To add to Morris's theory, black historians have also historically played a significant role in passing on "tradition of protest" historical epistemologies.

According to Kitwana, the hip-hop generation, with some exceptions of course, seems to be self-consumed, individualistic, and not willing to sacrifice for the advancement of "the tradition of protest." "For us," Kitwana contends, "achieving wealth, by any means necessary, is more important than most anything else, hence our obsession with the materialistic and consumer trappings of financial success." Kitwana adds that one of the greatest problems facing the hip-hop generation is the fact that we have abandoned the positive cultural values laid forth by our parents, elders, and ancestors. We have exchanged what Elijah Anderson has called "old head" values for ideals promoted by a capitalistic, individualistic, and racist society.[19] The "fact remains that when many hip-hop generation youth have to choose between personal financial success at the expense of what the older generation considers communal cultural integrity, individual gain comes first."[20]

Beyond what some might consider overgeneralizations, Kitwana's analysis is problematic in delineating such a large generation spanning nearly twenty years. As he admits in passing, his hip-hop generation could be further broken down into at least "three distinctive subgroups."[21] Nelson George and Todd Boyd have both discussed how being born at certain points during the Civil Rights Movement impacted their analyses of hip-hop. I would at minimum highlight that there is a significant difference between the ideologies of those born between about 1965 and the mid-1970s and those born in the late 1970s and the 1980s. Those young blacks born in the 1980s, for instance, are not being molded as adolescents and young adults by the same types of black cultural nationalist stimuli which shaped those of us born between about 1965 and the mid-1970s and socialized during the late 1980s and early 1990s, the "golden age" of hip-hop and rap music. I call those young blacks born between about 1965 and the mid-1970s Black Power (hereafter BP) era born hip-hop generationers. Those blacks born during the late 1970s and the early to mid-1980s constitute the post-Black Power (hereafter PBP) era born hip-hop generation. These young blacks have largely been socialized by "commercial" hip-hop culture. BP era born hip-hop generationers were shaped by social and cultural forces that were more conducive to black cultural nationalism than PBP era born hip-hop generationers. The gap in historical consciousness between the BP and PBP era born hip-hop generations exists and is noteworthy.

The most recent significant resurgence and upsurge of black cultural consciousness and nationalism occurred during the late 1980s and the early 1990s until perhaps as late as 1995 or 1996, marked by the Million Man March and the death of 2Pac, respectively. Though this period was not nearly as lively, widespread, and progressive as the well-known cultural revitalization of the Black Power era, during the late 1980s and especially the early 1990s there existed meaningful stimuli promoting black consciousness among the BP era born hip-hop generation. As Robin D.G. Kelley has attested, "The decade of the 1990s was a period of resurgent black nationalism."[22] Many examples in black popular culture demonstrate this.

Despite Nas's recent claim that "conscious" emceeing has become increasingly "trendy," non-underground, popular, "conscious," "nation-conscious," "reality rap," and analytical rap music was more common during the late 1980s and the early 1990s than it is today. In order to be a "conscious" rap artist, one must devote the majority of his/her lyrics to discussing "empowerment through politics and knowledge," social change, the problems facing the black communities in critical manners, and/or non-superficial aspects of Black history.[23] In the late 1980s and early 1990s—the "golden age" of hip-hop—there were many of these types of rap artists, including Public Enemy, KRS-One and Boogie Down Productions, De La Soul, Brand Nubians, at times Ice Cube, A Tribe Called Quest, Jungle Brothers, Goodie Mob, Paris, X-Clan, Black Star, Poor Righteous Teachers, Queen Latifah, and others. In one of his first articles on hip-hop culture written in 1989, Michael Eric Dyson highlighted the "historical revivalism" of rap during its golden years, arguing that it "retrieved historic black ideas, movements, and figures to combating the racial amnesia that threatens to relegate the achievements of the black past to the ash heap of dismemory." More important, Dyson asserted that this "renewed historicism" permitted members of the BP era born hip-hop generation to "discern links between the past and their own present circumstances, using the past as a fertile source of social reflection, cultural creation, and political resistance."[24] PBP era born hip-hop generationers are not being exposed to historically conscious "nationalist rappers" as BP era born hip-hop generationers were when we were coming of age.

Though variations of 1970s "blaxsploitation" films continued through the 1980s and 1990s, Spike Lee's films, particularly from 1988 until 1992, played a major role in socializing young blacks by addressing important and often controversial issues in young blacks' lives and Black history. In 2001, black film historian Donald Bogle commented that Lee's "Do the Right Thing" "remains the most controversial and provocative film by an African American filmmaker" and that "no other black film drew as much attention or had as great cultural impact as this drama."[25] In 1991, John Singleton produced "Boyz N the Hood" for the BP era born hip-hop generation. He openly discussed important issues facing black urban America during the Reagan years, such as HIV/AIDS, racism, black male-female relationships, community development, and black leadership. A decade later, for the PBP era born hip-hop generation he produced the much less analytical "Baby Boy."

There have been a few black films which PBP era born hip-hop generationers could have gravitated towards, but chose not to. Take, for instance, Spike Lee's "Four Little Girls" (1997) and "Bamboozled" (2000). These films failed to attract a large young black viewership. "Bamboozled," Lee's magnum opus, which he directed as an amateur, public historian, could have become a rite of passage cinematic experience for the PBP era born hip-hop generation. Instead, in 2002 the PBP era born hip-hop generation witnessed Halle Berry and Denzel Washington receive Oscars for Best Actress and Best Actor for their stereotypical roles in "Monster's Ball" and "Training Day," respectively. Berry's character had no redeeming qualities. She embodied the image of the black woman as the oversexed, promiscuous jezebel, a stereotype that, as Deborah Gray White has demonstrated, dates back to the days of slavery.[26] Denzel earned his Oscar for Best Actor forty years after Sidney Poitier earned the same award for his role in "Lilies of the Field." Washington played the role of a drug-using, corrupt black cop and deadbeat dad. This was especially interesting given the recent acts of police brutality against blacks at the hands of whites. Denzel could have very easily won an Oscar for Best Actor for his historically relevant roles in "Malcolm X" (1992) and "The Hurricane" (1999).

Afrocentrism, popularized by Molefi Kete Asante beginning in the 1980s, attracted a large following among the BP era born hip-hop generation. Afrocentric thinkers and black scholar-activists routinely lectured at major colleges and universities throughout the nation in the late 1980s and early 1990s. The roll call of these speakers is long, including Na'im Akbar, Jawanza

Kunjufu, "Dr. Ben" (Yosef ben-Yochanan), Ivan Van Sertima, Frances Cress Welsing, John Henrik Clarke, Oba T'Shaka, Asa Hilliard, Wade Nobles, Haki Madhubuti, Leonard Jeffries, Jr., Sister Souljah, and many others. Such types of speakers are not popular among the PBP era born hip-hop generation. During the late 1980s and the early 1990s, there was also a resurgence of interest in black scholarship among many college-going blacks. Africa medallions, *ankh* pendants, and all sorts of Afrocentric gear were in style and could be easily purchased in every major U.S. city. Imitating hip-hop video fashion, many members of the PBP era born hip-hop generation today wear the red-black-and-green wristbands without any knowledge of Marcus Garvey.

The popularization of Malcolm X was very important in fostering a black historical consciousness within BP era born hip-hop generationers. Malcolm X was resurrected by Boogie Down Production's album "By All Means Necessary" (1988) and by Spike Lee's lengthy film "Malcolm X" (1992, Warner Brothers, 201 minutes). In the 1990s, X hats, tee shirts with pictures of Malcolm and other black leaders, and other sorts of black memorabilia were popular and fashionable. Lee's film was critiqued by cultural critics such as bell hooks and by black activists who knew Malcolm, such as Dick Gregory. But, the film did spark within the BP era born hip-hop generation an intense interest in Malcolm X, Black history, and militant black ideologies. Using Malcolm X as a spiritual advisor and building upon the black student movement of the Black Power era, in the late 1980s and early 1990s thousands of black students at various predominantly white colleges and universities engaged in many meaningful, well-organized protests and sit-ins. In May 1989, black students at Michigan State University initiated one of the largest student protests of the decade which closely resembled the protests for Black Studies programs during the 1960s and 1970s. Nationwide, expressions of black student unity during the late 1980s and early 1990s resembled that of the Black Power era. The college students of the PBP era born hip-hop generation have collectively not been as active as previous generations. This is evidenced in the overall lack of critical response to The University of Michigan's and the Supreme Court's recent landmark decision concerning affirmative action.

The Million Man March on October 16, 1995, and even the death of 2Pac on September 13, 1996, marked the last stages in the steady decline of the black cultural pride movement that began in the late 1980s and early 1990s. While Farrakhan's "Holy Day of Atonement" did not solve the major problems facing black America and went against many of the fundamental principles of black economic nationalism espoused by Farrakhan and the Nation of Islam, it can not be denied that this spiritual event served as a turning point for many black men, raised black consciousness among young black men who attended it and heard first hand accounts, created a sense of black unity, and countered some of white America's racist stereotypes about black men. 2Pac's death also created a great void that arguably has yet to be filled in the "commercial" hip-hop music industry.[27]

The collective ethos of young blacks who were coming of age during the late 1980s and early 1990s seemed to draw upon Aldon Morris's black "tradition of protest" and historical consciousness in manners reminiscent of the Black Power era. Our consciousness was not something created independent of the external social forces. Those of us coming of age in the late 1980s and early 1990s were stimulated to get active by not only various forces in popular culture, but also by a host of post-Civil Rights Movement struggles.[28] The PBP era born hip-hop generation exists within an era that resembles what Rayford W. Logan called the "nadir" of black life (1877–1901) fifty years ago, especially in terms of health. Yet, unlike previous generations, they have not collectively responded, in mass, to black oppression or made distinctive contributions to the black "tradition of protest." Because racial oppression has become increasingly sophisticated and dangerously subtle to the layperson, critical thinking is needed more than ever before by the PBP era born hip-hop generation.

Despite the significantly different sets of circumstances that molded and socialized BP and PBP era born hip-hop generationers, today members of Kitwana's broad hip-hop generation appear to share a general lack of concern for and knowledge of Black history. Today, members of both hip-hop generations are existing in a time when it is far too easy to under-appreciate the value of African American history. Today's young blacks are distracted by a multitude of media-generated images and messages that no other previous generation of young blacks have had to deal with. While previous generations of black youth have drawn great knowledge and inspiration from Black history and cross generational dialogues, the hip-hop generation has largely failed to recognize the potential value of employing Black history. Those blacks born after the Civil Rights and Black Power eras need to study Black history in order to understand their unique status and position in the evolution of black America's struggle for advancement.

The Historicism of the Hip-Hop Generation's Magazines

What makes the hip-hop generation's current disregard for Black history especially perplexing is that, comparatively speaking, the hip-hop generation has more access to information on Black history than any other previous generation of African American youth. Today, there are countless books on Black history, numerous websites, and many very useful videos, especially those produced by California Newsreel and PBS. College and university students can regularly enroll in courses focusing on African American history. At the same time, in many ways, the internet, the most common form of information retrieval for the hip-hop generation, has replaced the art of reading as an active, creative process. If one does not have the critical skills and background to properly judge sources, which is often the case with high school and university students, the internet becomes a confusing reservoir of historical information, especially pertaining to African descendants. Among the repositories of knowledge, popular media significantly mold black youths' views of Black history. It is therefore useful to look at Black history as portrayed in popular magazines. Currently, the five most popular magazines among blacks between roughly 18 and 34 years old are *The Source*, *Vibe*, *Ebony*, *Jet*, and *Essence—The Source* and *Vibe* being the most widely read by the hip-hop generation. Many other hip-hop magazines are attempting to generate followings, such as *XXL*, Marc Ecko's *Complex*, *Urb*, *Ballin'*, *Owners Illustrated*, *Undercover*, *Scratch: The Science of Hip-Hop*, and a variety of internet magazines. The majority of these magazines ignore Black history and promote a materialistic ethos.

For fifteen years, *The Source* has detailed the lives, struggles, and music of countless hip-hop artists. The history of the magazine is nothing short of remarkable, a modern-day rags to riches story that embodies the struggles and successes of countless hip-hop artists who have drastically changed their qualities of life through struggle and timing. Founded as a one-page newsletter in 1988 by two young whites and one young black, by 1997 the editorial staff of the magazine was dominated by blacks and Hispanics and sold more than any other music periodical in the U.S.[29] In 2003, *The Source* boasted 9 million readers each month. The average issue is about two hundred pages and contains slightly more than one hundred advertisements per month. In 1988 *The Source* sold for $2.50. The price of placing an ad in *The Source* in 2003 was $32,000.00. According to its editors, its is "the most respected and most read" magazine for urban blacks between ages 18 and 34.[30] *Vibe* also makes the same claim. It is safe to say that *The Source* and *Vibe* are, give or take some thousand readers here and there, equally popular. *The Source*, however, seems to deal more critically with issues relevant to black America's status, past and present, than its chief competitor.

Writers for *The Source* have adroitly kept their readers abreast of the latest developments and drama within the community of hip-hop musicians. They often provide a forum for discussions relating to the state of hip-hop. In a few feature articles and in the "Ear to the Street" and "Central Booking" sections of the magazine, writers for *The Source* have critically addressed relevant aspects of African American life, past and present, as well as issues pertaining to the African diaspora, such as HIV/AIDS, female circumcision in Africa, reparations, Black Studies, police brutality, and black leadership. These commentaries, however, represent only a very small part of the magazine. *The Source* is non-historical for the most part, unless speaking about the not-so-distant history of hip-hop music and culture, the personal histories of hip-hop artists, and historical events and personalities in passing. The feature-length articles pertaining to Black history are uncommon. When the editors have decided to deal with historical issues, the results have often been positive. The potential for igniting historical consciousness among its readers is great and has been revealed in more than a few instances.

The March 2001 issue serves as a revealing example. This issue not only discussed the life of Gwendolyn Brooks based upon an interview with Haki Madhubuti, the history of police brutality in Oakland, California, and the life of former Black Panther Dhuruba bin Wahad, but also addressed the Detroit race riot of 1943. The six-page article featured rare photographs and easy-to-read historical prose. The author, Dan Frosch, traced the history of black resistance in Detroit, mentioning the city's Underground Railroad, blacks' newspaper *The Plain Dealer*, the Ossian Sweet case, the riots of 1943 and 1967, Motown, and the leadership of Coleman Young. One photo in the article was particularly shocking and instructional. Blown up to a full page under the heading "Horrifying scene from the 1943 riot," the article had a photo with a nicely dressed middle-aged black man bleeding profusely from the face and being held up by two young white men. Both were looking directly into the camera as if the photo was carefully posed. One of the white youths was wearing a U.S. Army sweatshirt and a pair of bloodstained khaki pants. In his right hand he held a bloodsoaked handkerchief of some sort that he had apparently used to wipe the victim's face. The other young man was smiling proudly, sporting a suit and tie.[31] More than previous black generations, the hip-hop generation relates to history as revealed through visual images. These images certainly helped *The Source's* black readers better understand the police brutality their community faced. Similar historically relevant articles are scattered throughout issues of *The Source*. More articles such as these are needed, especially as feature articles, since it is easy to overlook such knowledge among the onslaught of ads and distracting images.

Vibe is also an interesting case study. Founded in the early 1990s by Quincy Jones and Time-Warner, *Vibe* is more mainstream in its appeal than *The Source*. In 2002, *Vibe* beat out *The New Yorker*, *Jane*, *Wired*, and *Gourmet* in winning the General Excellence Award from the National Magazine Awards, sponsored by the American Society of Magazine Editors. According to *Vibe's* former Editor-in-Chief, Emil Wilbekin, "It's the first time a magazine that covers urban music, with a large African American audience, has won in the award's 37-year history."[32] *Vibe* focuses on hip-hop artists, fashion, and music and rarely delves into issues related to Black history and cultural consciousness in critical manners. Nationalist rappers such as dead prez and underground, "conscious" artists have received some coverage, but in comparison to the attention given to "commercial" artists, it is fairly insignificant.

In the one-page "What's Up" section of the magazine, which is easy to overlook, the editor-in-chief routinely discusses important issues relevant to the black community. In May 2002, Wilbekin called upon black men to stop emulating "the posturing, the clothing, the jewelry, the womanizing, and the lifestyle of the gangster high life," all dynamics that the magazine directly glorifies. He has critiqued hip-hop's self-destructive elements. In another instance, evoking history, Wilbekin asserted that hip-hop artists were not correctly laying the foundations for future generations as previous generations had. "Back in the day, hip hop had political consciousness…we need to get involved and make more powerful statements, as our forefathers did."[33]

However, such ideas are drastically contradicted by other views. When making references to Black history for inspiration and comparisons, there has been a tendency among the hip-hop generation to turn to the Black Power era. It is fresh in black America's collective memory since many of the activists from this period are still alive. The Black Power era is more appealing than the non-violent direct action strategies of the Civil Rights Movement and it provides an obvious form of militancy and radicalism with which many hip-hop generationers (especially those self-proclaimed "thugs" and "gangstas") can relate. In a 2002 issue, Wilbekin asserted:

> There's a new Black Power in America. Secretary of State Colin Powell and National Security Advisor Condeleeza Rice are the most powerful of any African-Americans in government. Russell Simmons is politicizing the hip hop nation...Tiger Woods, Venus and Serena Williams, Shaquille O'Neal and Kobe Bryant are flexing athletic prowess and reigning as champion...We won...but we need to keep on fighting, working, demanding equality...creating powerful music, and keeping our eyes on the prize.[34]

The brief commentary also featured a photo of Denzel Washington and Halle Berry with their Oscars in hand. Wilbekin's version of Black Power is anti-historical and cliché at best. Using Colin Powell and Condeleeza Rice as advocates and symbols of Black Power is especially inaccurate and misleading.

In the same issue of *Vibe*, another article equated Black Power with the economic gains and conspicuous consumption of a few hip-hop moguls. The photo accompanying the article is of a black male executive's clenched fist imitating the traditional Black Power symbol. It is easy to decipher the Rolex mark on the man's watch. The author, Audrey Edwards, opens by defining Black Power in a simple, misleading, anti-historical manner:

Back in the day, black power was about the symbols, not the benjamins. Black leather jackets and black beats. Dashikis and towering Afros...We marched and sat in. We had clear leaders then, diverse and often divided, but each with a following and a vision.

Edwards continued:

And though many of us never really thought about what black power actually looked like once we had it, we were always pretty clear on what it meant: the freedom to mix and mingle with whites as equals. To sit beside them in the classroom or on the bus or at a lunch counter, to live next to them in integrated neighborhoods, to work with them in racially diverse job settings.

Edwards's description of Black Power sounds more like an oversimplification of the Civil Rights Movement. The proponents of Black Power (the Black Panther Party, Stokely Carmichael, Malauna Karenga, Angela Davis, George Jackson, Amiri Baraka, The Republic of New Africa, D.R.U.M., and many others) did not see integration as their ultimate goal. Black cultural autonomy was central to Black Power activists. Further clouding the history of the Black Power era, Edwards claimed that "entertainment is driving American culture to black power."[35]

Popular magazines are not expected to provide deep historical analyses of Black history. This is the job of professional historians. But if widely-read magazines decide to delve into Black history they should be accurate in their presentation. Hip-hop generation historians need to be involved in actively promoting and popularizing the study of Black history among the hip-hop generation by tapping into the hip-hop ethos. A popular Black history magazine administered by hip-hop generation historians is long overdue. We are in need of an updated, hip-hop version of Woodson's *The Negro History Bulletin*, first started in 1937 as a means of broadening Black history's clientele.[36] *The Crisis*, founded by the NAACP and Du Bois in 1910, continues to address crucial issues relating to the African American community, past and present. However, it has not attracted a large following among the hip-hop generation. Published from October 1989 until June 2000, a magazine like *Emerge* needs to be reintroduced.[37] There currently exists one major, widely circulated magazine devoted to democratizing the complex study of Black history. A quarterly founded in 1998, *American Legacy: The Magazine of African-American History and Culture* is thorough, informative, reader-friendly, and covers a wide range of interesting topics in every issue. This magazine does not possess the political flavor that *The Crisis* does or that *Emerge* did, and unfortunately it does not seem to have attracted a large following within the hip-hop generation. Each issue of *American Legacy* does, however, contain informative, easy-to-read articles concerning vital issues of African American history. Such a magazine with a hip-hop culture flavor could help restore Black history's important function in black youth culture.

In the not-so-distant past, especially during and shortly after the Black Power era, *Ebony* and *Essence* were vital in promoting Black history. Their recent histories could help guide future hip-hop generationers' efforts. Lerone Bennett, Jr.'s numerous articles throughout the Civil Rights and Black Power movements not only exposed *Ebony* readers to important historical events and personalities, but he also challenged his readers to acknowledge their relationship to the past. In a paper delivered at an annual ASALH meeting, published in *Ebony* in 1980, Bennett declared: "We are responsible, totally responsible, not only for ourselves but for the whole of the Black experience. For it is only through us that the dreams of the past can be fulfilled. It is only through us that the first slave can reach the finish line."[38] During the 1970s, *Essence* featured informative articles on Africa and African culture, Black Studies, black male-female relationships, black literary figures, and Black history and culture in general. In the early 1970s, John Henrik Clarke published several articles on African Women's history more than a few years before it became a major sub-field for Africanists. During the mid to late 1970s, *Essence* featured a history section called "Family Tree." In July 1976, Anita King challenged her readership with a "Her-Story Quiz," proclaiming that throughout the course of history, black women "were not just standing on the sidelines cheering our men on."[39] This leading black women's magazine still continues to address issues pertinent to black women and other relevant issues. It deals with Black history from time to time, usually during Black History Month or in the forms of token tributes to famous black leaders and entertainers. Yet, overall it no longer possesses the political and historical flavor that it did during its formative years.

Whither "Historical Revivalism?": Recent Commercial Rap's Portrayal of Black History

Though Todd Boyd adamantly argues that the hip-hop generation cannot mimic the struggles and approaches of the Civil Rights Movement and that hip-hop better informs us about the present state of black America than the black historical record, he also acknowledges that "hip-hop is defined by a strong sense of historical identity," that it's "all about history."[40] Many of today's most popular hip-hop artists' modern Horatio Alger stories and personal histories are inspirational to black youth. Significant local and underground Black history-centered hip-hop exists, yet the rap music that dominates today's airwaves collectively does little to spark young blacks' interest in Black history. In previous generations, even during the so-called heyday of hip-hop from the 1980s until about the early–mid-1990s, young blacks could readily turn to non-underground black music for insightful discussions about the state of black people, past, present, and future. Prior to the Black Power era, music was especially functional in African American culture. Slave spirituals, Jazz, the Blues, Soul music, and R & B have all functioned in constructive, therapeutic manners in black communities.[41] Certainly, black musical expressions have been exploited for hundreds of years.[42] Yet, within the last decade, rap has reached unprecedented levels of commodification and commercialization, extolling "the virtues of conspicuous consumption."[43] In his insightful assessment of the "black popular music tradition" over the last fifty years, *What the Music Said*, Mark Anthony Neal identifies the recent shift in hip-hop's historicism:

> In less than a decade, hip-hop culture had been transformed from a subculture primarily influenced by the responses of black urban youth to postindustrialization into a billion-dollar industry in which such responses were exploited by corporate capitalist and the petit bourgeois desires of the black middle-class.

As a result, hip-hop has become disconnected from "the real communal history of the African American diaspora."[44] Recent widely-embraced, "commercial" rap is not concerned with Black history in meaningful senses. Several examples are revealing.

In "The Jump Off" from her *La Bella Mafia* album, Lil' Kim likened herself to the Black Panthers. She rhymed: "I'm the wicked bitch of the east, you better keep the peace/Or come out like the beast/We the best still there's room for improvement/Our presence is felt like the Black Panther movement." Though Lil' Kim is certainly a radical element in hip-hop, her connections with the Panthers is nonexistent. In his hit "Through the Wire," which recounts his October 2002 near-fatal car accident, Kanye West recounted: "And just imagine how my girl feel/On the plane scared as hell that her guy look like Emmett Till." West's personal triumph over tragedy is inspirational. Still, it would be refreshing if a major, rising mainstream hip-hop artist could discuss the brutal lynching of Till more directly. In a few more stanzas, West could have very easily schooled young blacks about what Till represents for the black struggle. In another track with Jay-Z on the 2003 "College Dropout" album, West mentions how his mother's and grandparents' sit-in activities influenced him. A more complete rap about the meaning and realities of the Civil Rights Movement's strategies is easily within West's range and would be very instructive to his young listeners. Mississippi native David Banner also alluded to Till in his "Cadillac on 22s" video when he sported a tee shirt paying tribute to the Civil Rights Movement martyr. Banner has the power to help reintroduce northern blacks to the history of the majority of African Americans in the South. History lessons, of course, have not been the purposes of West's and Banner's artistic expressions, and hip-hop artists certainly have the right to define their own agendas. But they clearly have the power and potential to influence many black youths by injecting Black history facts and symbols into their rhymes, which are ritualistically memorized by millions. Nelson George's observation from 1998 is still very relevant: "Hip-hop's major problem is that MCs are not social activists by training or inclination."[45]

Nas presents an interesting case. He was almost universally praised for his 2002 hit "I Can." One reviewer noted that in "I Can" Nas blows young blacks' minds with "a fact-filled verse about African empires and the dawn of European colonial aggression."[46] Given the state of commercial hip-hop, Nas's anthem was refreshing. Nas declares in a series of verses:

> Africa was almost robbed naked/Slavery was money, so they began making slave ships…Still goes on today, you see?/If the truth is told, the youth can grow/Then learn to survive and gain control/Nobody wants to be gangstas and hoes/Read more learn more, change the globe/Ghetto children, do your thing/Hold your head up, little man, you're a king.

The children's background vocals, like those that appear in Trick Daddy's thug anthem and Jaheim's "Fabulous," help draw in young listeners. Though inspirational, positive, and original, Nas's "I Can" contains a few factual inaccuracies about ancient African history. In other tracks from "God's Son," Nas demonstrated the ability to successfully include tidbits of Black history. He should also be applauded for his history-relevant lyrics on the re-mix of Jadakiss's "Why?" and his 2004 *Street's Disciple* double CD album that contains several conscious and historically relevant tracks.

In "These Are Our Heroes," Nas chastises the hip-hop generation's icons for not building upon the sacrifices of elder black entertainers and leaders such as Stokely Carmichael (Kwame Ture), Nikki Giovanni, Jim Brown, Fela Kuti, and Mariam Makeba. Echoing Spike Lee's tactics in "Bamboozled," Nas compares today's black entertainers with those of the past: "You Homey the Clown, bowtie, apple pie, Bo Jangles/But we love Bo Jangles, we know what he came through/But what's your excuse…?/…You don't ride for the facts…" In "U.B.R. (Unofficial Biography of Rakim)," Nas demonstrates his ability to clearly articulate the personal life history of a pioneer hip-hop artist. Such an approach would work well with all major personalities in African American history. In "Bridging the Gap," Nas delves into the history of black music, making relevant connections between himself and the past: "Bridging the gap from the blues to jazz to rap/The history of music on this track/The blues came from gospel, gospel from blues/Slaves are harmonizin' them ah's and ooh's/Old School, new school, know the rules/All these years I been voicin' my blues…." Nas resembles 2Pac in that his flow is impeccable, his passion prevails, and he has demonstrated the ability to produce mainstream, popular, historically conscious rap.

Yet, when compared to KRS-One's raps from the late 1980s and early 1990s about African and African American history, many of Nas's Black history-conscious tracks seem somewhat lagging behind what the times call for. KRS-One, who recently published an insightful study entitled *Ruminations* (2003) in which he discusses the meaning of Black history for the hip-hop generation, rapped about African and African American history in greater detail than any of today's mainstream rappers. His approach was clearly a byproduct of the black cultural rejuvenation of the late 1980s and early 1990s, his upbringing, and the pre-hypercommercial phase of hip-hop. In his hit "You Must Learn," from Boogie Down Production's *Ghetto Music: The Blueprint of Hip Hop* (1989), a nineteen-year-old KRS-One schooled his listeners:

> When one doesn't know about the other one's culture/Ignorance swoops down like a vulture/Cause you don't know that you ain't just a janitor/No one told you about Benjamin Banneker/A brilliant man that invented the almanac…Granville Woods made the walkie-talkie/Lewis Latimer improved on Edison/ Charles Drew did a lot for medicine/Garrett Morgan made the traffic lights/Harriet Tubman freed the slaves at night/Madame C.J. Walker made the straightening comb/But you won't know this you weren't shown/ The point I'm getting' at it might be harsh/Cause we're just walkin' around brainwashed…You must learn.

Though many of KRS-One's lyrics could have been expanded and refined, his ideas were much more historically relevant than Nas's at many levels and were more ahead of their times. A year later on his *Edutainment* album, KRS-One discussed facets of African American history in the form of brief lectures. He continues to lecture throughout he country and has shared the podium upon several occasions with Cornel West.

Those artists whose rhymes do contain detailed Black history-conscious lyrics exist today, such as Talib Kweli, dead prez, Common, Saigon, Immortal Technique, Mos Def, and others. Their music, however, does not receive the type of airplay and support needed to make large-scale impacts. The challenge becomes how to make Black history-conscious hip-hop without becoming too commercial. Rejecting the role model labels that are often placed upon them by American society, most hip-hop artists probably do not view themselves as being responsible for changing their listeners' consciousness, especially concerning Black history. But imagine if all the major "commercial" hip-hop artists agreed to devote at least one major track of every album to

Black history. Imagine if hip-hop artists agreed to collaborate with historians on a Black history album.

Embracing "Sankofa"[47] While Tapping into Hip-Hop Culture: The Necessity of Hip-Hop Generation Historians' Perspectives

Young black historians cannot simply imitate Woodson's and his co-workers' visions and efforts. I am not calling for the blind return to some utopian black historical past. Our efforts must be reflective of the distinct times in which we exist. Armed with our knowledge and distinct interpretations of history, we need to address a host of serious problems in the black community, all of which have concrete historical roots in a past marked by oppression and perseverance. Vincent Harding's eloquent articulation of the responsibilities of black scholars to "direct as much of their writing, their speaking, their teaching, and their singing" to the black community is instructive.[48] We need to embrace, engage, and speak to the young hip-hop generation whose culture is at the present time defining and directing youth culture movements across the globe. As pioneering hip-hop scholar Tricia Rose has convincingly argued, rap music and hip-hop culture have the potential to "revitalize American culture."[49]

Black historians, especially those of the hip-hop generation, need to consider creating effective, innovative, and appealing media with which to popularize and transmit Black history among black communities, especially among the hip-hop generation and the youth. The recent development of various on-line Black history websites, as well as the movement to publish easy-to-read textbooks, biographies, thematic studies, and juvenile literature, are necessary steps in making black history popular and relevant. Rap music, hip-hop culture's most characteristic creation, could serve as an effective transmitter of Black history. Cheryl Keyes has highlighted the relationship between emcees and griots (oral historians from bardic West African traditions), suggesting that modern rappers were influenced by their African oral historian predecessors.[50] Rose has defined the role of the rapper in the black community in a manner that is strikingly similar to the role of the black historian:

> Rap music is a black cultural expression that prioritizes black voices from the margins of urban America. Rap music is a form of rhymed storytelling accompanied by highly rhythmic, electronically based music…From the outset, rap music has articulated the pleasures and problems of black urban life in contemporary America…Rappers speak with the voice of personal experience, taking on the identity of the observer or narrator…Rappers tell long, involved, and sometimes abstract stories with catchy and memorable phrases and beats that lend themselves to black sound bite packaging, storing critical fragments in fast-paced electrified rhythms. Rap tales are told in elaborate and ever-changing black slang and refer to black cultural figures and rituals, mainstream film, video and television characters, and little-known black heroes.[51]

As academic emcees, hip-hop generation historians must continue to develop innovative ways to share with young blacks their communal history. We are, after all, competing with a very powerful group of musicians and artists. Of the utmost importance is that we approach our craft with the passion and energy characterizing hip-hop.

Scores of hip-hop scholars have acknowledged the pragmatism of embracing dimensions of hip-hop. Several elder scholars from a generation largely alienated from their progeny have transcended divisive generational boundaries and have also recognized this. In *Great Wells of Democracy* (2002), Manning Marable called for cross-generational dialogues and the usage of hip-hop "as a matrix for black empowerment."[52] On his debut 2001 CD, "Sketches of My Culture," Cornel West attempted to speak to the hip-hop generation by marrying hip-hop instrumentals to his intellectual discourse. Harvard's president Lawrence

Summers had no reservations in expressing his disappointment
with West's pragmatic approach to Black history and West's
album did not gain any following among the hip-hop generation.
Tapping into hip-hop culture, a centerpiece of many young black
adults' existence, could be very useful for upcoming generations
of black historians. Black historians could help restore hip-hop's
"historical revivalism." Hip-hop generation historians must help
the present and future hip-hop generations fully appreciate where
they fit in the black struggle. They should be routinely reminded
that their generation follows in the footsteps of a Black history
characterized by struggle.

A student of Black history himself, Malcolm X served as
the "archetype, reference point, and spiritual advisor in absentia"
for Black Power activists. Similarly, during the late 1980s and
early 1990s, especially following Spike Lee's 1992 film, young
blacks of the hip-hop generation looked to Malcolm X for great
inspiration. He believed adamantly that Black history was central
to blacks' collective identity.[53] While he was not a professional
historian, it is timely to reflect upon his straightforward ideas
pertaining to the significance of Black history in the black struggle for advancement. In a speech to members of the Organization
of Afro-American Unity a month before he was assassinated,
Malcolm X argued that blacks lacked a knowledge of their history, which contributed directly to their oppression. He defined
Black history in direct relation to the present:

> When you deal with the past, you're dealing with his-
> tory, you're dealing actually with the origin of a thing.
> When you know the origin, you know the cause. If you
> don't know the origin, you don't know the reason,
> you're just cut off, you're left standing in mid-air. It is
> so important for you and me to spend time today learn-

ing something about the past so that we can better understand the present, analyze it, and then do something about it.[54]

Chapter 2 of this book originally appeared elsewhere. It has been altered a bit for publication here. The author gratefully acknowledges permission to republish it. The original publication information is:

"'Of all our studies, history is best qualified to reward our research': Black History's Relevance to the Hip Hop Generation," *The Journal of African American History* Vol. 90, no. 3 (Summer 2005): 299-323.

Notes

Chapter 2

"Of all our studies, history is best qualified to reward our research": Black History's Relevance to the Hip-Hop Generation

[1] George Breitman, ed., *Malcolm X Speaks: Selected Speeches and Statements* (New York: Grove, 1965), 8.

[2] KRS-One, *Ruminations* (New York: Welcome Rain, 2003), 145, 154–155.

[3] Thorpe, *Black Historians*, 18. For discussions of the black historical profession, see Thorpe's study as well as Michael R. Winston, *The Howard Department of History: 1913–1973* (Washington, DC: The Department of History, Howard University, 1973); Franklin, "On the Evolution of Scholarship in Afro-American History," 13– 22; Meier and Rudwick, *Black History and the Historical Profession, 1915–1980*; Carter G. Woodson, "Negro Historians of Our Times," *The Negro History Bulletin* 8 (April 1945), 155–59, 166; Thorpe, *Negro Historians in the United States*; Benjamin Quarles, "Black History's Antebellum Origins," *American Antiquarian Society* 89 (1979): 89–122; John Hope Franklin, *George Washington Williams: A Biography* (Chicago: University of Chicago Press, 1985); Wilson Jeremiah Moses, *Afrotopia: The Roots of African American Popular History* (Cambridge: Cambridge University Press, 1998); Julie Des Jardins, *Women and the Historical Enterprise in America: Gender, Race, and Politics of Memory, 1880–1945* (Chapel Hill: University of North Carolina Press, 2003); Pero Gaglo Dagbovie, "Black Women Historians from the Late 19th Century until the Dawning of the Civil Rights Movement," *The Journal of African American History* 89 (Summer 2004): 241–261.

[4] Van Deburg, *New Day in Babylon*, 280.

[5] Meier and Rudwick, *Black History and the Historical Profession*, 161.

[6] Cruse, *The Crisis of the Negro Intellectual*, 565.

[7] Bazel E. Allen and Ernest J. Wilson, "Foreword," in Cruse, *The Crisis of the Negro Intellectual*, vi.

[8] Kendra Hamilton, "Making Some Noise: The Academy's Hip-Hop Generation," *Black Issues of Higher Education* 21 (22 April 2004): 35.

[9] Robin D.G. Kelley first addressed hip-hop in the 1990s. Other black historians have recently addressed hip-hop as well. These references, however, have been in passing in textbooks on the African American experience.

[10] Some of these books include: Steven Hager, *Hip Hop: The Illustrated History of Break Dancing, Rap Music, and Grafitti* (New York: St. Martin's, 1984); Houston Baker, Jr., *Black Studies: Rap and the Academy* (Chicago: University of Chicago Press, 1993); S.H. Fernando, *The New Beats: Exploring the Music, Culture, and Attitudes of Hip-Hop* (New York: Anchor, 1994), Tricia Rose, *Black Noise: Rap Music and Black Culture in Contemporary America* (Middletown: Wesleyan University Press, 1994); Russell A. Porter, *Spectacular Venaculars: Hip-Hop and the Politics of Postmodernism* (Albany: State University of New York Press, 1995); Nelson George, *Hip Hop America* (New York: Viking, 1998); Alan Light, ed., *The Vibe History of Hip Hop* (New York: Three Rivers, 1999). For a comprehensive list of sources dealing with hip-hop from the 1980s and 1990s, see the bibliography in Cheryl L. Keyes, *Rap Music and Street Consciousness* (Urbana: University of Illinois Press, 2002), 260–280.

[11] Hamilton, "Making Some Noise," 34.

[12] Untitled document, *Dergi: The Magazine*, <http://www.instanbulmuseum.org/muze/dergi/magazine/hiphp.htm>

[13] For instance, see Alonzo Westbrook, *Hip Hoptionary: The Dictionary of hip-Hop Terminology* (New York: Harlem Moon, 2002); Jim Fricke, *Yes Yes Y'all: The Experience Music Project Oral History of Hip-Hop's First Decade* (Cambridge: Da Capo, 2002); Todd Boyd, *The New H.N.I.C. (Head Niggas in Charge): The Death of Civil Rights and the Reign of Hip Hop* (New York: New York University Press, 2002); Murray Forman, *The 'Hood Comes First: Race, Space, and Place in Rap and Hip-Hop* (Middletown: Wesleyan University Press, 2002); Anthony Pinn, ed., *Noise and Spirit: The Religious and Spiritual Sensibilities of Rap Music* (New York: New York University Press, 2003); Oliver Wang, ed., *Classic Material: The Hip-Hop Album Guide* (Toronto: ECW, 2003); Todd Boyd, *Young, Black, Rich, and Famous: The*

Rise of the NBA, the Hip Hop Invasion, and the Transformation of American Culture (New York: Doubleday, 2003); Kevin Powell, *Who's Gonna Take the Weight?: Manhood, Race, and Power in America* (New York: Three Rivers, 2003); Ian Maxwell, *Phat Beats, Dope Rhymes: Hip Hop Down Under Comin' Upper* (Middletown: Wesleyan University Press, 2003).

[14] Rachel Raimist, "You Must Learn: Hip-Hop Academics Are Now on the Rise at Most Colleges," *The Source: The Magazine of Hip-Hop Music, Culture and Politics* 168 (September 2003): 57. Raimist appears to have coined the term "Hiphopology." On October 18, 2003, *The New York Times* featured a lengthy article on Rose in its "Arts and Ideas" section.

[15] Forman, *The 'Hood Comes First*, xix–xx.

[16] Robin D.G. Kelley and Earl Lewis, eds., *To Make Our World Anew: A History of African Americans* (New York: Oxford University Press, 2000), 613. Mark Anthony Neal has called what Kitwana calls the hip-hop generation "soul babies".

[17] Bakari Kitwana, *The Hip Hop Generation: Young Blacks and the Crisis in African-American Culture* (New York: Basic Civitas, 2002), xiii, 4.

[18] Aldon Morris, *The Origins of the Civil Rights Movement: Black Communities Organizing for Change* (New York: Free Press, 1984), x.

[19] For a more detailed discussion of "old head" black men, see Elijah Anderson, *Streetwise: Race, Class, and Change in an Urban Community* (Chicago: University of Chicago Press, 1990).

[20] Kitwana, *The Hip Hop Generation*, 6, 7, 8.

[21] Ibid., xiii, xiv.

[22] Kelley and Lewis, eds., *To Make Our World Anew*, 604.

[23] For a brief definition of "conscious" rap, see Yvonne Bynoe, "How Ya' Like Me Now?: Rap and Hip Hop Come of Age," in *Race and Resistance: African Americans in the 21st Century*, ed. Herb Boyd (Cambridge: South End, 2002), 89–99. Also see Keyes, *Rap Music and Street Consciousness*; Joseph D. Eure and James G. Spady, *Nation Conscious Rap* (Philadelphia: PC International, 1991).

[24] Michael Eric Dyson, *The Michael Eric Dyson Reader* (New York: Basic Civitas, 2004), 408–409.

[25] Donald Bogle, *Toms, Coons, Mulattoes, Mammies, and Bucks: An Interpretive History of Blacks in American Films* (New York: Continuum, 2001), 318, 319, 323.

[26] White, *Ar'n't I A Woman?*, 27–61.

[27] As a writer for *The Source* recently lamented, "From clothing lines to books, Pac's images are everywhere" and many have unsuccessfully "attempted to make a quick buck selling 'Tupac and me' projects." See Rob "Biko" Baker, "Tomb Raiders: Eight Years After His Death, the Music Industry Has Yet to Let Go of Tupac Shakur," *The Source* No. 180 (September 2004): 57.

[28] For a discussion of the harsh realities facing young blacks during the 1980s and 1990s, see Robin D.G. Kelley's essay, "Into the Fire," in *To Make Our World Anew*, ed. Kelley and Lewis.

[29] For a discussion of *The Source*, see George, *Hip Hop America*, 16, 17, 67, 71–72.

[30] <http://www.thesource.com>

[31] Dan Frosch, "Slum Beautiful," *The Source* 138 (March 2001): 174–179.

[32] Emil Wilbekin, "In It to Win It," *Vibe* (September 2002): 70.

[33] Emil Wilbekin, "No More Drama," *Vibe* (May 2002): 42; Wilbekin, "Follow the Leader," *Vibe* (June 2003): 26.

[34] Emil Wilbekin, "In It to Win It," 70.

[35] Audrey Edwards, "Black Power," *Vibe* (September 2002): 188.

[36] For a discussion of *The Negro History Bulletin* during Woodson's times, see Pero Gaglo Dagbovie, "Making Black History Practical and Popular: Carter G. Woodson, the Proto Black Studies Movement, and the Struggle for Black Liberation," *The Western Journal of Black Studies* 27 (Winter 2003): 263–274; and Chapter 5 of this study.

[37] *Emerge* was one of the most recent black magazines devoted to important issues, historical and contemporary, pertaining to the African American community, covering issues such as "affirmative action, economic empowerment, religion, the criminal justice system, civil rights, sexism, education, and much, much more." The articles in *Emerge* were at times hard-hitting, oftentimes historical, and could be easily digested and understood by lay members of the hip-hop generation. In

2003, former editor George E. Curry announced that he hopes to soon publish the magazine again. One did not need to search through advertisements, photos of half-naked models and hip-hop video "divas," celebrities' mansions and cars, as well as biographies of hip-hop artists, celebrities, and entertainers in order to find historically relevant articles, as seems to be the case with today's popular black magazines. See George E. Curry, ed., *The Best of Emerge Magazine* (New York: Ballantine, 2003).

[38] Bennett, "Listen to the Blood: The Meaning of Black History," 36, 38, 42.

[39] Anita King, "Her-Story Quiz," *Essence* 7 (July 1976): 20.

[40] Boyd, *The New H.N.I.C.*, 88. Throughout his diatribe, Boyd talks about how blacks of the hip-hop generation should not turn to the past for guidance. He argues that the hip-hop generation must create its own programs. At the same time, he claims, with limited evidence, that the hip-hop generation is also very historical in its orientation.

[41] For an interesting discussion of the history of black music, see Samuel A Floyd, Jr., *The Power of Black Music: Interpreting Its History from Africa to the United States* (New York: Oxford University Press, 1995).

[42] In every stage of African American history, expressions of black music have been commercialized and exploited in varying degrees. Several examples early in African American history demonstrate this. For instance, even during the middle passage it was not uncommon for African musicians to be used for entertainment purposes. Certain slaves with musical talents were identified and were often used to entertain the other slaves on the slavers, especially for aiding in daily exercise. Likewise, during the antebellum and post-bellum periods, minstrel shows and groups like the Fisk Jubilee Singers existed and were very popular.

[43] Bynoe, "How Ya' Like Me Now?: Rap and Hip Hop Come of Age," 93.

[44] Mark Anthony Neal, *What the Music Said: Black Popular Music and Black Public Culture* (New York: Routledge, 1999), 150, 154.

[45] George, *Hip Hop America*, 154–155. The lyrics of Kim, West, and all the other hip-hop artists cited in this chapter come from

<http://www.ohhla.com>, one of the most reputable websites for hip-hop lyrics.

[46] Akiba Solomon, "Record Report," *The Source* 161 (February 2003): 128.

[47] "Sankofa" (pronounced sang-ko-fah) belongs to a larger group of the Akan people's adinkra symbols. Beginning several hundred years ago, these symbols originally functioned as cultural signifiers in adinkra cloths often worn by the Akan peoples during funerals. The cloth was decorated with different adinkra symbols and "in a specific manner to convey a parting message to the deceased." Though not as prevalent as in pre-colonial times, adinkra symbols still function in their traditional capacity. They have been transformed, often reinterpreted, reconfigured, and incorporated into facets of Ghanaian, West African, and even African American popular culture. "Sankofa" means "go back to fetch it," "go back to the past in order to build for the future," and "we should not forget our past when moving ahead." In a popular version of this symbol, a bird with its head facing backward, often searching through its feathers, is used. These symbols should be embraced by African Americans, especially by members of the hip-hop generation. Black history and the strategies and philosophies of our ancestors should be a part of our daily lives, helping guide our actions, decisions, and thought in the present and future. For more detail on "Sankofa" and adinkra symbols in general, see W. Bruce Willis, *The Adinkra Dictionary: A Visual Primer on the Language of Adinkra* (Washington, DC: The Pyramid Complex, 1998).

[48] Vincent Harding, "Responsibilities of the Black Scholar to the Community," in *The State of Afro-American History*, ed. Hine, 279–281.

[49] Rose, *Black Noise*, 185.

[50] Keyes, *Rap Music and Street Consciousness*, 18–19.

[51] Rose, *Black Noise*, 2–3.

[52] Manning Marable, *Great Wells of Democracy: The Meaning of Race in American Life* (New York: Basic Books, 2002), 269–270.

[53] Van Deburg, *New Day in Babylon*, 2–10.

[54] Malcolm X, *Malcolm X on Afro-American History*, 4–5.

CHAPTER 3

Towards a Deeper Understanding of Black History Month: Revisiting Its Roots

Most Americans, regardless of their ethnic heritage, have probably heard of Black History Month but have not heard of Carter G. Woodson. It is hoped this will soon change, especially in Washington, D.C. where Woodson's former home will become a museum and a tourist attraction as a result of the passage of "a federal bill establishing the house as a National Historic Site."[1] As an undergraduate and graduate student during the 1990s, I used to routinely visit elementary and high schools during the month of February. I still engage in this type of outreach education from time to time, but now focus my energies on working with college students. As is the case with black scholars throughout the country, every February I am bombarded with invitations and requests to speak at various venues. I often remind educators, students, and institutions that Black history can be discussed during the other eleven months with equal effectiveness and relevance. Black History Month celebrations at many colleges and universities often become unproductive because administrators and students pack February with activities and keynote speakers to the point that it is impossible to check everything out. If such events were spread out between September and May, those interested could relax and soak in black culture. Spreading out events related to Black history would also

119

fulfill Woodson's ultimate goal: a pluralistic, multicultural interpretation of U.S. and world history.

Whatever the case may be, I usually begin my Black History Month presentations with the following question: *Who
founded Black History Month?* Regardless of the age of my audience, I am usually met with silence or hear the names of Martin Luther King, Jr., Malcolm X, Jesse Jackson, Rosa Parks, Harriet Tubman, Frederick Douglass, and Sojourner Truth blurted
out with confidence. Students enrolled in my introductory surveys in African American History also often initially share this
same type of historical ignorance. This lack of knowledge about
Carter G. Woodson, black historians, and Black history in general is not surprising. It is indicative of the failure of truly integrating the study of African Americans into American educational institutions and infrastructures. I myself did not know de-
tails about Woodson until first discovering him and other pioneering black historians as an undergraduate student in the early
1990s while reading Molefi Kete Asante's *The Afrocentric Idea*
and John Hope Franklin's important essay on the black historical
enterprise, "On the Evolution of Scholarship in Afro-American
History." As a graduate student, I then gradually began expanding my knowledge on Woodson by reading the scholarly works
of Lorenzo Johnston Greene, Charles H. Wesley, Rayford W.
Logan, L.D. Reddick, Earl E. Thorpe, Sister Anthony Scally,
August Meier and Elliott Rudwick, Jacqueline Goggin, and others.

The fundamental argument of this chapter is straightforward. I maintain that the Negro History Weeks of Carter G.
Woodson's times were much more practical and effective than
the Black History Months of more recent times. We need to return to the Woodsonian vision, adapt it to the present situation,
and make Black history practical, accessible, and something
truly interesting and valuable to the masses of black people, especially to the black youth and hip-hop generation. We could
achieve great things by meshing Woodson's vision with our cur-

rent knowledge and advanced state of technology. During the last decade or so, Black History Month (February), very much like Kwanzaa (December 26 through January 1) and Martin Luther King, Jr. Day (the third Monday of January), has become commercialized and in many ways co-opted by the materialistic and capitalistic ethos of American culture. In many regards, our annual Black History Month celebrations have been transformed into something that Woodson was opposed to back in his day. How did Black History Month come to be celebrated during the entire month of February? How has Black History Month been commercialized since its inception, and how does its process of co-optation resemble what has happened in recent years to Kwanzaa and Martin Luther King, Jr. Day? What were the Negro History Weeks of Woodson's days like? In what ways were they more productive than those of the present times? These are the chief questions that this chapter seeks to answer.

The Commodification of Black History Month, Kwanzaa, and Martin Luther King, Jr. Day

Since 1976, during the month of February—the shortest month of the year—Americans have routinely paid tribute to the contributions of African Americans to U.S. history in the form of what we call Black History Month. During America's Bicentennial celebration in 1976, the Association for the Study of Negro Life and History or the ASNLH (now the Association for the Study of African American Life and History or the ASALH) expanded Woodson's annual celebration of Negro History Week. In 1926, Woodson founded Negro History Week in order to celebrate African Americans' contributions to U.S. history and culture, instill blacks with pride and self-esteem, and integrate the study of blacks into all American schools' curricula. Woodson selected the second week of February for this celebration in order to acknowledge the births and contributions of Abraham Lincoln and Frederick Douglass. Douglass clearly was a freedom fighter, but many today would probably wonder why Woodson associated Lincoln with his celebration. Woodson certainly understood Lincoln's open anti-black attitudes, behavior, and actions; however, when placed within the context of U.S. presidents and the vast majority of whites, especially those in the South during his times, Lincoln could have been viewed as being pro-black. That is, he was assassinated because he remotely, and this should be stressed, inferred at times that he did not believe in white supremacy. Lerone Bennett, Jr. has published a thought-provoking study entitled *Forced Into Glory: Abraham Lincoln's White Dream* (1999) which challenges the conventional characterization of Lincoln as being "the great emancipator." Among other things, Bennett argues that when viewed side by side with various Radical Republicans and abolitionists such as John Brown, Lincoln was not an outspoken advocate of black freedom.[2] Woodson's times did not allow him to develop such a critical approach to Lincoln.

After fifty years of celebrating Negro History Week, in 1976 the ASNLH decided to push to expand the traditionally week-long celebration to incorporate the entire month of February. After the ASNLH strategically issued this call 200 years after the Declaration of Independence, the U.S. government supported it in the form of annual presidential proclamations and the celebration caught on and continued to grow. The exact point at which Black History Month became linked with American capitalism and commercial life is unknown, but is was an inevitable transition. Profit-seekers exploited the Negro History Weeks of Woodson's time. Black History Month was bound to become a pawn of American capitalism.

By the mid-1970s, many U.S. corporations capitalized on Black History Month and the vestiges of black cultural pride left over from the Black Power era. *Essence* magazine, founded during the peak of the Black Power movement, featured many advertisements that used Black history and Black History Month to target middle-class black spenders. United Airlines released an ad in *Essence* in 1975 and 1976 that told blacks to "celebrate yesterday's heroes" by visiting historical sites related to black historical figures such as Jean Baptiste Point Du Sable, Peter Salem, Bose Ikard, and Harriet Tubman. Several years later, in 1977, one of United's competitors, American Airlines, featured an ad featuring images of Frederick Douglass, James Beckworth, and Crispus Attucks. "Relive American History on an American Fly-Drive," American Airlines declared, "Now you can visit the historical places you've read and heard about. Places where great men spoke out for what they believed in." In the same year, the U.S. government urged *Essence* readers to purchase U.S. savings bonds in memory of Benjamin Banneker's surveying of the nation's capital. Chrysler used a brother with a big afro and dashiki to sell its vehicles. Bell telephone company marketed its products by claiming that they understood and respected blacks' unique history of communication and oral history, from the griots in West Africa to the present, and blacks' success in the motion picture and television industries. An obscure company named SOIL based in Mississippi offered *Essence* readers "genuine African earth encased in clear acrylic" "direct from Nigeria" for $10.50. This company claimed that the dirt was inspected by the U.S. government and represented "the soil on which trod the forefathers of Black America." Though educational, several companies, at least one of which was black-owned, marketed Black history board games in *Essence*. Similar ads also appeared in *Ebony*.[3]

By the mid-1980s, Black History Month was more directly being used by many corporations to sell products. In reality, these businesses cared little about black life and history. In the February 1986 issue of *Ebony*, there were several pages of "Black History Month Money Saving Coupons." Businesses such as Duncan Hines, Tide, Tylenol, Uncle Ben's Rice, Aunt Jemima, Artra Skin Tone Cream, Sinutab, LaxCaps, Carefree Panty Shields, and many others joined the Black History Month bandwagon by strategically offering coupons for their products on token salutes to famous black pioneers and inventors. *Essence* carried similar coupons. Since the mid–late 1980s, Philip Morris, Anheuser-Bush, Coors, McDonalds, Coca-Cola, Nissan, and many others have also been involved in Black History Month marketing. Some department stores have even had Black History Month sales. Several years ago during February, I recall seeing on top of gas pumps at Mobile cards saluting Black History Month.

Today, companies such as Campus Marketing Specialists, Inc. are seeking to make profits from the history of the African American struggle by mass marketing Black History Month posters, pens, notepads, buttons, key tags, bookmarks, stadium cups, and faux Kente cloth scarves. Some may believe that this publicity helps popularize Black history. Memorabilia can indeed help publicize Black History Month, but the millions of dollars made from this type of marketing should, as Woodson championed, be invested into the Black history movement and the black struggle. Black consumers should also be aware of these disrespectful marketing ploys.

During the 1990s, black historians and scholars voiced some of their concerns regarding the commercialization of Black History Month in a manner similar to how Woodson warned about the misuse of Negro History Week. In a mild critique of how Black History Month was losing its Woodsonian flavor, in a 1995 issue of *Ebony* John Hope Franklin, Robert L. Harris, Jr., Bettye J. Gardner, and Darlene Clark Hine declared that studying and celebrating Black history needed to be spread throughout the year and not simply relegated to February.[4]

In 1997, *The Journal of Blacks in Higher Education* (hereafter *JBHE*) initiated a scholarly forum on the meaning and usefulness of Black History Month. They asked a "group of distinguished African-American historians" whether Black History Month was still needed. The *JBHE* was openly opposed to Black History Month not because they were conservatives but because they believed that it had been "usurped by large corporations" and greedy book publishers.[5] They argued that Black History Month justified the marginalization of blacks' monumental contributions to U.S. history. In their view, this celebration during what Dick Gregory dubbed the month "with all them days missing" should have been substituted with the true integration of Black history into the overall American experience. John Hope Franklin chastised marketers and lecturers for capitalizing on the celebration. In overt Woodsonian fashion, an elderly Franklin commented:

> The commercialization of the 'month' provides the hucksters with a longer period in which to sell their trinkets and souvenirs, corporations a greater opportunity to display their special brand of 'civic awareness,' and lecturers the golden chance to show off their knowledge of black history.[6]

Franklin, however, did not share the *JBHE* writers' sentiments that Black History Month should be done away with. He believed that the month was partially successful in terms of educating people and vowed to continue to help spread the word.

Harold Cruse noted that the Negro History Weeks of Woodson's times profoundly impacted him, but he openly dissed contemporary black historians for offering "very little, if anything, in the way of new interpretations of the 'celebratory' factor already known at the black high school or college level." In his classic iconoclastic style, he challenged black historians to innovate new ways of conceptualizing Black History Month to suit the times. "The bulk of the new bunch of black historians has little to say that is really new, inventive, or revealing," [7] Cruse lashed out. Cruse's harsh and unsubstantiated indictment of black historians coming of age in the late 1990s could have very well represented an unresolved carryover from *The Crisis of the Negro Intellectual*. Yet, his criticisms are refreshing at one level. In post-Civil Rights era America, debates among black scholars seem to have decreased. Black scholars need to return to critically challenging each other so that we can push each other to more fully maximize our potential. Cross-generational debates are especially needed. Hip-hop generation historians should respond to Cruse's challenges by helping incorporate Black History Month into hip-hop culture. Making Black history practical and popular among the masses of black youth today—given America's overall anti-historical culture, unless the sanitized history bolsters patriotism—would certainly be something new, inventive, and revealing. In order to successfully accomplish this, the black historian needs to immerse him/herself in hip-hop culture enough to reach the youth. This immersion, however, must be monitored so as not to render oneself unproductive and disrespected as a historian.

Activist-columnist Earl Ofari Hutchinson has offered some refreshing views of Black History Month that synthesize many of the opinions offered during the 1990s:

> Seventy-four years ago, pioneer black historian Carter G. Woodson initiated what Woodson called Negro History Week. He wanted to rescue black people's accomplishments from the netherworld of American history and make them a source of pride for blacks and all Americans. Today Black History Month is an established tradition. Politicians designate special days, issue proclamations and sponsor tributes to African American notables. TV networks shove in most of their specials, documentaries and features on blacks. Then February ends, and it's back to business as usual. Black achievements vanish from the screen, the concert halls and the speeches of politicians. It's time to end this annual disappearing act. Black contributions to society should be celebrated every month...When the experience of blacks is accepted as central to the American story, black history will be what it always should have been—American history.[8]

Hutchinson's observations were right on track and speak accurately to the current times.

Similar critiques can be made of two other African American holidays and celebrations that were founded in the 20th century. Kwanzaa and Martin Luther King, Jr. Day have both been commercialized and watered down like Black History Month. Kwanzaa was founded by Malauna Karenga in 1966. During the Black Power era, Karenga advocated a cultural nationalist program. He believed that an important part of the black struggle was in the realm of culture. He and others called upon blacks to celebrate and take pride in their African roots and heritage. Karenga developed the Nguzo Saba—seven key principles and values that could, he reasoned, help blacks achieve psychological and material liberation. In 1966, he created Kwanzaa, a celebration that served as a substitute to how Americans traditionally approached Christmas. The first Kwanzaa was held mainly in Los Angeles from December 26, 1966 until January 1, 1967. In the words of Karenga, the holiday was created to "reaffirm and restore our rootedness in African culture," to "serve as a regular communal celebration to reaffirm and reinforce bonds between us as a people...to be an ingathering to strengthen community and reaffirm common identity, purpose and direction as a people and a world community," and to "introduce and reinforce the *Nguzo Saba.*"[9]

Since Karenga first created this holiday, it has been increasingly more commercialized and watered down. While there are many black cultural nationalists who still practice Kwanzaa in the traditional manner, the holiday has been co-opted at many levels by the American capitalistic system and has swayed from Karenga's ideal, original plan. By the early 1990s, when we witnessed a post-Black Power era increase in black cultural consciousness, Kwanzaa became more commodified and linked to American capitalism. This commercialization of Karenga's holiday has not gone unnoticed. In fact, since the 1990s there have been some ongoing debates concerning the transformations undergone by Kwanzaa since its inception.

In the early 1990s, even major white-run newspapers such as *The New York Times* discussed the concerns regarding "the marketing of Kwanzaa."[10] While publicizing Kwanzaa, their discussions tended to shift the focus away from the real significance of the holiday as an expression of black cultural solidarity, nationalism, and identity. In the mid-1990s, concerned black activists formed the Coalition to Preserve the Sacredness and Integrity of Kwanzaa in response to a Kwanzaa Holiday Expo in New York City. Many black journalists also pointed out the dangers in marketing Kwanzaa. For instance, one African American writer for the *Philadelphia Tribune* declared that "Kwanzaa is not a civil rights project. It is a Black Power project." It is not "aimed at integration," he continued, "but rather the national interest of African-Americans as a self-determining people...Let's not destroy it by exploiting its true meaning."[11] Expressing similar sentiments, a writer from the *New Pittsburgh Courier* lamented that the state of Kwanzaa in 1996 had drifted from Karenga's initial purpose. "By allowing large retailers to distribute our ethnic goods, we have, in a sense, opened the door to the commercialization of our heritage...We cannot cheapen our beautiful heritage because this devalues our history as a great people."[12]

Karenga joined in the debates during the late 1990s as well. He commented that he was not surprised that Kwanzaa had been commodified. Referencing what had been done to Christmas and Hanukah in the United States over the years, he viewed the marketing of Kwanzaa as being a natural development in a capitalist society. Karenga interpreted the media's focus on the economic viability of Kwanzaa as being detrimental because none of the mainstream newspapers unpacked the deeper meanings of Kwanzaa. Karenga's simple solution called upon blacks to "reaffirm and hold to the essential meaning of Kwanzaa and refuse to cooperate with the corporate drive to dominate and redefine it and make it simply another holiday to maximize sales."[13] Karenga's words are very relevant to the present state of Kwanzaa celebrations.

Today, there are Kwanzaa commercials and salutes on major television stations, Kwanzaa dolls are sold in toy stores, the majority of blacks who celebrate the holiday all over the world celebrate both Kwanzaa and Christmas, and companies continue to capitalize on black Americans' spending power during the holiday season. Since 1992, Hallmark has been mass-producing Kwanzaa cards. Hallmark is just one of many major U.S. corporations that produces Kwanzaa products. Other major corporations involved in marketing Kwanzaa include Anheuser-Bush; Pepsi Cola; Revlon; Wal-Mart; Chemical Bank; JC Penney; AT&T; Time/Life Books; Proctor and Gamble; Safeway grocery stores; Bed, Bath, and Beyond; K-mart; and countless others. Of course, we know that these companies are not down with the black struggle for equality and liberation. Collectively, they have all made a great deal of money from Kwanzaa. It was estimated that in 2000, when about five million African American families celebrated Kwanzaa, "more than $700 million was spent on Kwanzaa-related merchandise."[14] Perhaps the most tragic part of this transformation of Kwanzaa is that this trend is directly opposed to the essence of this "first fruits" holiday; it goes against the fourth principle, Ujamaa, cooperative economics. Not only are anti-black, racially ambivalent, and/or racially neutral capitalistic corporations reaping millions of dollars from Kwanzaa, but much of the merchandise, especially the unity cups and kinaras (candle holders) are being made in countries like China, Taiwan, and India by an exploited workforce. When Karenga created the holiday, participants were supposed to exercise Kuumba (creativity) by making the zawadi (the gifts). Today many purchase gifts from outside the black community. Young blacks from the hip-hop generation need to reclaim Kwanzaa, restoring it to its original state. In order to accomplish this, young blacks need to revisit African American history. The Black Power era, like all of the other periods of the black American experience, has a lot to offer the hip-hop generation. Given the militant tone of much of the hip-hop music, they should be able to gravitate towards this movement.

The fate of Martin Luther King, Jr. Day is similar to that of Kwanzaa and Black History Month. As Michael Eric Dyson pointed out in his controversial *I May Not Get There with You: The True Martin Luther King, Jr.*, the history behind King's birthday becoming a national holiday is interesting and reflective of the struggle that African Americans have faced for hundreds of years. On April 4, 1968, Martin Luther King, Jr. was assassinated. He was only 39 years old. Four days later, Michigan Congressman John Conyers declared that he wanted to introduce a bill to make King's birthday a federal holiday. Throughout the 1960s, 1970s, and 1980s, there was a great amount of debate concerning this issue. In 1971, the Southern Christian Leadership Conference (SCLC), got 3 million signatures of people supporting making King's birthday a federal and national holiday. They submitted their petition to Congress. They were unsuccessful at first. In the mid-1970s, several states, including Illinois, Massachusetts, Connecticut, and New Jersey created their state-wide celebrations to honor the life, work, and vision of King. Certainly, those in favor of the holiday faced significant resistance.

In 1979, Coretta Scott King testified before the Senate Judiciary Committee and before a joint hearing of Congress, declaring the importance of her husband's contributions to U.S. history and culture. A year later, in 1980, Stevie Wonder joined the struggle and released his famous hit "Happy Birthday." Many of us hip-hop generationers have perhaps listened to this jam without realizing that Wonder, a longtime activist, created this song to protest for the making of MLK, Jr. Day. With this hit, he raised money for the struggle. In 1981, The King Center decided to devote its energies to the cause, establishing a "holiday coalition." Coretta Scott King and Stevie Wonder then presented 6 million signatures to the Speaker of the House in favor of honoring MLK, Jr. In August 1983, the House of Representatives voted on the MLK, Jr. holiday bill—338 voted in favor of the bill and 90 were opposed. In 1979, during the Carter administration, the bill was voted against in the House of Representatives. In October 1983, the Senate, in response to a march in Washington, DC with nearly 1 million folks, "passed the bill by a vote of 78 to 22." On November 3, 1983, Ronald Reagan—known for his open stance against blacks' civil rights—signed the bill "establishing the third Monday of each January as the Martin Luther King, Jr. national holiday." Since then, as Dyson has highlighted, there have been many arguments against celebrating the life and work of King.[15]

While honoring King is great and much needed, the holiday established in his honor has been watered down and has lost much of its focus and purpose. During the first several months of January each month, we are bombarded with images of King delivering his famous "I Have a Dream" oration delivered in 1963. The post-1963 King who spoke about poor people across the nation and the horrors of war is never publicized by the white American media. At another level, the American public is not even exposed to the entire "I Have a Dream" speech. King said some quite radical things in this speech. In fact, he called for reparations without any apology. Before he went off on his "I have a dream..." tip, he called out the United States for its brutal mistreatment of African Americans. He also called for reparations. In his most well-known speech, after noting that 100 years after the Emancipation Proclamation the black was "an exile in his own land," he declared:

So we've come here today to dramatize a shameful condition. In a sense, we've come to our nation's capital to cash a check. When the architects of our republic wrote the magnificent words in the Constitution and the Declaration of Independence, they were signing a promissory note to which every American was to fall heir. This note was the prose that all men, yes, black men as well as white men, would be guaranteed the unalienable rights of life, liberty, and the pursuit of happiness.

It is obvious today that America has defaulted on this promissory note in so far as her citizens of color are concerned. Instead of honoring this sacred obligation, America has given the Negro people a bad check; a check which has come back marked "insufficient funds." We refuse to believe that there are insufficient funds in the great vaults of opportunity of this nation. And so we've come to cash this check, a check that will give us upon demand the riches of freedom and security of justice.[16]

Why are we not bombarded with these words from King on the third Monday of every January? King has been molded by the white American media in order to turn him into something that does not represent the totality of his character. King lived beyond 1963 when he delivered his "I Have a Dream" speech and, at another level, his messages were multilayered. As did Booker T. Washington from the 1880s through 1915, King simultaneously spoke to many different audiences and at many different levels. Though the holiday was born out of struggle and has done some positive things in terms of elevating a black leader in a manner that should happen more often in U.S. society, the King holiday has, like Kwanzaa and Black History Month, become watered down, misused, and has drifted from its original intentions. King's image has been marketed for profits. One of the most controversial examples was the advertisement from the French communications company Alcatel. They reconfigured original footage from King's "I Have a Dream" oration and erased the crowd of more 250,000 marchers. Alcatel straight up capitalized on King's holiday and image in popular American culture. There has been a great deal of debate pertaining to the

King family's willingness to market him.[17] David Garrow, Manning Marable, and many others have openly voiced their opposition to what they perceive as the King family's commercialization of Martin Luther King, Jr. Clayborne Carson, on the other hand, sees nothing new with Dexter King's commercialization of his father's legacy. He believes that he is merely seeking to gain control over a phenomenon which has been taking place for some time.[18]

Celebrating Black History Woodson Style

The Negro History Week celebrations of Woodson's times were much more practical, relevant, and influential than today's Black History Month celebrations. Those of us from the hip-hop generation really need to check out what Woodson was dealing with and sample from his programs. Armed with advanced technology, more access to education, greater mobility, and hip-hop music, we could convert Black history into a very powerful vehicle for practical social reform.

Several historians seem to agree that the concept of Negro History Week originated in 1920. In that year, Woodson delivered a speech entitled "Democracy and the Man Far Down" to members of the Omega Psi Phi fraternity in Nashville, Tennessee. During the presentation, Woodson commented that these fraternity members needed to become more active in promoting the study of black life and history. This Omega chapter responded by devoting one week out of every year to the study of Black history. They called their celebration "Negro History and Literature Week." Their efforts continued until 1925. Woodson did not acknowledge the Association's Negro History Week as an extension of the Omegas' efforts. He explained the reason behind Negro History Week in a pamphlet widely distributed months before the first celebration was to take place during the second week in February 1926, in commemoration of Frederick Douglass's and Abraham Lincoln's birthdays. Woodson told his readers that blacks knew "practically nothing" about their history and that without this knowledge "the race" could become "a negligible factor in the thought of the world" and stood "in danger of being exterminated."[19]

Woodson added that race prejudice, from segregation to violence, resulted from the widely accepted notion that black people had not contributed anything of worth to world civilization. He argued that if the historical record were set straight and that if in schools the history of black people were studied along with the achievements of others, not only would black youth develop a sense of pride and self-worth, but racism would be abolished. Woodson ended his plea:

> Let truth destroy the dividing prejudice of nationality and teach universal love without distinction of race, merit or rank. With sublime enthusiasm and heavenly vision of the Great Teacher let us help men rise above the race hate of their age unto the altruism of a rejuvenated universe.[20]

Today, part of Woodson's plan may seem naive and optimistic, especially the contention that exposing whites to Black history would eliminate prejudice. Yet, for the time, Woodson's thought was understandable. Like his predecessors, he attempted to explain why blacks had been dehumanized for centuries.[21]

Negro History Week was the first major achievement in popularizing Black history and one of the few movements in the broader Black history movement to prioritize and focus on the youth. Woodson realized that the mis-education of black people began in their homes, communities, and elementary schools. He therefore targeted these sites aggressively, focusing on the schools. Woodson's strategy of gradually introducing Black history as a supplement to white American history has been deemed conservative by some. To the contrary, it was pragmatic and, at the same time, very radical when analyzed in the broader context of his agenda. Woodson knew that if he had demanded that

Black history be integrated into the American educational system all at once, his plan would have been too easily dismissed. Woodson concluded that a modest week-long celebration during the winter season was much less threatening to the white public, philanthropists, and to those "highly mis-educated Negroes" whom he sought to convert into devout black nationalists.[22]

The meaning of Negro History Week had deeper implications for Woodson. This week in February was to serve as a steppingstone toward the gradual introduction of Black history into the curricula of educational institutions, from the elementary school years through college, throughout American communities, black and white. He wanted Negro History Week to evolve into Negro History Year. Routinely, Woodson instructed those observing the week that they needed to prepare for the celebration months in advance and that after mid-February they should not ignore the role of African descendants in world history. "Negro History Week should be a demonstration of what has been done in the study of the Negro during the year and at the same time as a demonstration of greater things to be accomplished," Woodson instructed school teachers. "A subject which receives attention one week out of the thirty-six will not mean much to anyone."[23]

According to Woodson, soon after he mailed out his first "Negro History Week Circulars" to various educational institutions, presses, fraternal and social welfare organizations, literary societies, and radio stations, "there was a stir in the direction of active participation." He boasted that "there were few places in the country where this celebration did not make some impression."[24] Woodson offered to those interested a concrete program along with research and promotional materials that highlighted black achievements, from ancient times in Africa to contemporary times. People who decided to take part in the celebration had autonomy over the week's activities, Woodson reassured. Woodson did, however, offer a host of suggestions.

In pamphlets and *Negro History Bulletin* articles, he routinely instructed participants to organize committees for the celebration months before Negro History Week. He outlined the critical steps to success: involving the board of education in their area to introduce black history books into school curricula, advertising the events extensively, recording oral testimonies from elders within the community, persuading libraries to order Black history books, setting aside one day of every week as a "Book and Picture Fund Day" to raise money to purchase Black history books for the community, sending in any relevant historical documents into the Association so that they could be properly maintained, organizing Black history clubs, and creating a pageant highlighting the struggles of black Americans. He added special suggestions to school teachers about maximizing the involvement of the youth in practical ways.[25]

During the celebrations there were banquets, breakfasts, speeches, parades, exhibits, and lectures that were usually held in churches, black colleges and universities, and community centers. Woodson insisted that all the meetings and events be free to the public. For this week, Woodson stressed that speakers and organizers must donate their time to the cause. School teachers, mainly black women, were vital Negro History Week organizers. They raised funds in their communities; they had their students compose essays on famous blacks and events in Black history; and some had their students act in historical plays and pageants, taken largely from an anthology written for elementary students called *Plays and Pageants for the Life of the Negro*.[26]

After its inception in 1926, Negro History Week continued to expand. In his Annual Reports of the Director, Woodson noted that every year Negro History Week drew a greater following. In many volumes of the *Journal* after 1926, Woodson devoted brief articles to describing the success of the various programs. He was very pleased that Negro History Week had eventually made its way into the black churches, self-help organizations, public schools, and even to rural areas. In 1932, he also noted that Negro History Week was finding its way into white schools, facilitating better "inter-racial relations." These changes pleased Woodson, who commented two decades after Negro History Week began that "when only Negroes are reached only half the battle has been won." With each passing year, the black and occasionally the white press advertised local and national events. The most active presses in helping publicize Woodson's movement early on included *The Philadelphia Tribune, Baltimore Commonwealth, Chicago Defender, The Palmetto Leader, The Tampa Bulletin, The Washington Eagle,* and the *Norfolk Guide and Journal.* Later, they were joined by other more widely distributed newspaper publishers. Various radio stations were instrumental in publicizing and broadcasting Negro History Week events.[27]

By the 1940s, Negro History Week celebrations were increasingly popular, even abroad. Woodson developed elaborate programming schedules. In November 1948, in order to help rural schools with little or no resources, Woodson introduced Negro History Week Kits at $2.00 apiece. At first, the kits included writings and speeches by famous blacks as well as a play depicting Black history. Two years later, they were revised by Woodson to also include many photos of famous blacks as well as a list of books for further research. The cost for this edition was $2.50.

The Negro History Weeks of Woodson's times differed drastically from most Black History Month celebrations of the current era. For Woodson, it was of the utmost importance for the people themselves, especially the children, to create their own unique, personalized celebrations. While Woodson offered many suggestions, he challenged those interested in discovering the value of their past to do the uncovering themselves. In October 1941, he offered the following advice to school teachers:

Do not call in some silver-tongued orator to talk to your school about the history of the Negro. The orator does not generally have much in his head. His chief qualification is strong lungs—a good bellows. He knows very little about things in general and practically nothing about the Negro in particular except how to exploit the race. Let the children study the history of the race, and they will be the speakers who will put the spellbinder to shame.[28]

As Negro History Week became more popular, Woodson believed that there was a class of people that was exploiting the celebration for its own benefit. In the pages of the *Journal* and the *Bulletin*, he routinely warned his readers about "the disastrous methods of pseudo-historians among Negroes exaggerating in spectacular fashion facts of minor importance" in order to capitalize on a movement and transform it into a commercial venture. He was especially enraged with those "impostors" and "mis-informants," mainly entertainers, who, under the name of the ASNLH, made large profits during mid-February. At one point, he even demanded that they turn over their earnings to the Association, and he called upon Negro History Week organizers to boycott those "mischievous orators" and instead call upon one of the many historians whom Woodson trained.[29] Today, countless black scholars, personalities, and motivational speakers get paid because of Black History Month. If Woodson were still alive, he would demand that the money made by these speakers be invested in the Black history movement and that the youth themselves act as the researchers and speakers. As Afrocentric critic Manu Ampim has convincingly argued, we have invested too much in the notion that lecturing alone will help create social change. "Monetary interests" have clearly influenced more than a few black intellectuals to become professional lecturers.[30]

Woodson was still disturbed by the fact that as late as 1945 most students and teachers celebrated Negro History Week by calling up some black historian to secure some tidbits of information that they could in turn regurgitate to others. He was vexed that most school books on the black past "found their way to some shelf where they serve mainly to catch a portion of dust raised in that room." In one sense, he admitted the shortcomings of Negro History Week to penetrate into the psyche of American society. "It is evident then," he noted five years before he died, "that our supplementary books on the Negro supplement nothing in most of our schools."[31]

Despite Woodson's frequent pessimism, which counterbalanced his unrelenting faith that his people could humanize American culture, Negro History Week was a monumental movement. Yet, assessing the impact of Negro History Week celebrations on black working-class and youth consciousness from 1926 until 1950 is a difficult task. We can assume that many of those blacks who took part in these events felt great pride in their heritage and that some open-minded whites who witnessed and helped sponsor such events may have changed their views of Black history and culture.

School children were probably the most highly transformed by these events. They learned by doing, researching the lives of famous blacks, and acting in plays that depicted the African-American past. Woodson went out of his way to detail specific things children should do during Negro History Week. In the February 1938 issue of the *Bulletin*, for instance, Woodson instructed children to "make a study" of their school's history; to collect newspaper articles on "prominent" blacks in their county, city, or state; to explore the history of blacks in the professions; and to create a play or pageant that represented "every phase of life and every phase of struggle through which the race has come."[32]

Throughout the late 1930s and 1940s, *Bulletin* readers, especially female school teachers, wrote to Woodson, sharing with him, often in great detail, how they conducted their Negro History Week celebrations and how the process had influenced them and the other participants. Woodson often published these commentaries in the *Bulletin*. Many testified that Negro History

Week had helped transform their cultural and political consciousness. Carrie E. Johnson, a school teacher from Troy, Alabama, told Woodson that his work "has been my greatest inspiration in making me want to devote all my time to the study of my race."[33]

Many of Woodson's colleagues also believed that Negro History Week was his "most characteristic creation." One of Woodson's most devoted Negro History Week promoters, Luther Porter Jackson, called Negro History Week "the feeder for every other activity of the Association." In paying tribute to the Association founder, L.D. Reddick noted that "his greatest influence upon the public mind came through Negro History Week." Reddick believed that the effect of Negro History Week on African Americans' self-confidence, poise, desire to achieve, and morale "defies measurement." This "mass education program" and "God-send for the Association," he noted, pleased Woodson to "no end" and upon several occasions he deemed it the Association's most valuable contribution to reconceptualizing black life and history. Woodson extended himself during this month. In 1933, during the peak of the Great Depression, Woodson spent not only the week of Negro History Week lecturing at various venues, but the next month "in the field," lecturing and helping people organize throughout the country. [34] "By far," Woodson noted in the early 1930s, "the greatest stimulus given to the educational work of the Association in recent years has been the observance of Negro History Week."[35]

The impact of Negro History Week went beyond the African American community during Woodson's lifetime. In 1949, Morris U. Schappes, a member of the American Jewish Historical Society, wrote Woodson that at their annual meeting in February they decided to observe Jewish History Week from April 24 until April 30. He told Woodson that their decision was influenced by the success of Negro History Week. Woodson took pride in this wide-reaching impact of the Association's work and told blacks that they could learn a lot from the cultural national-ism of their Jewish counterparts.[36]

Many black historians, scholars, intellectuals, teachers, children, laypersons, and communities embraced Woodson's celebration. It was not, however, free from criticism during and after his lifetime. According to Harold Cruse, during the late 1940s and early 1950s black journalists debated the significance of Negro History Week. Writers for *The New York Amsterdam News* declared that it was "time to get rid of Negro History Week celebrations" because it supposedly isolated the black experience from U.S. history. *The Baltimore Afro-American* welcomed Negro History Week as one of the most important vehicles of Black history.[37] More than a decade later, Malcolm X, who praised Woodson in his autobiography, concluded that Negro History Week had been co-opted by white America: "It doesn't remind us of past achievements, it reminds us only of the achievements we made in the Western hemisphere under the tutelage of the white man." Malcolm believed that Negro History Week celebrations ignored black America's glorious African past and background. He was also opposed to calling the celebration *Negro History Week*. Malcolm proclaimed:

> As long as you call yourself a Negro, nothing is yours. It attaches nothing to you…They take you out of existence by calling you a Negro…It's a person who has no history; and by having no history, he has no culture. Just as a tree without roots is dead, a people without history or cultural roots also becomes a dead people.[38]

This brief history of the deeper roots of today's Black History Month celebrations demonstrates that the Negro History Weeks of Carter G. Woodson's times were complex, well-organized, systematic, and quite successful. Woodson's main goals were to: expose blacks to their history and culture in order to promote racial pride and self-esteem, expose whites to Black history in hopes of getting rid of racial prejudice and in turn promoting racial harmony, and integrate the study of Black history into American educational institutions. While a variety of audiences were targeted, black children and youth were his primary targets. Many different activists helped Woodson instigate an interest in Black history in various communities across the nation, and black female schoolteachers were the most important promoters of this cause. The historical record strongly suggests that the Negro History Weeks of Woodson's times were more serious and effective than the Black History Months of more recent times. We could learn many valuable lessons by exploring these early efforts at popularizing the study of Black history in practical, meaningful ways. The creative hip-hop generation needs to return to Woodson's vision. If we aren't careful, before we know it Black History Month could become yet another money-making device for capitalists and just another token, month-long tribute to one of America's underrepresented ethnic groups.

Notes

Chapter 3

Towards a Deeper Understanding of Black History Month: Revisiting Its Roots

[1] "Congress Makes Home of Carter G. Woodson a National Historic Site," *Jet* 104 (22–29 December 2003): 4, 6.

[2] Lerone Bennett, Jr., *Forced Into Glory: Abraham Lincoln's White Dream* (Chicago: Johnson Publishing Company, 1999).

[3] The ads that I have discussed here appeared in *Essence* and *Ebony* from about 1975 until 1979.

[4] "How to Celebrate Black History Month 12 Months of the Year," *Ebony* 50 (February 1995): 62–66.

[5] "Black History Month: Education or Tokenism?," *The Journal of Blacks in Higher Education* 3 (Spring 1994): 30–31; "Black History Month: Serious Truth Telling or a Triumph in Tokenism?," *The Journal of Blacks in Higher Education* 18 (Winter 1997–1998): 87.

[6] "Black History Month: Serious Truth Telling or a Triumph in Tokenism?," 88.

[7] Ibid., 90.

[8] Earl Ofari Hutchinson, "Black History is U.S. History: It's Time to Put the Role of Blacks on Center Stage," *San Francisco Chronicle*, 8 February 1999.

[9] For a detailed discussion of Kwanzaa, see the "Official Kwanzaa Web Site" organized by Malauna Karenga, <http://www.officialkwanzaawebsite.org>

[10] Douglas Martin, "The Marketing of Kwanzaa," *The New York Times*, 20 December 1993, p. B1.

[11] Will Conrad, "Kwanzaa Belongs to Us, Don't Let Them Commercialize It," *Philadelphia Tribune*, 25 January 1994, p. 7-A.

[12] Marc Cummings, "The Commercialization of Our Soul," *New Pittsburgh Courier*, 24 January 1996, p. A-7.

[13] Malauna Karenga, "Kwanzaa and Corporate Commercialism," *Philadelphia Tribune*, 24 December 1999, p. 7A.

[14] "Kwanzaa Becomes $700 Million Business," *Ebony* 56 (December 2000): 42; Genea Webb, "Kwanzaa Founder to Address Holiday's Meaning: Says Blacks Should Resist Commercialization," *New Pittsburgh Courier*, 23 December 2000, p. A1.

[15] For Dyson's insightful discussion of the King holiday, see Michael Eric Dyson, *I May Not Get There With You: The True Martin Luther King, Jr.* (New York: The Free Press, 2000), 286–306. Also see the February 2000 issue of *Emerge: Black America's Newsmagazine*, which includes a provocative essay by Dyson.

[16] James Melvin Washington, ed., A *Testament of Hope: The Essential Writings of Martin Luther King, Jr.* (New York: Harper and Row, 1986), 217.

[17] Brent Staples, "Putting a Price Tag on the Legacy of Martin Luther King," *The New York Times*, 28 November 2001, p. A24.

[18] John Christensen, "Scholars Fear King's Legacy Is Fading: 'Commodification' of Civil Rights Leader Blamed." 6 April 1999 <http://www.cnn.com/SPECIALS/1999/mlk.legacy/>

[19] For a discussion of the origins of Negro History Week, see Patricia Watkins Romero, "Carter G. Woodson: A Biography" Ph.D. dissertation, The Ohio State University, 1971; "Carter G. Woodson, "Negro History Week," *JNH* 11 (April, 1926): 238–242.

[20] Woodson, "Negro History Week," 238–241.

[21] Woodson's predecessors included antebellum era black historians dating back to the writings of William Cooper Nell, George Washington Williams, and even W.E.B. Du Bois. For further discussions of black historians before Woodson, see Franklin, "On the Evolution of Scholarship on Afro-American History;" Thorpe, *Black Historians*; Benjamin Quarles, "Black History's Antebellum Origins." Also see Chapter 4 of this study.

[22] Carter G. Woodson, *The Mis-Education of the Negro* (New Jersey: African World Press, 1990); "How Shall We Celebrate Negro History Week," *NHB* 8 (January 1945): 91. For a provocative discussion of Woodson's relationship with white philanthropists, see Darlene Clark

Hine, "Carter G. Woodson: White Philanthropy and Negro Historiography," in Hine, *HineSight*, 203–222.

[23] "Starting Right," *NHB* 1 (February 1938): 12; "Renew Your Subscription," *NHB* 9 (1946): 188.

[24] "The Annual Report of the Director," *JNH* 11 (October 1926): 551.

[25] In the February volumes of the *NHB*, Woodson always offered his strategies as how to best celebrate Negro History Week.

[26] Routine brief discussions of Negro History Week events can be found in Woodson's annual assessments of the celebration in *The Journal of Negro History*.

[27] Every year after the founding of Negro History Week in 1926, Woodson reviewed the status of the celebration. See, for instance, "Negro History the Fourth Year," *JNH* 14 (April 1929), 109–115; "Negro History Week the Eighth Year," *JNH* 18 (April 1933): 107–113; "Negro History Week the Eleventh Year," *JNH* 21 (April 1936): 105–110.

[28] Carter G. Woodson, "Start Now Negro History Year in Order to Have a Negro History Week," *NHB* 5 (October 1941): 24.

[29] "Negro History Week the Eleventh Year," 106–107.

[30] Manu Ampim, *Towards Black Community Development: Moving Beyond the Limitations of the Lecture Model* (California: Advancing the Research, 1993).

[31] Woodson, "Supplementing Nothing," *NHB* 8 (March 1945): 144.

[32] Carter G. Woodson, "What Children Should Do in Observing Negro History Week," *NHB* 1 (February 1938): 12.

[33] "Negro History Week Nation-Wide," *NHB* 12 (March 1949): 135.

[34] "Negro History Week the Eighth Year," 107–113.

[35] L.D. Reddick, "Twenty-Five Negro History Weeks," *NHB* 13 (May 1950): 178–188; "Annual Report of the Director," *JNH* 18 (October 1933): 362.

[36] "Negro History Week Nationwide," *NHB 12* (March 1949): 136; "Jewish History Week," *NHB 12* (June 1949): 194.

[37] Cobb, ed., *The Essential Harold Cruse*, 203.

[38] Malcolm X, *Malcolm X on Afro-American History*, 15–16.

CHAPTER 4

Before Carter G. Woodson:
The Roots of the
Black Historical Profession

Before Woodson earned his Ph.D. in history in 1912, co-founded the Association for the Study of Negro Life and History in 1915, and launched *The Journal of Negro History* in 1916, there existed many different types of black historians. When looking at these early pre-Woodson black historians, the conventional term "historian" must be modified some. The first black to become a professional historian by earning a Ph.D. in the field was W.E.B. Du Bois in 1895. But, before Du Bois, there were many blacks, going back to their African ancestors, who wrote history, passed on history in the form of oral tradition, used history in their day-to-day lives, and, in essence, played the roles of historians by critically interpreting and discussing things done and said in the past and by writing history. Before Woodson came on the scene, there existed many important historians in African American culture. While Woodson may not have considered himself directly descended from them, they indirectly paved the way for his success in creating the early Black history movement.

In this chapter, I discuss many issues: the role of history and historians in the traditional African cultures from which African Americans' ancestors came; the meaning and use of history by enslaved African Americans; blacks who wrote history during the days of slavery, the Civil War era, and Reconstruction; George Washington Williams; black women historians from the

1890s until the early 1900s; and W.E.B. Du Bois's and Booker T. Washington's early contributions as historians.

The Meaning of History in Pre-Colonial, Traditional, Sub-Saharan African Cultures

When dealing with African American history and culture, it is imperative to begin by using Africa as some sort of starting point. All black Americans have some type of African roots. It is therefore only logical that we begin by looking at how African Americans' African ancestors may have viewed history. Cultural traits that African descendants brought with them from Africa to the various destinations where they were taken during the brutal, inhumane enslavement process are known as Africanisms. Some of these cultural carryovers, such as those found in language, foods, hairstyles, clothing, music, dance, artistic expression, and religion are not too difficult to locate and identify. On the other hand, philosophical Africanisms are harder to measure. Getting into the minds of the masses of Africans during pre-colonial times is a challenge. Linking these inner thoughts to Africans' descendants in America is equally challenging. Nonetheless, it is possible that the evolution of the African American historical enterprise was impacted by their African ancestors' views of history.

Blacks in the United States hail from a range of different ethnic groups mainly from West and Central Africa. Scholars have debated the specific ethnic backgrounds of African Americans for decades. It is safe to say that African Americans come from a wide range of cultures and ethnic groups (many of which today have different designations) including Mandingo, Yoruba, Fanti, Dahomean, Bambara, Melinke, Whydah, Igbo, Mende, Congo, Akan, Ewe, and hundreds of others. The middle passage and early stages of slavery in North America forced these various African peoples to unite to some degree. As Sterling Stuckey has argued, "It is greatly ironic, therefore, that African ethnicity, an obstacle to African nationalism in the twentieth century, was…the principle avenue to black unity in antebellum America." Stuckey continued:

> During the process of becoming a single people,
> Yorubas, Akans, Ibos, Angolans, and others were present on slave ships to America and experienced a
> common horror…As such, slave ships were the first
> real incubators of slave unity across cultural lines, cruelly revealing irreducible links from one ethnic group
> to the other.[1]

At the same time, while it must be stressed that the Africans from whom African Americans descended were a very diverse peoples, there existed, and still do to some degrees, common cultures in Africa. "In the cultures of West Africans, and Sub-Saharan Africa in general, it is considered the opinion of many Africans that there are basic cultural threads that bind together these societies," Desai Ram has asserted. Another scholar, Mervyn C. Alleyne reiterated what Ram observed. "Clearly Africa is a continent with a vast number of peoples and cultures. However, Sub-Saharan Africa, as Black Africa, has certain unique traits that set it apart from the rest of the world." Alleyne added:

> The notion of 'African culture' does not mean that all
> inhabitants of the Sub-Saharan region share a common
> set of cultural traits or institutions in which they all
> equally participate. It merely means that they have
> more in common with each other than with any other
> human groups.

Afrocentric pioneer Molefi Kete Asante has more recently articulated these scholars' ideas in his notion of the "composite African," which he shares with C.T. Keto.[2] Among the cultural attributes that many West and Sub-Saharan African peoples held and hold in common are similar ideas concerning family, work, social and political structures, economics, religion, art, oral tradition, community, time, and respect for elders. Notions of history could also be added to this group of cultural ideals.[3]

In pre-colonial, traditional, Sub-Saharan (hereafter PTS) African societies, history was usually functional and pragmatic in nature. According to Adebayo Oyebade, in PTS African societies

> history was not an abstract concept. It was not a purposeless acquisition of knowledge of past and present events. Rather, history was relevant, having a purpose necessary for the survival of a community's traditions. History primarily served as a socializing agent, playing a vital role in day-to-day living, particularly in the education of the individ-ual...History, therefore, constituted the pivot of the socialization process. It was a means through which every person was educated in the codes of conduct of the society, in the norms, values, and ethics of the culture. It was through the knowledge of history that each community defined itself and its relationship to other communities.[4]

Oyebade is among the few historians to discuss the role of history in PTS Africa. He makes some important points. In PTS African societies, history was part of folks' daily lives, not something compartmentalized and "academicized" as it often is in European and American cultures.

Africans routinely remembered history in order to help them in the present and future. In PTS African societies, it was not uncommon for parents to name their children after deceased elders and historical figures. Among the Yoruba in Nigeria, "the name of Babatunde means 'father returns.' It is given to a male child born immediately after the death of his grandfather. For a girl, it is Yetunde, 'mother returns.'" [5] This ensured that the names, personalities, and legacies of their ancestors were constantly invoked, presentized, and used as guides for the future. PTS Africans often poured libations for their ancestors as well.

R. Kelley's pouring out some liquor to his deceased "nigga" in his "I Wish" video is nothing new.

Another concrete example of the pragmatism of history in PTS Africa is revealed by *Sundiata: An Epic of Old Mali*. This classic historical legend features Mandingo griots, those who conserve tradition and teach it and personify and demonstrate the role of history in shaping the community's attitudes, actions, and views of the future. The griots often held some of the most important positions in pre-colonial West African societies. According to D.T. Niane, "Generally, in every village of old Mali there is a griot family which conserves historical tradition and teaches it."[6] They committed their kingdom's and people's history to memory and passed it on to each succeeding generation. Though the griots are almost always described as being males, there existed in pre-colonial times African women who also functioned in this role with different titles. Elder African women socialized their communities by participating in the culture of oral tradition. African women operated as vital oral historians by telling legends, myths, folktales, proverbs, stories, riddles, and by singing praise songs. They also played essential roles in various ceremonies that were linked to the past, especially those invoking the memories, guidance, and the spirits of the ancestors. They kept their children and communities aware of their collective past, in turn setting forth a roadmap for the future. In PTS African societies, history was a practical, functional, relevant concept.

The Significance of History to Enslaved Africans

The various processes of enslavement were destructive and indeed traumatic. As Na'im Akbar has passionately argued in *Chains and Images of Psychological Slavery* (1984), the psychological impact of these experiences cannot be downplayed. While the vast majority of those Africans enslaved were most often farmers, all classes of Africans were enslaved. Court poets, griots, elders, storytellers, local historians, the custodians of family histories, priests, musicians, male and female, were enslaved most likely as a result of slave raiding and warfare instigated by political conflicts. In the baracoons and the forts, the ideas, thoughts, and beliefs of these preservers of their peoples' past must have surfaced in some form or another. What function did history play in these settings? What role did history play during the horrific voyage known as the middle passage? Did these Africans blend their individual and group histories into one common history? Did history help Africans explain their harsh realities? Did it help them strive to be free, since nothing like this had ever happened to them before? What roles did the former court poets, griots, and storytellers play? Did their visions help Africans survive? Given our lack of sources, such questions are abstract and hard to answer, yet deserve serious speculation.

The various phases of the enslavement process did not sever Africans' culture, including their notions of history. The millions of slaves who endured the middle passage—the horrific voyage across the Atlantic—from the mid-fifteenth century through well into the nineteenth century most likely used history and memory as a social force, a tool of survival. It is safe to assume that many certainly reflected upon their lives and upbringings in Africa while crossing the Atlantic. In his award-winning *Middle Passage* (1990), novelist Charles Johnson creatively approached what enslaved Africans may have thought during the middle passage. The ship logs of slavers often recounted slaves becoming seriously ill from melancholy or depression. These feelings of helplessness were probably enhanced by being so far removed from their land and their recent past. Knowledge of history, particularly the memories of their past lives as free people, could have influenced Africans to commit suicide, organize revolts, survive, and engage in other acts of resistance during the middle passage. Their knowledge of their past achievements and ways of life could have encouraged their efforts. During the early stages of the Atlantic slave trade, it was not totally uncommon for African women housed on the decks of the slavers to commit suicide by jumping overboard. These acts of self-determination were in part guided by those Africans' memories of their past.

They often possessed deep desires to return to the way things were, their not so distant history. As Vincent Harding has eloquently argued, the black struggle for freedom on the countless slavers constituted a movement to "repossess our history and our future."[7]

In New World settings, Africans' beliefs about history were modified and adjusted in order to suit the realities of slavery and a society in which blackness was made into a badge of inferiority. As a vital facet of African American culture, in the North American setting, as elsewhere, history was transformed into a mode of survival, a tool of resistance. A handful of enslaved Africans' memories of Africa were probably shaped and manipulated by their masters as was the case with Phillis Wheatley (c. 1753–1784) who in her poetry belittled Africa, asserting once that "twas mercy that saved me from my Pagan land." Other generations of African-born slaves probably used their memories of their recent history as a source of power and pride through the colonial era, the American Revolution, and the early stages of America as a "new nation." During the mid to late 1700s when many Africans were being imported into the United States, they certainly brought with them the knowledge of their past and culture. These "salt water" Africans reintroduced American-born slaves to their African roots and past.

History was important to slaves in North America. Within the slave community, black men and women continued their roles as storytellers and elders armed with knowledge and memories of the past. Many enslaved African Americans had a clear sense of history, which was rooted in their African background. "Before African Americans were aware of history as a profession or discipline, our keepers of culture were griots—family and community elders who passed knowledge and values" and a sense of history down to the succeeding generations. "This communal view of history transcended our bondage in America by reaching back to embrace the values and cultural mores rooted in" the various cultures from which African Americans originated. John E. Fleming argued:

The sense of history that was passed on by African-American griots incorporated 'survival tools,' capturing the vision of the American ideal that brought black people out of slavery and through the crucible of intolerance, discrimination, and racism in the nineteenth- and early twentieth-century United States.[8]

Enslaved black women quilters played a very important role in socializing slave communities. They acted as informal historians. Often consciously and subconsciously drawing from their African cultural heritage, they encoded important, complex, and symbolic messages in their quilts, which often served as historical roadmaps for their families and communities. "Quilting gave many enslaved women, and later freedwomen, a mechanism with which to transmit and preserve 'cultural memory.'" It was, and still is, a common practice for quilts to be carefully passed on from generation to generation. Generations of African American quilters made familial, individual, and collective histories practical and accessible to their entire communities. All of those who possessed and viewed these quilts could have received some historical knowledge, regardless of their education.

This was an important approach since roughly five percent of slaves could read and write. A material possession like a quilt was in many cases more meaningful to blacks in the late 1800s and early 1900s than many books. The one who inherits the quilt, like the griots in traditional Mandingo cultures, had the responsibility to make certain that the historical tapestry is passed on to the next generation. Black women quilters were also important because they sometimes provided "the only physical evidence or historical testament revealing aspects of the inner lives and creative spirits of many otherwise obscure and unknown Black women."[9] In this sense, though they might not have recognized it, they symbolically laid the foundations for the Black Women's history movement that surfaced most concretely in the 1970s and continues to thrive. Today, these quilts can best be used as vital "resources in reconstructing the experiences of

African-American women. They provide a record of their cultural and political past."[10]

Black Writers of History During the Antebellum Era or the Days of Slavery

During the period of slavery in the U.S., history was an important component of African American culture and clearly there were blacks who did record the history of their peoples. During the period of U.S. slavery (1789-1865), many black abolitionists, journalists, leaders, ministers, and educators advocated that black people chronicle, know, and create Black history. Equally important, they also indicted U.S. society and culture for excluding the contributions of African Americans from standard American historical diatribes.

After the United States gained its independence and became a recognized nation, two African Americans wrote brief history books, Paul Cuffee and Prince Saunders. Cuffee (1759–1817), a free-born black activist who advocated the mass emigration of blacks back to Africa and who sailed with a total of 38 people to Sierra Leone in December 1815, wrote a brief history of Sierra Leone. Cuffee's *Brief Account of the Settlement and Present Situation of the Colony of Sierra Leone in Africa* (1812) is only twelve pages and "can scarcely be called history," Earl E. Thorpe noted, but it still demonstrated an early effort to chronicle history by an African American. In 1816, Prince Saunders, a free-born black who ventured to Haiti in 1807, wrote a history of Haiti, *Haytian Papers: A Collection of Very Interesting Proclamations and Other Official Documents, Together with Some Account of the Rise, Progress and Present State of the Kingdom of Haiti*. Gaining its independence in 1804, Haiti was a common topic for black historians during the antebellum era. Like the work of Cuffee, Saunder's book was short and contributed only "a small account of actual history."[11] Nevertheless, these two free blacks demonstrated that there were some blacks during the early years of America's new nationhood who wanted to convey

important messages to others through historical writings, however short, informal, and makeshift.

Before the 13th Amendment, which abolished slavery in
1865, there were about a half dozen black intellectuals who
wrote Black history books. From 1836 to 1863, the major texts
were Robert Benjamin Lewis's *Light and Truth: Containing the
Universal History of the Colored and Indian Race* (1836, 1844),
James W.C. Pennington's *A Text Book of the Origins and His-
tory of the Colored People* (1841), William Cooper Nell's *Col-
ored Patriots of the American Revolution* (1855), Martin R. De-
lany's *The Condition, Elevation, Emigration and Destiny of the
Colored People of the United States* (1852), James Theodore
Holly's *A Vindication of the Capacity of the Negro Race for Self-
Government and Civilized Progress* (1857), and William Wells
Brown's *The Black Man: His Antecedents, His Genius, and His
Achievements* (1863).[12]

Though these abolitionists, writers, and activists dealt with
different issues in their books, they addressed a range of common themes and concerns. Foremost, these antebellum era historians sought to challenge the racism so prevalent in the United
States during the early years of the United States. Throughout
the days of slavery in the U.S., it was a widespread belief among
whites that blacks were inferior and had no history. These anti-
black thoughts date back to antiquity, as pointed out by Joseph
E. Harris in *Africans and Their History*, and were expanded upon
in the United States side by side with racist expressions in
Europe. In 1768 philosopher David Hume claimed that blacks
and Africans were "naturally inferior to the white." He continued, "There was never a civilized nation of any other complex-
ion than white, nor even any individual eminent either in action
or speculation. No ingenious manufacturers amongst them, no
arts, no sciences." In his famous book *Philosophy of History*,
German philosopher Georg Hegel (1770–1831) shared Hume's
beliefs:

> It is manifest that want of self-control distinguishes the
> character of the Negroes. This condition is capable of

no development or culture, and as we have seen them at this day, such have they always been...At this point we leave Africa, not to mention it again. For it is no historical part of the world; it has no movement or development to exhibit.[13]

Echoing and mirroring Hume's and Hegel's sentiments, Thomas Jefferson was one of the key "founding fathers" of pseudoscientific and academic racism. This is especially interesting given the fact that between 1790 and 1808 Jefferson fathered at least seven children with Sally Hemmings, his slave and mistress. Jefferson's racial ambivalence has been explored by many historians. Jefferson originally composed his famous *Notes on Virginia* in the early 1780s. While in France in 1785, Jefferson had 200 copies of this book published and distributed to his friends. At first, it appears that he did not plan on having the book published on a mass scale or circulated in the United States. By the late 1780s and the early 1800s, the book was available in greater numbers. Most people recognize the original publication of this text in the U.S. as being about 1804. In "Query XIV," Jefferson made many comments about blacks being inferior. He asserted that the only two blacks who could come close to competing with whites on intellectual levels were Phillis Wheatley and Benjamin Banneker. He also stressed many so-called inherent physical and biological differences between blacks and whites, even insinuating that black women were chosen as sexual partners by "the Oranootan." He believed that blacks had no history. Jefferson, credited with creating one of the first methods of determining and breaking down a black person's blackness and racial identity, was a "founding father" of racist scholarship.[14]

The first group of black historians writing during the days of slavery challenged such racist ideas. They practiced what Manning Marable has deemed the "corrective" principle of the African American intellectual tradition. This stream of thought has attempted to challenge and critique the racist stereotypes that have dominated the mainstream discourse of Euro-American academic institutions. This part of the black intellectual tradition has rigorously condemned and disputed theories that espouse the genetic, biological, and cultural inferiority of black people...It has challenged Eurocentric notions of aesthetics and beauty, which all too often are grounded in an implied or even explicit contempt for the standards of blackness.[15]

A second important thrust of the earliest group of black historians was that they create history texts that could empower their black readership and audiences. Though the vast majority of their fellow blacks could not read or write, they wanted to instill pride, self-esteem, and hope within their few black readers who could in turn pass on the knowledge "through the grapevine." They discussed issues such as the Haitian Revolution, blacks' role in the American Revolution, the contributions of famous Revolutionary era blacks such as Wheatley and Banneker, and blacks' overall essential roles in building the United States. Their histories "depict black people as shapers of their own destiny." In the books they wrote:

Blacks are not passive. They resist slavery, become free, acquire property, build institutions, and fight in America's wars...That they had participated in these struggles, blacks thought, proved that they were the equals of whites.[16]

Literate blacks who read their books, they reasoned, would be inspired by the strength, perseverance, and monumental achievements of their ancestors, going all the way back to their biblical and ancient African roots. They probably hoped that their messages would trickle down to the masses of their people. Literate blacks, they surmised, could and did break them down and pass them on to their various black audiences in formal and more grassroots settings. Listening to an informal lecture on Black history from the mouth of a black abolitionist could have had the same effect as reading a book. Even most free blacks during the days of slavery did not enjoy the leisure time to read a lot. At another level, these early "chroniclers of the black past" viewed themselves as laying the foundations for future generations of their bothers and sisters. In the mid-1830s, Maria W. Stewart, abolitionist, political activist, and one of the first American women to engage in public political debates, called upon black women to create history for the future generations: "O, ye daughters of Africa! What have ye done to immortalize your names beyond the grave? What examples have ye set before the rising generations?"[17]

A third significant thing that these pioneering black historians did was highlight early African history, while often simultaneously calling upon their African brothers and sisters at home and abroad to embrace Christianity. They recognized that Europeans justified the enslavement and overall mistreatment of their ancestors by claiming that Africans had no history. Drawing upon mythology and the Bible, many of these early black writers of history maintained that Africans had a glorious past. They argued that they descended from a people who possessed high civilizations. They sought to "establish the unity of humankind."[18]

These historians also celebrated blacks' contributions to America's wars in hopes of proving to white America that blacks, because of their patriotism, deserved equal rights and justice. William Cooper Nell's history of black participation in the American Revolution and the War of 1812 is a perfect example of this. He laid before the public the many ways in which they served their country. This theme would continue through the modern era with the scholarship of Benjamin Quarles about blacks in the American Revolution and the Civil War.

Overall, this pioneering group of black writers of history during the antebellum era sought to help get rid of racism in American society, while simultaneously empowering blacks in psychological ways. In terms of mechanics and writing style, these writers were not formally trained, wrote incidentally at times, drew inspiration quite often from the Bible, were nonanalytical in their approach, and often wrote in narrative styles with many biographical sketches. In *Deromanticizing Black History*, Clarence Walker claimed that it was not until W.E.B. Du Bois's *Black Reconstruction* that black historians broke with this "form of historical writing which was largely idealist in its conceptualization." Benjamin Quarles, Earl E. Thorpe, Elizabeth R. Bethel, W.D. Wright, and Ahati N.N. Toure have argued otherwise, stressing antebellum era black historians' vital contributions to the Black history movement. "Despite their shortcomings, much is owed to this first group," Thorpe argued.

> They started the movement which was later to bear such commendable fruit with the work of Du Bois, Woodson, and others...It was this group which pointed up for the first time...neglected aspects of American history... Without their works, many sources of black history would probably be unavailable today.[19]

W.D. Wright went a step further and asserted that

> while early Black historians lagged behind early white historians in research and narrative skills, Black historians had a keener insight into American history than many lay and professional white historians, even many professional white historians today.[20]

Black Historians from Emancipation Through George Washington Williams's *History of the Negro Race*

Between emancipation in 1865 and the 1882 publication of George Washington Williams's *History of the Negro Race from 1619 to 1880* (called the first "coherent" Black history book by John Hope Franklin), black writers of history continued to develop and their foci began to shift. These historians were very similar to their predecessors in terms of the quality of their writing, their motivations, their philosophies, and their overall approaches. They were, however, profoundly impacted by the aftermath of the Civil War, emancipation, and Reconstruction. A significant part of their scholarship sought to "justify emancipation by showing that some members of the race had committed distinctive acts in the past, and that the numbers of such individuals could be multiplied many times by giving the race better opportunities."[21]

They sought to prove to their white readers that blacks had earned the right to be free and did not deserve to be mistreated during the era of Reconstruction (1865–1877) and the "nadir" (1877–1901 or 1923). The major Black history books published from 1865 to 1882 included William Still's *The Underground Railroad* (1872), William Wells Brown's *The Rising Son* (1874), and Joseph T. Wilson's *Emancipation: Its Course and Progress, from 1481 B.C. to A.D. 1875* (1882). The most popular book of these was probably Brown's 555-page *The Rising Son*. Though it was "almost devoid of documentation" and even "below the standards of scholarship which many scholars of the period were producing,"[22] the book sold more than 10,000 copies in its first year of publication. This is quite significant considering the time. It would be interesting to know how many of these copies were purchased by blacks. Whites sympathetic to the black cause probably purchased significant numbers of Brown's third historical study on African Americans. Many middle-class, educated blacks certainly found solace in Brown's book. Courses in Black history in the early twentieth century were taught at Black colleges and universities such as Atlanta University, Fisk University, and Howard University. It is quite possible that some black students at historically Black colleges and universities read Brown's and others' historical studies.

Benjamin Quarles, Earl E. Thorpe, and more recently Ahati N.N. Toure argued that the first distinctive group of African American historians emerged during the antebellum era. John

Hope Franklin, on the other hand, has suggested that George Washington Williams (1849–1891) holds the honor of being the first African American historian, the first person to publish a "coherent" history of black America. During the "nadir," Williams published two major historical studies, *History of the Negro Race in America from 1619 to 1880* (1882, 1883, 1885) and *A History of the Negro Troops in the War of the Rebellion, 1861–1865* (1887). Williams was a self-taught historian who conducted meticulous research from the mid-1870s through the mid-1880s. Franklin argued that Williams joined the ranks of the American historical profession because he went to great lengths to acquire historical documents, pioneered methods of oral history, extensively used newspapers, sought advice from established American historians, critiqued his sources, maintained an overall objective approach, and in 1883 called for the creation of an African American historical society.[23]

Williams, a free-born Civil War veteran, first developed an interest in history while studying at Newton Theological Institution near Boston from 1869 until 1874. Then, in 1874 while a pastor at Boston's Twelfth Baptist Church, he wrote a history of his church. His study was "well written, despite the haste." Later, as a journalist and pastor in Cincinnati, Williams often incorporated history into his articles and sermons. Franklin suggested that at least one of his sermons "laid the groundwork for the history of his race he was to write some years later." After serving a term in the House of Representatives of the Ohio General Assembly (1880–1881), Williams decided "to devote his time to historical research and writing."[24]

Several years later, he published *History of the Negro Race*, a comprehensive history of African Americans from their African origins until 1880. Williams proclaimed:

> I became convinced that a history of the colored people in America was required, because such a history would give the world more correct ideas of Colored people, and invite the latter to greater effort in the struggle of citizenship and manhood. The single reason that there

was no history of the Negro race would have been a sufficient reason for writing one.[25]

Williams's second historical monograph, *A History of the Negro Troops in the War of the Rebellion, 1861–1865*, stressed the role of black soldiers in the Civil War within a broader historical context. In highlighting the achievements of black soldiers, Williams, like William Cooper Nell and others, sought to demonstrate to the American public that the African American experience was marked by patriotism, a dedication to America that should have translated into equal rights in society. While it is hard to measure the impact of Williams's scholarship, it was for the most part positively reviewed by white scholars. [26] His *History of the Negro Race* was also instrumental in influencing Woodson to write *The Negro in Our History* (1922) and Franklin to write *From Slavery to Freedom* (1947).

W.E.B. Du Bois: The First Professionally Trained Black Historian

In the years between the 1882 publication of *History of the Negro Race from 1619 to 1880* and the emergence of Woodson as "The Father of Black History," there was a host of black writers of history who contributed to the development of the Black history movement. During this period, one of the greatest accomplishments in the evolution of the black historical enterprise was Du Bois becoming the first black to earn a Ph.D. in history from Harvard in 1895. In 1913 in an essay entitled "The Negro in Literature and Art" (1913), W.E.B. Du Bois humbly announced that George Washington Williams was "the greatest historian of the race."[27] This generous compliment was a great overstatement. From the mid-1890s until Woodson earned his Ph.D. in 1912 and co-founded the Association for the Study of Negro Life and History in 1915, Du Bois, recognized by many as primarily being a sociologist, was black America's most high-ranking historian. While he was truly multidisciplinary in his intellectual approach, "it was along history's pathway that he made his literary route to the present and the future."[28] By earning his Ph.D. from Harvard, Du Bois not only added a sense of legitimacy to the African American historical profession, but he also possessed the necessary credentials for significantly challenging racist historical scholarship.

From the mid-1880s until the mid-1890s, Du Bois studied history at Fisk, Harvard, and the University of Berlin. He earned his M.A. from Harvard in history in 1891. His study was published in the Annual Report of the AHA as "The Enforcement of the Slave Trade Laws." In the same year, Du Bois became the first African American to participate in an AHA convention.[29] A year after earning his Ph.D., he published his dissertation as *The Suppression of the Atlantic Slave Trade to the United States of America, 1638–1870* (1896). From 1897 until 1914, Du Bois taught economics and history at Atlanta University and coordinated the annual Atlanta University Studies and Conferences and edited its publications, all of which incorporated historical analyses. "These studies with all their imperfections were widely distributed in the libraries of the world and used by scholars," Du Bois recounted.

> It may be said without boasting that between 1896 and 1920 there was no study of the race problem in America which did not in some degree depend upon the investigations made at Atlanta University; often they were widely quoted and commended.[30]

In 1899, Du Bois published *The Philadelphia Negro*, "one of the first major works to combine the use of urban ethnography, social history, and descriptive statistics." Du Bois devoted two brief chapters to exploring the history of black Philadelphians from 1638 until 1896, yet sections of many other chapters possessed historical analyses.[31] Du Bois' opus *The Souls of Black Folk* (1903) is by far his most famous and celebrated book to this day. Taken together, the fourteen essays in this volume constitute a mélange of writing styles and academic vantage points:

history, social science, political theory, cultural studies, psychology, and spirituality.[32] History enters almost every discussion, particularly in dealing with the Freedman's Bureau and the evolution of black education, black leadership, and southern race relations.

After *The Souls of Black Folk*, Du Bois's next major piece of historical scholarship was his biography of John Brown, a historical figure whom he greatly admired. Although Du Bois said that this was one of his favorite books, *John Brown* did not do well, selling less than 700 copies.[33] In 1909, Du Bois delivered his second presentation at the American Historical Association (AHA). In doing so, he was the only African American to present a paper at an AHA conference until the World War II era. In 1910, in the pages of *The American Historical Review*, Du Bois challenged U.S. historians to rewrite Reconstruction in "Reconstruction and Its Benefits." Du Bois's optimistic-sounding title masked the overt critiques that he offered about the period. While he identified increased black political participation and the Freedman's Bureau as benefiting blacks, he oversimplied the failures of Reconstruction. This article, which laid the foundations for his exhaustive *Black Reconstruction* (1935), was the only article by a black historian to appear in the *American Historical Review* until 1979.[34]

He opened his article in a revisionist tone: "There is a danger that between the intense feeling of the South and the conciliatory spirit of the North grave injustice will be done the negro American in the history of Reconstruction." Du Bois placed black agency at the forefront, asserting that African Americans drew upon a tradition of self-determination during a period of "nothing more nor less than slavery in daily toil." Du Bois empowered those blacks who were active during Reconstruction and the "nadir," in one instance citing a lengthy speech by Thomas E. Miller, one of the six African Americans of the South Carolina Constitutional Convention of 1895. Du Bois indicted the United States for not empowering the Freedman's Bureau and creating a true program of equal opportunity for African

Americans. He also provided examples of what the United States could have done to have provided a more comprehensive program of Reconstruction.[35]

From 1910 through 1934, as director of publishing and research for the NAACP, Du Bois served as editor of the *Crisis*. He routinely explored issues relating to Afro-diasporic histories in this widely circulated magazine. Before Woodson began to be recognized as the key figure in the early Black history movement, Du Bois published one major historical study devoted to African descendants, *The Negro* (1915). David Levering Lewis has posited that "*The Negro* was a large building block in an Afrocentric historiography that has achieved credibility through the writings of scholars such as Basil Davidson, Martin Bernal, and Chiekh Anta Diop." Though Molefi Kete Asante and other leading Afrocentric scholars would challenge Lewis's interpretation of Afrocentricity, Lewis's point is clear.[36] Du Bois predated modern Afrocentric thinkers in stressing the blackness of ancient Egypt.

Challenging the Aryan view of ancient Egypt, Du Bois noted:

> Of what race, then, were the Egyptians? They were certainly not white in any sense of the modern use of that word—neither in color nor physical measurement, in hair nor countenance, in language nor social customs. They stood in relationship nearest to the Negro race in earliest times...Egyptians show distinctly Negro and mulatto faces...The Egyptians themselves... affirmed that they and their civilization came from...black tribes.[37]

Du Bois's *The Negro*, though brief, was the first scholarly history book of its kind on Africans in the diaspora. He himself asserted that by 1915 there was "no general history of the Negro race" and he called his work "a complete history of the Negro people." Du Bois wrote *The Negro* in order to dispel the "widespread assumption throughout the world that color is a mark of inferiority," that "black men are and always have been naturally slaves."[38] While Du Bois drew from the available leading scientific scholarship of his times, his work is also openly celebratory. He argued that the "Negroes are the best and keenest tillers of the ground" and "perhaps no race has shown in its earlier development a more magnificent art impulse than the Negro."[39]

Du Bois's study is subdivided into twelve sections, eight of which deal with Africa. In separate chapters, he also treats the slave trade, blacks in the Caribbean, the African American experience, and Pan-Africanism. His chapter on the African American experience is less than thirty pages, yet covers the most important dimensions of Black history from the colonial era through the turn of the century. Du Bois stressed the progress that African Americans made from when they were "freed as a penniless, landless, naked, ignorant laborer" until the aftermath of emancipation.[40] Du Bois concludes his study with an optimistic observation:

> In a conscious sense of unity among colored races there is to-day only a growing interest. There is slowly arising not only a curiously strong brotherhood of Negro blood throughout the world, but the common cause of the darker races against the intolerable assumptions and insults of Europeans has already found expression. Most men in this world are colored. A belief in humanity means a belief in colored men. The future will, in all reasonable probability, be what the colored men made it.[41]

Du Bois was clearly the preeminent black historian from the mid-1890s until 1915, but there was a host of other significant black historians active during these years. In *Black Historians: A Critique*, Earl E. Thorpe called this group "historians without portfolio." This cadre of black historians "represent that group of non-professional persons...feeling that their life experiences peculiarly fit them for chronicling some historical events."[42] In the 1890s, several history books were published on black America by black writers. In 1891, Edward A. Johnson published *School History of the Negro Race in America from 1619 to 1890* and became the first person to publish a school text book on African American history. In 1897, William H. Crogman authored his first Black history book, *Progress of a Race*. In the early 1900s before Woodson founded the ASNLH in 1915, there was a handful of other books written in the field of Black history, including Booker T. Washington's two volume *The Story of the Negro* (1909), Monroe Work's *Negro Year Book* (first published in 1912), Benjamin Brawley's *A Short History of the American Negro* (1913), John W. Cromwell's *The Negro in American History* (1914), and John R. Lynch's *The Facts Reconstruction* (1915). These works were significant but were overshadowed by Du Bois's scholarship. Of these works, Washington's study was probably the most widely read, especially by whites.

Exploring Booker T. Washington's Underappreciated Role as a Historian

Arguably the most powerful and influential African American leader of the Progressive era, Booker T. Washington viewed history as an important element in the black struggle for advancement and a vital component of his own leadership strategies. Not only did he write a two-volume history of African Americans from their African origins until the early twentieth century, *The Story of the Negro: The Rise of the Race from Slavery* (1909), but Washington also injected his philosophy of history into his famous 1895 speech, *Up From Slavery*, and other major publications. While Earl E. Thorpe and John Hope Franklin noted the existence of Washington's historical writings, Louis R. Harlan, Washington's recognized chief biographer, dismissed Washington's intellectual capacities. In his first biography on Washington, Harlan argued:

> Those who try to understand Washington in ideological terms, as the realistic black philosopher of the age of

Jim Crow, or as the intellectual opposite of W.E.B. Du Bois, miss the essential character of the man. He was not an intellectual, but a man of action. Ideas he cared little for. Power was his game, and he used ideas simply as instruments to gain power.[43]

Washington did indeed use much of his historical writings as a means of gaining support from influential sectors in white America. Yet, the largely uncontested Harlan view of Washington ignores his intriguing philosophy and approach to history. In his rhetoric and writings, Washington used history to win over his white audiences, instill pride within his black followers, and explain the peculiar status of contemporary black America.

In his famous 1895 Atlanta Exposition address, dubbed the "Atlanta Compromise" by Du Bois, Washington manipulated Black history and the myth of the "Old South" in order to gain the support of his southern white listeners. He portrayed slavery as being a benevolent institution:

> You can be sure in the future, as in the past, that you will be surrounded by the most patient, faithful, law-abiding, and unresentful people that the world has seen. As we have proved our loyalty to you in the past,...so in the future...we shall stand by you.[44]

He continued to mythicize the black historical experience in his most famous book, *Up From Slavery* (1901). Building upon the sentiments expressed in his 1895 Atlanta oration, Washington portrayed slaves as being loyal before and during the Civil War; slavery as being a "school" for enslaved blacks; and Reconstruction as benefiting blacks. Because he knew nothing of his own personal history, he viewed himself as being a history-maker. "Years ago I resolved that because I had no ancestry myself I would leave a record of which my children would be proud, and which might encourage them to still higher effort."[45] While *Up From Slavery* mythicized the antebellum era, in his first autobiography, *The Story of My Life and Work* (1900), which was "written primarily for blacks," Washington historicized slavery with more painful memories. "The thing in connection with slavery that has left the deepest impression on me was the instance of seeing a grown man, my uncle, tied to a tree early one morning, stripped naked, and someone whipping him with a cowhide," Washington recounted.[46] As was the case with his social and political programs, Washington molded his view of history to suit his particular audience.

The Tuskegee principal offered his more philosophical thoughts about history in his nonautobiographical books featuring his programs concerning racial uplift, *A New Negro for a New Century* (1899), *The Future of the American Negro* (1899), and *The Story of the Negro* (1909). In *A New Negro for a New Century*, Washington prioritized a knowledge in Black history as being an important element of blacks' struggle. He acknowledged the oppression in Black history and defined the role of the black historian as being directly linked to social reform. "As a surgeon must harden his heart while he probes the wound, that he may apply a healing lotion; so the historian must record the facts however heart-rending, that he may perchance suggest a remedy."[47] Unlike in *Up From Slavery*, he also openly criticized the United States' slaveholding past. In an uncharacteristically unpatriotic manner, Washington declared: "We read of no greater inconsistency or more indefensible farce, than to call this the land of freedom, when millions of her people were slaves, including some of the most gallant defenders of this country or their descendants."[48]

In *The Future of the American Negro*, while Washington perpetrated the myth of slavery as laying the foundations for blacks' education, he also articulated that "the race" needed to "have the element of hero-worship in it." Echoing the American Negro Academy and foreshadowing Woodson, Washington called upon blacks to proactively study and document their history:

> We have reached a period when educated Negroes should give more attention to the history of their race,

should devote more time to finding out the true history of the race, and in collecting in some museum the relics that mark its progress...We should have so much pride that we would spend more time in looking into the history of the race, more effort and money in perpetuating in some desirable form its achievements, so that from year to year,...we can point to our children the rough path through which we grew strong and great.[49]

In addition to his historical biography on Frederick Douglass published in 1906, Washington published *The Story of the Negro* in 1909. Washington advertised this work as a "straight forward" history of African Americans from their African origins until the dawning of the twentieth century. Robert E. Park, one of Washington's ghostwriters from 1905 to 1914, and his Tuskegee Institute co-worker Monroe N. Work helped Washington write and conduct research for this study.[50] Preceding John Hope Franklin, Washington called Black history a history "from slavery to freedom." Writing *The Story of the Negro* significantly molded Washington's philosophy of Black history. "The story of the Negro, in the last analysis, is simply the story of the man who is farthest down; as he raises himself he raises every other man who is above him."[51] Certainly, many of Washington's contemporaries offered much more sophisticated analyses of African American history than he did. Yet, Washington's use of history in his multidimensional program for black uplift is important, adding further complexity to understanding his strategy. Washington's descriptions of his ancestors' history and its function were largely dictated by his role as black America's leading spokesperson. While introducing his white readers to the black past, he embraced the myth of the "Old South." At the same time, he stressed to blacks that they use their history of perseverance over oppression as a source of pride and inspiration. At bottom, Washington viewed his own Horatio Alger-like life as articulated in *Up From Slavery* and other writings as "an epitome of the history of my race."[52]

Black Women Historians Who Were Active
Before Woodson Came on the Scene

Earl E. Thorpe should be applauded for including "historians without portfolio" and laymen in his conceptualization of black historians. Yet, he basically ignored black women lay historians. He mentioned the work of only one non-formally trained black woman historian, Laura Eliza Wilkes, who published *Story of Frederick Douglass* (1898) and *Missing Pages in American History, Revealing the Services of Negroes in the Early Wars of America* (1919). Thorpe's failure to deal with black women and gender issues in greater detail is understandable. His work was written before Black Women's History emerged as a distinct field of study. Black women historians active during the "nadir" of black life made significant contributions to the black historical enterprise. Restricted by the prevalent gender conventions of their times, pioneering black women historians overcame a different set of barriers than their male counterparts in earning their doctorates, publishing, securing employment, receiving professorial promotions, and gaining respect in academia. Though in 1925 Anna Julia Cooper became the first African American woman to earn a doctorate in history from the Sorbonne in Paris, France and she was one of the leading black women intellectuals through the Civil Rights Movement, her direct impact on the black historical profession was symbolically important, but limited in more tangible terms.[53] In 1940, Marion Thompson Wright became the first African American woman historian to earn a Ph.D. in the United States.

The significant lapse in time between Du Bois earning his doctorate in 1895 and Anna Julia Cooper and Marion Thompson Wright receiving theirs is neither surprising nor difficult to explain. Historically, black women have faced significant opposition from various fronts in pursuing and attaining education, especially in higher academia. When Du Bois and Woodson emerged as leading historians, black women were widely and often systematically excluded from participating in U.S. and African American academic culture.[54] From the 1880s through the

1950s, as historian Stephanie Shaw argued in *What a Woman Ought to Be and Do*, black women professionals were carefully socialized to work in the "feminized professions—as social workers, librarians, nurses, and teachers."[55] Black women in the historical profession and academia as a whole during these times faced multiple forms of oppression, including sexism and racism, and in some cases class discrimination. In response to this environment, Paula Giddings suggested that black female intellectuals have historically possessed a certain desire to persevere, a drive that was supposedly unattainable by men. "Since education is the key to the more attractive occupations, black women intellectuals have possessed a certain history of striving for education beyond what their gender or their color seemed to prescribe," Giddings observed. "Black men have not had the same motivation, historically, because they had a greater range of options."[56]

Giddings's fundamental theory that environment dictates behavior patterns is provocative and deserves further elaboration. It is indeed clear that African American women as a group have historically struggled to acquire an education and join the ranks of professionally trained scholars in white and black communities.[57] Especially during the "nadir," they reacted to the pervasive exclusionary policies of the broader white society by promoting an ideology and strategy of self-help. At the same time, black women scholars responded to the stifling gender conventions within the black community. African American female historians of the "nadir," in turn, created a range of coping strategies, survival mechanisms, and alternative ways to approaching and writing history. Fewer than ten black women earned doctorates in history before the mid-1950s, thereby gaining access in some form to academic sanctioning. However, before Anna Julia Cooper or Marion Thompson Wright, many non-Ph.D.-holding black women published scholarly historical works and engaged in the craft of historians.

The history of early black women historians active during the period between Williams's *History of the Negro Race* (1882) and the founding of the ASNLH in 1915, constitutes a dynamic narrative, challenging us to revisit the lives and works of lesser-known black women scholars, re-conceptualize conventional definitions of what makes one a historian, and rediscover insightful scholarly vantage points. I have identified two major groups of black women historians during this period: novelists and amateur historians.

Around the time that Williams died in 1891, several black women writers used their novels as history texts. Recently deceased literary critic Claudia Tate convincingly argued that post-Reconstruction "black domestic melodramas" written by African American women were "symbolically embedded" with "cultural meaning, values, expectations, and rituals of African Americans of that era." Tate explored

> how black women authors of the post-Reconstruction era used domestic novels, as did other politically excluded writers, as entry points into the 'literary and intellectual world as a means of access to social and political events from which [as black women were] ...largely excluded.[58]

Tate's theory can be applied to black women as writers of history as well.

Black women novelists, namely Frances Ellen Watkins Harper (1825–1911) and Pauline Hopkins (1859–1930), wrote "female-centered," seemingly unthreatening, "domestic novels" that critically addressed controversial issues and events in U.S. history such as slavery, the Civil War, and Reconstruction. "Without an historicized interpretive model, the black domestic novels seem maudlin, inconsequential, even vacuous," Tate has warned us.[59] In post-Reconstruction America, black women intellectuals who sought to write conventional historical texts may have faced more resistance than they did as novelists. They tapped into a literary genre perhaps more accessible to them as black women. In line with their pragmatic worldview, they also probably reasoned that novels had a much broader appeal than history texts among black and white middle-class readers.

Harper and Hopkins, two of the most influential black women writers of the turn of the century, challenge us to broaden traditional definitions of historians.

In 1892, at the age of sixty-seven, Harper, a former full-time antebellum-era reformer, poet, lecturer, teacher, and novelist, published her most famous book, *lola Leroy, or Shadows Uplifted*. Harper's novel "was probably the best selling novel by an Afro-American writer prior to the twentieth century." Her book had "wide appeal." As she had done decades earlier in her poetry on slavery, Harper critically revisited America's past in hopes of generating debate among her wide readership. While Harper's novel addressed many of the intricacies surrounding slavery, the wartime South, emancipation, and Reconstruction, it was also a historical discussion of the role and social responsibility of educated, privileged blacks. Harper explored various issues in African American history until Reconstruction, and her message was applicable to the times in which she wrote. She made connections between the period of slavery and the present for pragmatic, political purposes. In analyzing *Minnie's Sacrifice* and *lola Leroy*, Melba Joyce Boyd argued that "these novels provide a connection between the past horrors of slavery and the present terror of lynching. The radical history Harper preserves in both novels," Boyd continues, "is a time continuum essential to a liberated vision in the future. In both instances, the works are written for the black reading audience." Harper acknowledged the complex inner workings of slave culture long before the slavery studies of the 1960s and 1970s argued that recognizing slaves' agency was essential. In *lola Leroy*, Harper identified slaves "as participants in the struggle for liberation" and contrabands of war, the diversity within slave societies, and "the complex dynamics that characterize the master/slave relationship." Harper's discussion of slavery, though couched in a work of fiction, was revisionist in nature, yet sensitive to historical objectivity. "Harper's portrayals of the enslaved contradict popular opinion, manifesting vital, thriving voices of resistance. At the same time, Harper does not romanticize the slaves to benefit a counterargument." In dealing with Reconstruction, Harper also highlighted the significance of rebuilding the family for blacks in the South.[60]

Through history, Harper dictated a program for African American social uplift. In the novel, protagonist lola, who had been living as a white person until her adult years, immediately accepted her African heritage upon discovering that her mother was "a quadroon." During the Civil War and following emancipation, this "Southern lady, whose education and manners stamped her as a woman of fine culture and good breeding," devoted her life to the black masses of the South as a model race woman. For lola, being a servant and leader of the race "is a far greater privilege than it is to open the gates of material prosperity and fill every house to sensuous enjoyment." In response to a white physician's desperate plea that she no longer serve her oppressed people and marry him, lola passionately asserted:

> It was through their unrequited toil that I was educated, while they were compelled to live in ignorance. I am indebted to them for the power I have to serve them. I wish other Southern women felt as I do...I must serve the race which needs me most.[61]

Harper stressed that African American professionals owed a collective debt to the historically rooted African American struggle for survival.

Like Harper, Pauline Hopkins used her historical scholarship to help her people in the struggle for liberation. In the Preface of her first and only novel published in the form of a book, she proclaimed: "In giving this little romance experience in print, I am not actuated by desire for notoriety or for profit, but to do all that I can in an humble way to raise the stigma of degradation from my race."[62] During the late nineteenth century and the early 1900s, Hopkins was one of black America's most productive journalists. "The single most productive black woman writer at the turn of the century," this multi-talented scholar was just as prolific as the leading male writers of her time such as Paul

Laurence Dunbar, Charles W. Chesnutt, and Sutton Griggs.[63] From 1900 until 1905, Hopkins published four novels (one in book form), seven short stories, one brief self-published historical booklet, two dozen biographical sketches in the *Colored American Magazine*, and many essays, columns, and editorials. She has been called by one scholar a "performer, playwright, orator, novelist, journalist, short story writer, biographer, and editor."[64] She was also an active historian. She published many important historical pieces, including *Contending Forces* (1900), serialized novel *Winona* (1902), two dozen biographical sketches on "famous" African American men and women in the *Colored American Magazine* from 1900 until 1902, and a brief thirty-one-page booklet, *A Primer of Facts Pertaining to the Early Greatness of the African Race and the Possibility of Restoration by Its Descendants—with Epilogue* (1905).

While Frances Ellen Watkins Harper couched her historical commentaries in prose and novels, Hopkins was a self-proclaimed historian. She introduced her best-known novel as being a historical study grounded in rigorous research. "The incidents in the early chapters of the book actually occurred." Hopkins openly challenged her readership to verify her sources for *Contending Forces*. "Ample proof of this may be found at Newberne, N.C., and at the national seat of the government, Washington, D.C." In the Preface of her romance novel, Hopkins also argued that history was instructive because of its direct connection with the present and future. She viewed the present as being part of a larger historical continuum, part of a vast body of interconnected ideologies and events. Though she "tried to tell an impartial story," Hopkins was forthright in the need for black authored revisionist historical accounts.

> No one will do this for us; we must ourselves develop the men and women who will faithfully portray the inmost thoughts and feelings of the Negro with all the fire and romance which lie dormant in our history, and, as yet, unrecognized by writers of the Anglo-Saxon race.

Hopkins's plea was quite modern and advanced, foreshadowing by nearly a century Vincent Harding's notion that black historians must passionately chronicle the pain, humanity, and reality of black people, and Manning Marable's theory of the "descriptive" principle of African American Studies and the black intellectual tradition.[65]

Making history political and pragmatic, Hopkins stressed that the conditions facing blacks during the "nadir" were essentially the same as those of the antebellum era. She rejected the notion of black progress from emancipation and Reconstruction widely celebrated by the majority of black spokespersons, asserting:

> Mob rule is nothing new. Southern sentiment has not been changed; the old ideas close in analogy to the spirit of the buccaneers, who formed in many instances the first settlers of the Southland, still prevail, and break forth clothed in new forms to force the whole republic to an acceptance of its principles. Let us compare the happenings of one hundred—two hundred years ago, with those of today. The difference between then and now, if there be, is so slight as to be scarcely worth mentioning. The atrocity of the acts committed one hundred years ago are duplicated today, when slavery is supposed no longer to exist.[66]

In writing her serial novel *Winona*, set in Kansas during the turbulent 1850s, Hopkins echoed her strategies as a lay historian in *Contending Forces*. Hopkins may have selected this pivotal historical setting, highlighting the struggles of John Brown, in order to "justify the need in 1902 for the kind of organized resistance to racist violence led by the anti-slavery leader John Brown in 1856." Thus, Hopkins interpreted the historian's role not simply in terms of recounting past events, but, more important, as a source of motivation and direction for the future. Like *Contending Forces*, *Winona* drew from historical sources. In discussing John Brown, she relied on the available scholarship.[67] Since the late 1980s, scholarly interest in Hopkins's life and work has blossomed and at least one scholar has noted her function as a historian. "Throughout her tenure at *CAM* (1900–1904), Hopkins acknowledged her obligation not simply to cultivate but to create an audience for her revisionist race history," C.K. Doreski asserted, "She assumed the authority of race historian and mediated the issues of race and gender to incite a readership to pride and action." Hopkins's historical approach as an editor and journalist for the *Colored American Magazine* was essentially pragmatic. Decades before Woodson decided to dedicate himself to writing popular African American history, Hopkins attempted to translate "representative lives into authentic history" and compose "history from exemplary lives in the hope of elevating the image of the entire race." She translated the two dozen biographical sketches of "famous" black historical figures into "participatory exemplary texts."[68] At the same time, Hopkins attacked the widespread racism of the Gilded Age by educating her significant white *Colored American Magazine* readership, comprising about one third of her total readership.[69] In this sense, she preceded Woodson's ideal yet substantive philosophy that by educating whites about black history, racial prejudice and discrimination could be reduced.

Several years after Williams's death, in 1894 Gertrude E.H. Bustill Mossell (1855–1948), editor, journalist, and feminist, became the first African American woman to publish a major nonfiction book on African American history, *The Work of the Afro-American Woman*, a historical and contemporary assessment of black women intellectuals' and activists' monumental accomplishments since the era of the American Revolution. Joanne Braxton posited that this volume "was, for the black woman of the 1890s, the equivalent of Giddings' work of the 1980s—in sum, a powerful and progressive statement." *The Work* is subdivided into various sections, "original essays and poems...part intellectual history, part advice book, and part polemic." Mossell introduced her scholarship as being a vehicle of race pride and inspiration. "The value of any published work, especially if historical in character, must be largely inspirational," Mossell argued. "This fact grows out of the truth that race instinct, race experience lies behind it, national feeling, or race pride always having for its development a basis of self-respect."[70] In the first two essays of *The Work*, Mossell discussed a variety of black women historical figureheads and also offered some provocative thoughts on the deeper meanings of history to African Americans. Mossell highlighted the achievements of her contemporary "industrious" black women social activists, the struggles waged by Phyllis Wheatley, Sojourner Truth, and Harriet Tubman, and the contributions of obscure black women such as Revolutionary War participant Deborah Gannet, former slaves Elizabeth Freeman and Jessie Slew, and Kate Ferguson, a former slave who opened one of the first successful Sunday schools for blacks in New York City.[71]

In another "tribute to black womanhood" entitled "A Sketch of Afro-American Literature," Mossell outlined her philosophy of history and stressed the uniqueness of African American history:

> The intellectual history of a people or nation constitutes to a great degree the very heart of its life. To find this history, we must search the fountain-head of its language, its customs, its religion, and its politics expressed by tongue or pen, its folklore and songs. The history of the Afro-American race in this country may be divided into three epochs—the separation from native land and friends, and later arrival in this land of forced adoption.

Mossell added:

> Next follows two hundred and fifty years of bondage and oppression mitigated only through the hope thrown upon life's pathway by the presence of hundreds of freemen of the race eking out an existence hampered on all sides by caste prejudice. Later, an era of freedom

covered by twenty years of emancipation, holding in name citizenship, but defrauded of its substance by every means that human ingenuity could devise. Again, the intellectual history of a race is always of value in determining the past and future of it. As a rule, a race writes its history in laws and in its records.[72]

Mossell viewed history as being one of the most important and encompassing aspects of a people. In analyzing African American history, she stressed the necessity of focusing on the specific, oppressive historical contexts that shaped black America's historical realities. She viewed herself and other African Americans engaged in writing literature as contributing to the history of black people, as leaving behind concrete records for their people. Foreshadowing Woodson, Mossell recognized the importance of using history within the African American community as a guide for the future. Equally important, she acknowledged the struggle faced by blacks in chronicling their past and therefore determining their future.

Less than a decade after Mossell published *The Work*, in 1902 Susie King Taylor (1848–1912) published the only black woman's account of the Civil War. In *Reminiscences of My Life in Camp with the 33rd U.S. Colored Troops, Late 1st South Carolina Volunteers*, Taylor recounted her experiences as a laundress, teacher, and a nurse behind Union lines from about 1862 until 1865. Taylor, whose mother was a domestic slave, learned to read and write while living as a free person in Savannah with her grandmother. Nearly four decades following the end of the war, Taylor self-published *Reminiscences* while living in Boston. Thomas Wentworth Higginson introduced Taylor's book, noting that *Reminiscences*, "delineated from the woman's point of view," constituted an important contribution to U.S. military history.[73] Taylor began her account by tracing her family roots back to the Revolutionary era. She devoted her account to discussing the day-to-day experiences of the 33rd U.S. Colored Troops, renamed the First S.C. Volunteers. Though she glorified Lincoln's Emancipation Proclamation, she challenged the anti-black accounts of the Civil War era. Taylor wrote:

> These white men and women could not tolerate our black Union soldiers, for many of them had formerly been their slaves; and although these brave men risked life and limb to assist them in distress, men and even women would sneer and molest them whenever they met them.

Taylor also celebrated the role of black women during the Civil War. Though her statements were brief, they were ahead of their time. "There are many people who do not know what some of the colored women did during the war," Taylor asserted.

> There were hundreds of them who assisted the Union soldiers by hiding them and helping them escape. Many were punished for taking food to the prison stockades for the prisoners...These things should be kept in history before the people.[74]

Taylor's account of the Civil War is not very critical. Instead, there is an understandable patriotic tone to her account. She separated history from polemics, saving her most scathing critiques of white America for a later chapter, "Thoughts on Present Conditions." She critiqued the mistreatment endured by blacks during the "nadir," stressing the similarity between contemporary and past racial oppression. A refreshing part of Taylor's account is her plea that younger generations remember and study history. Taylor proclaimed in a way that Woodson would several decades later:

> We do not, as the black race, properly appreciate the old veterans. I look around now and see the comforts that our younger generation enjoy, and think of the blood that was shed to make these comforts possible for them, and see how little some of them appreciate

the old soldiers. My heart burns within me, at this want of appreciation.[75]

In 1912, another Washington DC educator and reformer, Leila Amos Pendleton, published *A Narrative of the Negro*, a brief work that she described as being "a sort of 'family history'" for the "colored children of America."[76] In 1915, Du Bois called his *The Negro* the first major study of African descendants throughout the diaspora.[77] Though not as scientific and analytical as Du Bois's work, Pendleton's study is encompassing, addressing Africans' lives from ancient times through the era of colonialism, blacks in Haiti, Brazil, Jamaica, and Bermuda, and black American life from the colonial era through the "nadir." Rejecting the constraints of objectivity, Pendleton's tone was militant. She critiqued King Leopold of the Belgium Congo and the violent nature of the colonial conquest, called slavery "evil," and condemned the "long series of brutal outrages, murders, maimings, beatings, burnings" and "barbarous lynchings" of African Americans.[78] The majority of Pendleton's study addressed African American history from the American Revolution through the "nadir," and in the tradition of African American juvenile literature relied heavily on many brief biographical sketches of a range of black leaders. Renowned Harlem Renaissance novelist and *Crisis* literary editor (1919–1926), Jessie Fauset praised Pendleton's book. "Now, at last, it would seem, we have an historian," Fauset proclaimed, "who has arisen in answer to our need."[79]

A wide range of black writers of history from the days when slavery flourished in the United States through the early 1900s laid the foundations for the emergence of the modern Black history movement under Carter G. Woodson and his protégés and co-workers. Today, it is easy to critique pre-Woodson black historians for their style, research methodologies, selection of information, optimism, or religious piety. Many historians, especially those of the hip-hop generation, perhaps consider the ideas of these pioneering historians archaic, boring, and difficult to relate to. Their scholarship must be analyzed within the sociohistorical context in which it was produced. When we acknowledge this, their efforts are best understood and appreciated. Their unwavering passion and commitment could help hip-hop generation historians and future generations of black historians remain grounded. A combination of past passions with contemporary, advanced scholarly approaches could result in a potent genre of Black history. Indeed, each generation of black historians must write its own history and must conceptualize Black history to suit its situation. At the same time, each generation of black historians has the responsibility—which becomes bigger every year with each new publication and idea generated—to critically reflect upon their predecessors' approaches, scholarship, and philosophical reasoning. Writing history then becomes a productive, never-ending discussion between generations of historians.

Notes

Chapter 4

Before Carter G. Woodson:
The Roots of the Black Historical Profession

[1] Sterling Stuckey, *Slave Culture: Nationalist Theory and the Foundations of Black America* (New York: Oxford University Press, 1987), 3.

[2] Desai Ram, *African Society and Culture* (New York: M.W. Lads, 1968); Mervyn C. Alleyne, *Roots of Jamaican Culture* (London: Pluto, 1989); Molefi Kete Asante, "The Afrocentric Metatheory and Disciplinary Implications," in *The African American Studies Reader*, ed. Norment, 413.

[3] Vincent B. Khapoya, *The African Experience: An Introduction* Second Edition (New Jersey: Prentice Hall, 1998); Festus Ugboaja Ohaegbulam, *Towards an Understanding of the African Experience from Historical and Contemporary Perspectives* (New York: University Press of America, 1990); Toyin Falola, ed., *African Cultures and Societies Before 1885: Volume 2* (North Carolina: Carolina Academic Press, 2000). All of these authors' studies discuss issues pertaining to pre-colonial, traditional African culture.

[4] Adebayo Oyebade, "The Study of Africa in Historical Perspective," in *Africa, Volume I: Africa to 1885*, ed. Toyin Falola (Durham: Carolina Academic Press, 2000).

[5] John S. Mbiti, *Introduction to African Religion* Second Edition (London: Heinemann, 1991), 18, 28, 92–95, 130.

[6] D.T. Niane, *Sundiata: An Epic of Old Mali* (England: Longman, 1990), vii.

[7] Harding, *There Is a River*.

[8] John E. Fleming, "African-American Museums, History, and the American Ideal," *The Journal of American History* 81 (December 1994): 1020–1021.

[9] Darlene Clark Hine, "Quilts and African-American Women's Cultural history," in *African American Quiltmaking in Michigan*, ed.

Marsha L. Macdowell (East Lansing: Michigan State University Press, 1997), 13, 15.

[10] Floris Barnett Cash, "Kinship and Quilting: An Examination of an African-American Tradition," *The Journal of African American History* 80 (Winter 1995): 30.

[11] Thorpe, *Black Historians*, 31, 32.

[12] Most of the historians whose works deal with antebellum black historians assert that Robert Benjamin Lewis and William Cooper Nell were the most important writers of this group. Elizabeth R. Bethel offers a different view. She contends that Pennington provided the first major Black history text that "stretched across time and space to ancient Africa, forging a heritage or raw material of popular belief, mythology, and popular lore." See Elizabeth R. Bethel, *The Roots of African-American Identity: Memory and History in Free Antebellum Communities* (New York: St. Martin's, 1997), 167–183.

[13] Joseph E. Harris, *Africans and Their History* Revised Edition (New York: A Mentor Book, 1987), 19–20.

[14] Thomas Jefferson, *Notes on the State of Virginia* (New York: Harper and Row, 1964). There are many books that detail Jefferson's ideas about blacks and slavery. See, Robert McColley, *Slavery and Jeffersoniam Virginia* Second Edition (Urbana: University of Illinois Press, 1978); Winthrop D. Jordan, *The White Man's Burden: Historical Origins of Racism in the United States* (New York: Oxford University Press, 1974), 165–193; Barbara Chase-Riboud, *Sally Hemmings: A Novel* (New York: Viking, 1979); Christopher B. Booker, *African-Americans and the Presidency: A History of Broken Promises* (New York: Franklin Watts, 2000); Jan Ellen Lewis and Peter S. Onuf, eds., *Sally Hemmings and Thomas Jefferson: History, Memory, and Civic Culture* (Charlottesville: University Press of Virginia, 1999); Shannon Lanier and Jane Feldman, *Jefferson's Children: The Story of One American Family* (New York: Random House, 2000). One of the most recent studies in which author Gary Wills discusses Jefferson's life "as a protector and extender of the slave system" is *"Negro President": Jefferson and the Slave Power* (Boston: Houghton Mifflin, 2003).

[15] Manning Marable, "Black Studies and the Black Intellectual Tradition," *Race and Reason* 4 (1997–1998): 3.

[16] Clarence Walker, *Deromanticizing Black History: Critical Essays and Reappraisals* (Knoxville: The University of Tennessee Press, 1991), 92.

[17] Quarles, "Black History's Antebellum Origins," 93.

[18] Walker, *Deromanticizing Black History,* 90.

[19] Thorpe, *Black Historians,* 31.

[20] Wright, *Black History and Black Identity,* 25.

[21] Ibid., 29.

[22] Ibid., 41–42.

[23] Franklin first explored Williams' contributions in a 1946 article in *The Journal of Negro History.* For an extensive treatment of Williams, see Franklin, *George Washington Williams.*

[24] Ibid., 10, 17, 39, 100.

[25] George Washington Williams, *History of the Negro Race in America from 1619 to 1880: Negroes as Slaves, as Soldiers, and as Citizens* (New York: G.P. Putnam's Sons, 1883), v. For extensive discussions of Williams's study, see Franklin, *George Washington Williams,* 100–133; Thorpe, *Black Historians,* 46–55.

[26] See George Washington Williams, *A History of Negro Troops in the War of the Rebellion, 1861–1865* (New York: Harper and Brothers, 1887, 1888). Franklin overviews how white scholars reviewed Williams's scholarship. See *George Washington Williams,* 116–133.

[27] W.E.B. Du Bois, "The Negro in Literature and Art," in *W.E.B. Du Bois: A Reader,* ed. Meyer Weinberg (New York: Harper Torchbooks, 1970), 234.

[28] Charles H. Wesley, "W.E.B. Du Bois: The Historian," in *Black Titan: W.E.B. Du Bois; An Anthology by the Editors of Freedomways,* ed. John Henrik Clarke, Esther Jackson, Ernest Kaiser, and J.H. O'Dell (Boston: Beacon Press, 1970), 82. There are many biographies on Du Bois that address his career as a historian. For more specific assessments of this part of his intellectual persona, see the following articles: Herbert Aptheker, "The Historian," in *W.E.B. Du Bois: A Profile,* ed. Rayford W. Logan (New York: Hill and Wang, 1971), 249–273; David W. Blight, "W.E.B. Du Bois and the Struggle for American Historical Memory," in *History and Memory in African-American Culture,* ed.

Genevieve Fabre and Robert O'Meally (New York: Oxford University Press, 1994), 45–71.

[29] Meier and Rudwick, *Black History and the Historical Profession*, 5.

[30] Herbert Aptheker, ed., *The Autobiography of W.E.B. Du Bois: A Soliloquy on Viewing My Life from the Last Century of Its First Century* (New York: International Publishers, 1968), 218–219.

[31] Elijah Anderson, "Introduction to the 1996 Edition of The Philadelphia Negro," in W.E.B. Du Bois, *The Philadelphia Negro: A Social Study* (Philadelphia: University of Pennsylvania Press, 1996), ix.

[32] For an interesting discussion of *The Souls of Black Folk*, see Arnold Rampersad, *The Art and Imagination of W.E.B. Du Bois* (Cambridge: Harvard University Press, 1976).

[33] David Roediger, ed., *W.E.B. Du Bois, John Brown* (New York, 2001).

[34] Meier and Rudwick, *Black History and the Historical Profession, 1915–1980*, 29.

[35] W.E.B. Du Bois, "Reconstruction and Its Benefits," *American Historical Review* 15 (July 1910): 781–783, 793–795.

[36] David Levering Lewis, *W.E.B. Du Bois: Biography of a Race, 1868–1919* (New York: Henry Holt, 1993), 462. Though Asante considers himself a disciple of Diop, he does not consider Davidson and Bernal as being key members of the Afrocentric intellectual school of thought. See Molefi Kete Asante, *The Afrocentric Idea* (Philadelphia: Temple University Press, 1987); Asante, *Kemet, Afrocentricity and Knowledge* (New Jersey: Africa World Press, 1990); Ama Mazama, ed., *The Afrocentric Paradigm* (New Jersey: Africa World Press, 2003).

[37] W.E.B. Du Bois, *The Negro* (New York: Oxford University Press, 1970), 17, 21.

[38] Ibid., 6, 15.

[39] Ibid., 64, 80.

[40] Ibid., 136.

[41] Ibid., 3, 146.

[42] Thorpe, *Black Historians*, 144.

[43] Thorpe, *Black Historians*; Franklin, "On the Evolution of Scholarship in Afro-American History;" Louis R. Harlan, *Booker T. Washington: The Making of a Black Leader, 1856–1901* (New York: Oxford University Press, 1972), "Preface."

[44] Booker T. Washington, *Up From Slavery* (New York: Dover Publications, 1995), 107.

[45] Ibid., 17

[46] Charlotte D. Fitzgerald, *"The Story of My Life and Work*: Booker T. Washington's Other Autobiography," *The Black Scholar* 21 (1992): 35; Booker T. Washington, *The Story of My Life and Work* (Atlanta: J.L. Nichols and Company, 1900), 18–19.

[47] Booker T. Washington, *A New Negro for a New Century* (Chicago: American Publishing House, 1899), 164.

[48] Ibid., 118.

[49] Booker T. Washington, *The Future of the American Negro* (New York: Haskell House Publishers, 1968), 182.

[50] Park helped Washington write *The Story of the Negro* and *My Larger Education* as well as many articles, speeches, and letters. Alphonsus Orenzo Stafford also helped Washington write *The Story of the Negro*. Washington sent Park his writings and at one point even instructed Park to add what he thought was needed. For discussions of Park's role as a ghostwriter, see Louis R. Harlan and R.W. Smock, eds., *The Booker T. Washington Papers: Volume 8, 1904–6* (Urbana: University of Illinois Press, 1979), 203.

[51] Booker T. Washington, *The Story of the Negro: The Rise of the Race from Slavery, Volume I* (New York: Negro Universities Press, 1969), 400, 399.

[52] Ibid., 3.

[53] Cooper's impact on the black woman's historical profession was limited because she received her degree outside of the United States, at the University of Paris, the Sorbonne; she did not focus her intellectual energies on practicing the historian's craft; she did not have the opportunity to work with other black women in the field; and in 1925, at the age of sixty-six, Cooper was approaching the end of her scholarly career. See Louise Daniel Hutchinson, *Anna Julia Cooper: A Voice From the South* (Washington, D.C.: Smithsonian, 1981), 138–

143; Dagbovie, "Black Women Historians from the Late 19th Century Until the Dawning of the Civil Rights Movement."

[54] Rayford W. Logan, *The Negro in American Life and Thought: The Nadir, 1877–1901* (New York: Dial, 1954); William M. Banks, *Black Intellectuals: Race and Responsibility in American Life* (New York: W.W. Norton, 1996). For discussions of how black male leaders of the Progressive era often openly opposed African American middle-class women's political activism and social commentaries, see Beverly Guy-Sheftall, *Daughters of Sorrow: Attitudes Toward Black Women, 1880–1920* (New York: Carlson, 1990); Patricia Morton, *Disfigured Images: The Historical Assault on Afro-American Women* (New York: Greenwood Press, 1991); Deborah Gray White, *Too Heavy A Load: Black Women in Defense of Themselves, 1894–1994* (New York: W.W. Norton, 1999); Floris Barnett Cash, *African American Women and Social Action: The Clubwomen and Volunteerism from Jim Crow to the New Deal, 1896–1936* (Westport, Connecticut: Greenwood, 2001); Alfred A. Moss, Jr., *The American Negro Academy: Voice of the Talented Tenth* (Baton Rouge: Louisiana State University Press, 1981), 78. For a discussion of black men's views of black women that differs from these works, see Rosalyn Terborg-Penn, "Black Male Perspectives on the Nineteenth-Century Woman," in *The Afro-American Woman: Struggles and Images*, ed. Harley and Penn, 28–42.

[55] Stephanie Shaw, *What a Woman Ought to Be and Do: Black Professional Women Workers During the Jim Crow Era* (Chicago: University of Chicago Press, 1996), 3.

[56] Paula Giddings, *When and Where I Enter: The Impact of Black Women on Race and Sex in America* (New York: Morrow, 1984), 7.

[57] One of the first Black women to earn a B.A. degree, Mary Jane Patterson (1840–1894), received her diploma in 1862 from Oberlin College. In 1891, Anna J. Cooper noted in The Southland that only twenty-nine black women earned B.A. degrees. See, Anna Julia Cooper, "The Higher Education of Women," in *Black Women in Higher Education: An Anthology of Essays, Studies, and Documents*, ed. Elizabeth L. Ihle (New York: Garland, 1992), 58. By 1900, Du Bois noted that about 250 black women had joined her in earning B.A. degrees from a range of colleges and universities, especially Black colleges and universities. Though black women did join the teaching staffs of Black colleges and universities in significant numbers by the late

nineteenth century, these positions did not gain black women entry into academia within the African American community and certainly not within the dominant white culture's academic circles. For a discussion of black women teachers in the South during the Progressive era, see Cynthia Neverdon-Morton, *Afro-American Women of the South and the Advancement of the Race, 1895–1925* (Knoxville: University of Tennessee Press, 1989), 78–103. In the 1920s, the first four black women earned Ph.D.'s. In addition to Cooper, the fourth black woman to earn a Ph.D., this pioneering group included Georgiana R. Simpson, Eva B. Dykes, and Sadie T.M. Alexander. During the first half of the twentieth century, the presence of black women doctorates in all fields combined was very limited. According to Harry Washington Greene, between 1876 and 1943, 381 African Americans received "the degree of Doctor of Philosophy or its corresponding equivalent." Horace Mann Bond updated Greene's study and estimated that roughly 820 African Americans earned doctorates from 1866 through 1949. See, Greene, *Holders of Doctorates Among Americans*, 22–29; Horace Mann Bond, *Black American Scholars: A Study of Their Beginnings* (Detroit: Balamp, 1972), 27. While Bond does not provide information concerning his subjects' sex, Greene does. According to his research, forty-six to forty-eight black women received Ph.D.s by 1943. The vast majority of these women were engaged in education in some manner.

[58] Claudia Tate, *Domestic Allegories of Political Desire: The Black Heroine's Text at the Turn of the Century* (New York: Oxford University Press, 1992), 5.

[59] Ibid, 19.

[60] Frances Smith Foster, "Introduction," in Frances E.W. Harper, *lola Leroy, or Shadows Uplifted* (New York, 1988), xxvii; Melba Joyce Boyd, *Discarded Legacy: Politics and Poetics in the Life of Frances E. W. Harper, 1825–1911* (Detroit: Wayne State University Press, 1994), 172, 174, 175, 176, 177.

[61] Harper, *lola Leroy*, 199, 57, 219, 235, 246.

[62] Pauline Hopkins, *Contending Forces: A Romance Illustrative of Negro Life in the North and South* (New York: Oxford University Press, 1988), 13.

[63] Richard Yarborough, "Introduction," in Hopkins, *Contending Forces*, xxviii.

[64] John Cullen Gruesser, "Preface," in *The Unruly Voice: Rediscovering Pauline Elizabeth Hopkins*, ed. Gruesser (Urbana: University of Illinois Press, 1996), ix.

[65] Hopkins, *Contending Forces*, 14; Vincent Harding, "Responsibilities of the Black Scholar to the Community," in *The State of Afro-American History*, ed. Hine, 277–284; Manning Marable, "Black Studies and the Black Intellectual Tradition," *Race and Reason* 4 (1997–98): 3.

[66] Hopkins, *Contending Forces*, 14–15.

[67] Among other sources she consulted was Franklin B. Sanborn's *The Life and Times of John Brown* (1885). See, Martha H. Patterson, "kin' o' rough jestice fer a parson': Pauline Hopkins's Winona and the Politics of Reconstructing History," *African American Review* 32 (1998): 445.

[68] C.K. Doreski, "Inherited Rhetoric and Authentic History: Pauline Hopkins at the Colored American Magazine," in *The Unruly Voice: Rediscovering Pauline Elizabeth Hopkins*, ed. Gruesser, 72, 74, 82.

[69] According to Martha H. Patterson, of a total circulation of 15,000–16,000 per month, about 5,000 issues of the *Colored American Magazine* were purchased by whites. See Patterson, "kin' o' rough jestice fer a parson," 458.

[70] Joanne Braxton, "Introduction," in Mossell, *The Work of the Afro-American*, xxvii, xxix; Mossell, *The Work of the Afro-American Woman*, 9.

[71] Ibid., 26.

[72] Ibid, 48–49.

[73] Thomas Wentworth Higginson, "Introduction," in *Susie King Taylor, Reminiscences of My Life in Camp with the 33rd U.S. Colored Troops, Late 1st South Carolina Volunteers*, ed. Patricia Romero (New York: M. Wiener Publishers, 1988), 23.

[74] Romero, ed., *Susie King Taylor, Reminiscences of My Life in Camp with the 33rd U.S. Colored Troops, Late 1st South Carolina Volunteers*, 107–108; 141–142.

[75] Ibid., 119–120.

[76] Leila Amos Pendleton, *A Narrative of the Negro* Electronic Edition (Chapel Hill, 1999), 3.

[77] Du Bois, *The Negro*, 3.

[78] Pendleton, *A Narrative of the Negro*, 46, 59, 90, 93.

[79] Jessie Fauset, "What to Read," *The Crisis* 4 (August 1912): 183.

CHAPTER 5

Carter G. Woodson (1875–1950): "The Father of Black History"

Carter G. Woodson earned his Ph.D. in history from Harvard in 1912. Three years later, in 1915, he co-founded the first major African American historical organization, the Association for the Study of Negro Life and History. In 1916, he founded the first major black historical journal, *The Journal of Negro History*. Then, in 1926 he founded Negro History Week. These accomplishments, along with the fact that he mentored many younger scholars and published more than 20 books, earned him the title "The Father of Black History." Who was Carter G. Woodson? How did his early life and struggles influence his decision to devote his life and work to the study, promotion, and popularization of Black history? How were African Americans viewed by the U.S. historical profession when Woodson came of age as a historian during the Progressive era? In what ways did he exemplify the life of a scholar-activist? How did he popularize Black history, making it practical and understandable to the youth and the masses of his people? What is Woodson's legacy? How can we perhaps learn from his life, work, contributions, and philosophy as we enter the 21st century? These are the major questions this chapter seeks to answer.

The Makings of a Black Historian, 1875–1912

Carter G. Woodson was born in New Canton, Virginia on 19 December 1875, towards the end of the Reconstruction period. Both of Woodson's parents were former slaves and shared with him first-hand histories of life during slavery. His father, James Henry, told his son how he had physically overpowered his master to take his freedom. He instilled within his son a sense of rebelliousness. Later in his life, Woodson commented that his father's stories sparked his later interest in documenting the stories of ex-slaves. As a professional historian, Woodson stressed the importance of documenting and recording the personal life histories of everyday people. Like many blacks of his time, he came from a large family, nine children in total. Woodson's literate mother, Anne Eliza (Riddle), and his father instilled "high morality," "a strong character," and a "thirst for education" in their children. In 1932, Woodson recounted that his father raised him never to accept insult, compromise his principles, mislead his fellow man, or to betray his people. Woodson's father taught his children to "be polite to everyone," but insisted that they demand the "recognition as a human being." He also instilled within his children race pride and racial solidarity. "Do not do for the traducer of the race anything he will not do for you," he told his children.[1]

A year before Woodson's birth, his parents settled in New Canton, Virginia, buying a farm of twenty-one acres. As a child, Woodson grew up on his father's farm and like nearly every black school-goer attended school for only four months out of the year. His family had to work hard in order to make ends meet. He worked on the family farm until he was about fifteen and then he stepped out and secured a job as a farm laborer and a jack-of-all-trades in Buckingham County, Virginia. Two years later, Woodson moved to Fayette County, West Virginia to work in the coal mines. In his late sixties, Woodson, looking back on his life, described this period as very significant to his intellectual development. In the coal mines, he met a black Civil War veteran named Oliver Jones. "He was well educated," Woodson recalled, "but could neither read not write." Jones allowed many of the coal miners to use his home as a center for social interaction and political discourse. Being the sole literate worker of the group, Woodson read newspapers to his co-workers as he had done and would later continue to do for his father. Jones also had a valuable library of books containing classic works by pioneering black scholars such as George Washington Williams, J.T. Wilson, and W.J. Simmons. Woodson drew great inspiration from these scholars' works. Woodson credited Jones with igniting his interest in research. "I learned so much because of the more extensive reading required by him than I probably would have undertaken for my own benefit," Woodson recounted. "My interest in penetrating the past of my people was deepened and intensified." The years in the coal mines also inevitably reinforced the value of hard work in Woodson's mind. In his late teens, Woodson was becoming a critical thinker with an interest in history, who was not opposed to working hard with his hands.[2]

At the age of twenty, around the time when W.E.B. Du Bois completed his Ph.D. dissertation, Woodson returned to West Virginia and decided to attend Frederick Douglass High School, for which he would later serve as principal from 1900–1903. It took him two years to finish the requirements for graduation. In the fall of 1897, he ventured to Berea College in Kentucky. It took him more than five years to receive a B.A. from Berea because he was searching for his purpose in life and devoting his energies to the uplifting of the race. For financial reasons, he left Berea in the 1897–98 academic year. From 1898 until 1900, he worked as a teacher for a school in Winona, West Virginia where he educated the children of black miners. Based upon an amendment in the West Virginia constitution, by 1899 the opportunities for ordinary blacks to attend basic schools increased.

In 1922, Woodson remarked that black West Virginians became excited in education during his teaching days in Winona, that "often Negro children in groups of only four or five were thus trained in the backward districts, where they received sufficient inspiration to come to larger schools for more systematic training."[3] Woodson was one of those teachers who helped inspire this thirst for learning. This work was an extension of the services he provided for his co-workers in the Fayette County coal mines. From 1900 until 1903, he returned to his high school alma mater, teaching history and serving as the principal. Woodson was in his mid–late twenties and was already the principal of a high school. No doubt he drew upon these administrative experiences later in launching and running the ASNLH. Woodson also remained close to his parents during these years. He helped his folks around the house and eagerly received the family's oral traditions.

Woodson received a Bachelor's degree in Literature from Berea in 1903. From mid-December of 1903 until early February of 1907, Woodson traveled abroad extensively. For roughly five years, under the auspices of the United States War Department, he went to the Philippines "to train the Filipinos to govern themselves," teaching English, health, and agricultural classes. He arrived in Manila sometime in late December 1903. He was first assigned to work in a country town in Nueva Ecija Province "among simple people tilling the soil and growing crops." In June, he was reassigned to another province, Pangasinan, where he trained Filipino teachers. He enjoyed this work very much and remained there until he resigned due to sickness early in 1907.[4]

Woodson did not talk extensively about his experiences in the Philippines. His most detailed account is in *The Mis-Education of the Negro*. Woodson believed that the best way to educate the Filipinos was based upon their own history and culture. He went to the Philippines not as a typical missionary, but as a culturally sensitive reformer. It seems that Woodson applied his early philosophy of using history as a source of pride to the conditions of natives of the Philippines. After leaving the Philippines in early 1907, Woodson briefly traveled around the world and spent roughly half a year in Europe. He briefly attended the Sorbonne. There he studied European history, which helped widen his scope of knowledge, preparing him for the University of Chicago, Harvard, and later for the writing of many book reviews dealing with European subject matter in *The Journal of Negro History*.

After returning from Europe, Woodson enrolled in the University of Chicago and a year later, in the summer of 1908, he received the M.A. degree in History, Romance Languages, and Literature. Woodson then enrolled in Harvard University as a doctoral student. In 1909 he left Cambridge and settled down in the Washington, D.C. area in order to teach French, Spanish, English, and History at the prestigious M Street High School. Professors in Harvard's history department did not share Woodson's passion for Black history. Woodson's first advisor was Edward Channing. He was soon replaced by Albert Bushnell Hart, Du Bois's former advisor. Woodson finished his course work in less than two years and submitted the first draft of his dissertation in the spring of 1910. His committee, consisting of Hart, Channing, and Charles Haskins, made many suggestions for revisions. By January 1911, he finished the revised draft. After finally passing his American history comprehensive examination in April 1912, Woodson completed his Ph.D. dissertation, entitled "The Disruption of Virginia." Woodson's study was worthy of publication, but he did not receive the necessary support to do so.[5]

Scholars have offered a range of explanations as to what sparked Woodson's decision to devote his life to the study and promotion of Black history. According to Lorenzo Johnston Greene, his experiences at Harvard were pivotal. It was there, Woodson told his protégé, where he received, "in a negative way, the inspiration for life's work." While attending one of Channing's classes, "he listened in amazement at the eminent Professor who told the class that the Negro had no history." Woodson told Greene that he challenged Channing and declared that "no people lacked a history." According to Greene's account, Channing then told Woodson to prove him wrong. Woodson then "accepted the challenge" and "resolved to ascertain whether he or Channing was correct."[6]

Racism and the U.S. Historical Profession
During the Progressive Era

It must be emphasized that Woodson began seriously studying history at a time when American historians were quite racist.
African American historians during the Progressive era or "nadir," professionally trained and amateurs, faced unique sets of
obstacles. They were challenged to develop delicately balanced,
innovative, and defensive approaches. Foremost, they defended
"the race" from the prevalent, deeply-rooted racist scientific history of their time. In assessing the U.S. Progressive era historical
enterprise, August Meier and Elliott Rudwick argued that "there
was always a degree of pluralism within the profession" and that
"there were a few white historians—ambiguous though their own
racial attitudes sometimes were—who perceived the significance
of the blacks' role and of race as a moral issue in American history and who were supportive of study in this area."[7]
Still, between 1890 and 1920, many leading U.S. historians
were racists, promoted the notion of African American inferiority, or ignored African Americans' contributions altogether.[8]
Harvard historian Albert Bushnell Hart, one of the few white
historians who was at times openly supportive of African American history and historians, was ambiguous in his attitudes towards blacks. While he occasionally praised certain exceptional
African Americans and challenged overt white supremacist
scholarship, he still held that African Americans were inferior.
"Race measured by race," he concluded in one section of *The
Southern South* (1910), "the Negro is inferior, and his part in
history in Africa and in America leads to the belief that he will
remain inferior in race stamina and race achievement."[9] Earl
Lewis has detailed the "pivotal role" of *The American Historical
Review* in promoting African American history during its first
century.[10] Nonetheless, it is clear that "outwardly racist" essays
were published in this journal during the early twentieth century.[11] According to Peter Novick, historians such as John F.
Rhodes, J.W. Burgess, William A. Dunning, and Ellis Paxson
Oberholtzer were "systematically racist," and a "consensual" and

"near unanimous" racism united white historians from the North and the South during the "nadir."[12] Despite their claim to being nontraditional, innovative, and pluralistic in scope, James Harvey Robinson's "New History" disciples and proponents ignored the race problem, implying that it was not a "primary force" and assuming that "race problems would be solved automatically in the course of progressive developments."[13] African American historians during Woodson's formative years accepted the responsibility of writing blacks into American history and correcting racist scholarship. Embracing the "corrective" principle of the black intellectual tradition, Du Bois and Woodson challenged U.B. Phillips's famous *American Negro Slavery* (1918). The first two African American doctorates in history critiqued Phillips's portrayal of African Americans as being "ignorant," "unenterprising," "barbaric," and "childlike and credulous" in the "ways of civilization."[14]

Unlike the vast majority of white historians during the Progressive era, pioneering African American historians such as Woodson were more directly challenged to democratize and popularize the study of history. For them, providing their African American readership with the basic rudiments of African American history was important. Positive portrayals of the African American experience could, they reasoned, provide blacks with self-esteem, positive role models, and recognition of their ancestors' central contributions to the modernization of the United States. African American historians during the "nadir" faced the dual challenge of producing two particular brands of scholarship: scientific scholarship and popular history for mass consumption. Certain white Progressive era historians faced a similar dilemma, but the situation was markedly distinct. John Higham chronicled how, following the professionalization of history in the mid- to late-1890s, American historians found it difficult to market their scholarship to the general public. Amateur historians, who in the formative years of the AHA dominated the organization, were gradually being removed from the ranks of professional historians and American historians increasingly shifted from writing for laypersons to writing for their colleagues.[15] African American historians continued to serve various distinct audiences within the black community: lay, academic, professional, working-class, middle-class, male, and female.

The scholarship of Progressive era African American historians was also political in a different manner than that of those who followed, for instance, the "commonwealth" history practiced by Benjamin Shambaugh and others.[16] White Progressive era historians often critically analyzed America's past and offered more complex and dynamic interpretations than their nineteenth-century predecessors. Their criticisms, however, rarely directly indicted Americans for their consistent mistreatment of African Americans. When white Progressive era historians did chastise racism and racial oppression, they tended to blame others for this problem. Eggleston and J. Franklin Jameson, for instance, indicted the British for forcing the slave trade and slavery on their ancestors, while others chastised southern slaveholders for slavery.

As members of a comparatively privileged group within the black community, African American historians faced the challenge of converting their profession into a viable, pragmatic vehicle of liberation. While they criticized the United States for dehumanizing African Americans and for not living up to the ideals of the "Founding Fathers," they avoided being unpatriotic. Like their counterparts who served in the U.S. armed forces during an age of empire building, African American historians of the Progressive era believed that their patriotism could help them gain access to certain rights and resources as well as respect for black people. They therefore often couched their critiques of white U.S. society in scientific methods, facts, and objectivity.

The Maturation of Woodson as a Historian of His People

The mid- to late-1910s were vital years in Woodson's career as a historian. In the spring of 1915, at the age of forty,

Woodson published his first monograph, *The Education of the Negro Prior to 1861,* a densely footnoted monograph that he had worked on during and following his doctoral studies. According to one historian, *The Education of the Negro Prior to 1861* was one of Woodson's "most scholarly from the standpoint of documentation and general objectivity." Woodson analyzed the educational opportunities for African Americans in the antebellum era in two major periods: the introduction of slavery to 1835, and 1836 through about 1861. For Woodson, the history of African Americans and education during a great portion of the nineteenth-century is largely a story of the "reactionary" tendencies of whites to blacks' struggles for education. Woodson's first book was reviewed positively in more than a dozen journals.[17]

On September 9, 1915 Woodson co-founded the Association for the Study of Negro Life and History (ASNLH) in Chicago with George Cleveland Hall, James E. Stamps, and Alexander L. Jackson. "It proclaimed as its purpose," Woodson recounted in 1925, "the collection of sociological and historical data on the Negro, the study of peoples of African blood, the publishing of books in this field, and the promotion of harmony between the races by acquainting the one with the other."[18] The ASNLH was much different from other professional historical associations of the Progressive era. Unlike the American Historical Association (AHA) or the Mississippi Valley Historical Association (MVHA), Woodson opened the doors of the ASNLH to lay historians, ministers, secondary and elementary school teachers, businessmen, and the African American community as a whole. Early on, the Association developed connections to the heart of black communities. Every year during Woodson's lifetime, the Association meetings were held in black churches, community centers, colleges and universities, and high school auditoriums throughout the country. Churches were most often used because they could accommodate many people and they constituted the centers of the black community. The first time that an Association meeting was held in a major hotel was in 1964 in Detroit.[19]

In 1916, without the consent of the other co-founders, Woodson launched the first issue of *The Journal of Negro History*, the first major historical journal of the black American experience. Closely resembling the *American Historical Review*, the *Journal* addressed a wide range of issues pertaining to Afrodiasporic histories. Many of the articles in the *Journal*, authored by professional and amateur scholars, helped sparked the historical scholarship in various sub-fields that would emerge in African American historiography after the dynamic 1960s. Woodson also used the pages of the *Journal* to discuss the developments of the study of African peoples, especially black America, and to regularly challenge racist scholarship in book reviews. By 1919, the *Journal* reached 4,000 people. In 1919, Woodson maintained that there were 1,648 subscribers, that 600 copies were sold at newsstands, and that 500 bound copies, including all four volumes in a single volume, were sold.[20]

While a teacher at Armstrong Manual Training High School, he published his second major monograph, *A Century of Negro Migration* (1918). Less objective in its tone than his 1915 monograph, this study explored the chief reasons why African Americans "struggled under adverse circumstances to flee from bondage and oppression in quest of a land offering asylum to the oppressed and opportunity to the unfortunate." Foreshadowing revisionist black migration studies of the 1980s and 1990s, Woodson argued that from the Civil War through 1918, migration was a "form of resistance to racial and class oppression." This study was much more political than Woodson's previous work. During an era of widespread anti-black violence, he brought charges against white southerners for the "barbarism" of their culture. On another level, for Woodson one of the greatest dilemmas of migration was the exodus of educated African Americans from the South. "The Southern Negroes," he declared, "have been robbed of their due part of the talented tenth." He understood why black intellectuals left the South, but at the same time he wanted them to stay connected to the masses. A substantial part of Woodson's study was aimed at dispelling the myths surrounding black migration during World War I. Woodson did not offer a monocausal explanation. He noted that blacks of various classes left and were leaving the South because they were violently terrorized, oppressed in political, social, and economic arenas, and because of various environmentally linked problems. Towards the conclusion of this study, Woodson also predicted that race riots would take place in America as the migration of black people from the South continued.[21] This study, unlike his previous scholarship, was written in laymen's terms. He wanted to attract a mass readership.

Early on in the Association's history, Woodson sought to popularize and democratize the study of Black history by gaining a mass following. By 1919, he employed J.E. Ormes, formerly in the business department of Wilberforce University, as a field agent. Ormes' role was to increase membership of the Association, appoint agents to sell books and subscriptions to the *Journal*, and organize Black history clubs. In the early years, Woodson called upon any interested individuals to join his cause. In 1919, Woodson announced that "any five persons desiring to prosecute studies" in Black history could organize a club. Each club was required to pay the Association $2.00, a small fee that entitled the club to a year's subscription to the *Journal* and access to Woodson, by mail, for advice and the necessary instruction. He often sent clubs bibliographies and outlines for study. Woodson required only that the clubs elect a president, a secretary, a treasurer, and an instructor—the group's "most intelligent and the best informed member."[22]

In 1919, Woodson completed his third monograph, *The Negro in Our History*. "While it is adapted for use in the senior high school and freshman college classes," Woodson noted, "it will serve as a guide for persons prosecuting the study more seriously." Woodson planned to send field agents to "Negro schools of secondary and college grade" in order to arouse interest in this first major textbook in African American history. However, because of what Woodson called a "printer's strike," *The Negro in Our History* was not published until 1922.[23] The foundations for Woodson's devotion to the Black history movement were laid during the Progressive era. By the early 1920s, Woodson fully dedicated himself to the ASNLH and the promotion of African American history.

While Woodson was laying the foundations for the early Black history movement, he was also active as a teacher of history. In 1918, Woodson became the principal of Armstrong Manual Training School, Washington, D.C. where he advocated vocational and classical education. Like Booker T. Washington, he also inaugurated an adult education program. From 1919 until 1920, he served as the Dean of Howard University's School of Liberal Arts. He also introduced and taught Black history at Howard. He was known among students for his seriousness and high expectations. Woodson did not see eye-to-eye with the white-dominated administration and left after one year of work. Many of his indictments of black colleges in *The Mis-Education of the Negro* (1933) originated from his experiences at Howard. From 1920 until 1922, he served as a Dean at West Virginia Collegiate Institute, the place where Woodson's protégé, Luther Porter Jackson, would later work tirelessly to place the ASNLH on the national map and popularize Black history. In the year he was appointed Dean, Woodson joined the Friends of Negro Freedom, an organization founded by Chandler Owens and A. Philip Randolph that stressed alleviating the economic problems facing black America. While he was Dean, he also published his third major monograph, *The History of the Negro Church* (1921).

Woodson advertised this study as the first serious historical study on the black church. He explored what he deemed "the greatest asset of the race" from the times when missionaries first converted blacks until the black church of the early twentieth century. The Association founder stressed that the black church and religion was a central cornerstone of black American culture. He argued that the greatest factor in the uplift of his people could have come from the ministry. *The History of the Negro Church* represents a significant shift in Woodson's scholarship. It is the first of his published monographs devoid of documentation and even a bibliography. Woodson also makes more generalizations in this study than in previous works. Woodson may have been increasingly realizing that a rigid scientific approach was no longer necessary. During the early 1920s, Woodson was busy with other tasks. He was directing the ASNLH, editing a journal, and managing the Associated Publishers, which he founded in 1921. He founded this press because white-owned presses largely ignored publishing works by black scholars, especially if they dealt with black subject matter.

In 1922, Woodson published *The Negro in Our History*. Woodson advertised this study as a textbook written for students of Black history at various levels, from secondary school students to college students. Woodson hoped that the book would find its way into the classrooms in black and white schools throughout the country. This text, which underwent nineteen editions during Woodson's lifetime, can be interpreted as one of Woodson's first major efforts to broaden his readership to non-scholars, since *The Journal of Negro History* was not widely circulated among lay persons or the black youth. By 1922, Woodson also decided to devote his life to the Association. He resigned from his position at West Virginia Collegiate Institute and moved to Washington, D.C. where he firmly established the ASNLH. For the next twenty-eight years he devoted his life to maintaining the Association, to the scientific study of black America, to training a cadre of black historians, to democratizing and popularizing the study of Black history, and to an overall quest for equal rights and justice for his people.

In many respects the 1920s, as Darlene Clark Hine has posited, were "golden years" for the Association. During this decade he received thousands of dollars from the Carnegie Foundation, the Julius Rosenwald Foundation, and from three Rockefeller trusts. These funds allowed him to hire young black scholars— including A.A. Taylor, Langston Hughes, Lorenzo J. Greene, Myra Colson Callis, Laura G. Glenn, and Charles Wesley—to conduct and publish cutting-edge historical and sociological research. During this age, Woodson also completed many key studies, including *Free Negro Owners of Slaves in the United States* (1924), *Free Negro Heads of Families in the United States in 1830* (1925), *The Mind of the Negro As Reflected in Letters Written During the Crisis,. 1800–1860* (1926), *Negro Orators and Their Orations* (1926), *African Myths Together With Proverbs* (1928), and *The Negro As Businessman* (1929). Even though the Association was rooted in black community infrastructures after its founding, by the mid-1920s Woodson more actively strove to open the Association's doors more widely to the black masses. By the early 1930s, after white philanthropists withdrew their support from the Association, Woodson relied upon black communities throughout the country, especially those in Washington, D.C., to maintain the Association's activities.

Woodson's Strategies of Popularizing Black History

One of Woodson's most important contributions to the early Black history movement was his mission and ability to transform Black history into a practical and popular medium for uplifting blacks and challenging racial prejudice. He revolutionized the American historical profession and democratized the study of Black history by extending the discipline to various nonprofessional groups of trained scholars. In adopting this approach, he did not de-emphasize the role of rigorous scholarship in the "life-and-death struggle" for black liberation. On the other hand, he maintained that in addition to being founded on rigorous research, the study and dissemination of Black history should extend to the working-class and youthful sectors of the black community. Woodson reasoned that the knowledge of African American history was, after all, one practical, though non-material, way in which black people could become liberated and empowered. Between 1915 and 1950 (increasingly more by the 1920s), he strove to enlighten the black masses, popularizing Black history in a variety of ways. He extended himself as a resource to black communities throughout the country. Woodson opened the doors of the Association meetings and activities to lay historians, ministers, secondary and elementary school teachers, businessmen, and the black community as a whole. He initiated Negro History Week and other extension services. And he published *The Negro History Bulletin*, an essential, yet often overlooked, outlet for not only Woodson himself but countless black thinkers representing a wide spectrum of the black community.

After earning his doctorate, Woodson began publishing a genre of historical scholarship that was accessible to a wide range of readers. In fact, Woodson wrote in such a simple language that some of his modern critics have considered him unsophisticated. Historians August Meier and Elliott Rudwick claimed that "Woodson, unlike Du Bois, did not produce monographs that are read and admired to this day," that he "did not function as an influential historian through his own monographs."[24]

Woodson, however, published several brands of scholarship: in the vindicationist tradition, rigorous, scientific scholarship to combat racist scholarship; polemical commentaries in order to address black America's contemporary status in American society; and books aimed at attracting a wide readership from elementary school students to university students. This last collection of books included *The Negro in Our History* (1922), *Negro Makers of History* (1928), *African Myths Together with Proverbs* (1928), *The African Background Outlined* (1936), and *African Heroes and Heroines* (1939). The unfinished *Encyclopedia Africana* was also written in very simple language. Woodson was very clear as to the purpose behind this last brand of scholarship. Several years before it was actually published, Woodson advertised *The Negro in Our History* as a study for use in Black history clubs, elementary and high schools, and colleges and universities. A high priority for him was reaching out to those reading and thinking at basic levels. Woodson told *Journal* readership:

Just as soon as this book has come from the press, the
Association will send to all Negro schools of secondary and college grade a field agent to interest them in
the effort to inculcate in the mind of the youth of African blood an appreciation of what their race has
thought and felt and done.[25]

It is difficult to discern how these various publications impacted their readers. The recently compiled *Papers of Carter G.
Woodson and the Association for the Study of Negro Life and
History, 1915–1950* contain elaborate records of books sold by
the Association from the 1920s on. While there are countless
receipts and orders, the Associated Publishers struggled throughout its existence. According to Lorenzo Johnston Greene, in the
middle of 1930 boxes of the Association's books were literally
collecting mildew in the Association headquarters' basement.
During Woodson's lifetime, there was not a high demand for
Black history books among the general black populace. Poet
Sterling Brown declared in the early 1940s that the hardest task
facing black authors was "developing a critical but interested
reading public."[26] Working-class blacks, especially during the
lean years of the Great Depression, did not place a high priority
on purchasing hard-cover scholarly literature. As Lorenzo
Greene testified during his book-selling campaigns, members of
the black professional class usually purchased the Association's
literature. *The Negro in Our History* was Woodson's most popular book. By March 1941, Woodson noted that 40,000 copies of
his text had been sold.[27]

Unlike any other academic organization of its time, the
ASNLH welcomed non-holders of Ph.D.s into its ranks and even
into its leadership positions. A perusal of the *Journal* from 1916
through Woodson's death indicates that at every annual meeting,
school teachers of various levels and community activists, including many club women, presented papers and in many cases
even had their essays published in the pages of the *Journal*
alongside the research of leading black and white scholars. In

doing so, Woodson sought to democratize the black scholarly community.

As discussed in Chapter 3, Woodson's most famous and perhaps most effective effort at attracting a mass following and popularizing the study of Black history was through Negro History Week celebrations, but before 1926 when he inaugurated this celebration, Woodson took Black history to the people in other ways. Between the founding of the ASNLH and his death, Woodson and his entourage were among the most sought-after lecturers in the black community nationwide. Woodson himself spoke at various venues throughout his lifetime. Many times when honoraria were not available, he accepted collections taken or he agreed to speak for lodging, food, and travel expenses. Woodson made such sacrifices because he was determined to spread his message to those willing to listen. The record indicates that he left a great impression on his audiences. L.D. Reddick, for instance, recounted that during his childhood in Jacksonville, Florida, Woodson was easily "the most impressive speaker" that he had heard. The manner in which he handled himself before his audience, his electricity, and his dedication to "the cause," influenced the young Reddick to join the "Negro History Movement."[28] Woodson also corresponded with countless men and women from around the world who were interested in Black history. He answered their questions, commented on papers, and mailed them information pertaining to the subject. Since its inception, the Association had functioned as a "free reference bureau" regarding the study of black life and history. Before Negro History Week, Woodson also attempted to stir interest in Black history among the youth with financial incentives. In 1924, for instance, in collaboration with the American Folklore Society, the Association offered a $200.00 prize "for the best collection of tales, riddles, proverbs, sayings, and songs, which have been heard at home by Negro students of accredited schools."[29]

In 1927, a year after the founding of Negro History Week, Woodson established the Association's Extension Division in order to expose more people to Black history through public lectures and correspondence study. The Home Study Department was necessary in Woodson's view because not enough teachers were qualified to teach the black youth about their history and because "various classes of citizens" needed to know their history. In a tone reminiscent of Booker T. Washington when he advertised Tuskegee Institute's Movable School or Jesup Agricultural Wagon, Woodson asserted that the Home Study Program took the school to the student. Woodson's program offered courses at introductory and advanced levels. Only those with a high school education and the desire to "profit by the work" were encouraged to apply for admission. While Woodson sought to make the study of Black history and life more accessible, he refused to de-legitimize the scholarly endeavor by abandoning standards. One had to apply for admission and pay a $5.00 matriculation fee. Tuition for one course was $20.00. Two classes could be taken for $35.00 and three classes could be taken for $52.00. Students had a maximum of one year to finish the requirements for each course, including the passing of a final examination. Woodson encouraged students to complete the assigned work in two to three months.[30]

Each introductory course was accompanied by a series of lessons with specific readings and suggestions. After completing these lessons, the student would answer some questions and mail the "recitation paper" back to the instructor who would then review it and mail it back to the student with the appropriate comments. Advanced courses were offered to college graduates. More flexible in nature than their introductory counterparts, classes were arranged with input from both the students and the professors. Woodson assured the public that the standards of the Home Study Department were equal to those of "accredited colleges and universities," that "nothing is hastily done," and that "every student is guaranteed personal attention." A brochure for the Home Study Department offered Anthropology, Art, English, History, Literature, and Sociology. The teaching staff boasted leading scholars in the African American community, including

Woodson himself, Charles H. Wesley, Alain Locke, E. Franklin Frazier, Luther Porter Jackson, James Hugo Johnston, and Charles Johnson. At the end of the course, each student received a certificate noting the amount of work that was accomplished. Full credit was granted only to those who passed the final examination.[31]

According to several of Woodson's biographers, the Home Study Department was not successful in terms of enrollment. It did not spread its roots into the black community like Negro History Week. While Woodson noted that the second year of the Home Study Department went "remarkably well," a year later he admitted to the *Journal* readership that the enrollment was very low mainly because of the fees and the standards of admission. Woodson still had a positive outlook, noting that those who did manage to finish were prepared to instruct others.[32] Such efforts demonstrate that central to Woodson's philosophy was the democratization of American academic culture. For Woodson, the field of Black history belonged not only to scholars, but to all black Americans and to the world.

Besides Negro History Week, another form of major extension work undertaken by the Association Director was the founding of *The Negro History Bulletin*. By the mid-1930s, Woodson realized that the contents of the *Journal* attracted only a certain class of black American readers and he wanted to increase his regular readership among black youth, the black working-class, black elementary and secondary school teachers, and among nonacademics in general. The *Journal* was also inaccessible to many because of its price. While white scholars such as Edward Channing told Woodson that the price of the *Journal* was too little, some black scholars told Woodson otherwise. W.H. Crogman, once president of Clark University in Atlanta, wrote to Woodson in a letter written in April 1927 of his regret that "for some reason I did not come into touch with your 'Journal of Negro History' until about three years ago. I subscribed to it one year, and discontinued my subscription because of the terribly hard times and high prices."[33]

The *Bulletin* had many functions. Written in simple language to help black teachers who had little or no knowledge of Black history, it supplemented standard American history textbooks at the time. The *Bulletin* was the vehicle by which school teachers and other concerned citizens could help Woodson take Black history into the homes of the black masses. The magazine served as an advertising mechanism for the Association's activities, especially for Negro History Week. It also served as another vehicle in which blacks, from elementary school children to community activists to school teachers to professional scholars, could openly discuss and even publish their thoughts pertaining to Black history and the study of it. Woodson stressed to potential contributors that only serious articles dealing with Black history would be considered. The *Bulletin* was not an entertainment magazine. Woodson also used the *Bulletin* as another of his ideological platforms.

The first issue of the *Bulletin* was introduced in October 1937 and, like the rest of the volumes during Woodson's lifetime, appeared nine times throughout the year, coinciding with the months of the school year. Until the late 1940s, a year's subscription was $1.00 (or 12 to 15 cents a copy) and for some time clubs of five people or more could secure the magazine for only 45 cents a year. Woodson also offered bulk rate discounts. By Woodson's death in 1950, the subscription price had only risen to $2.00 a year or 25 cents a copy. Woodson kept the price low and in fact sold the *Bulletin* at a loss in order to maintain a high readership. Though Woodson was the managing editor, the editorial and managing boards were dominated by black women. They wrote many of the articles, organized and ran the magazine, and encouraged children to begin their studies early. Individual issues of the *Bulletin* focused on certain topics and themes in black American history. Woodson adopted this approach so that regular subscribers would have "a brief illustrated history of the Negro" at the end of the year. He also sold back issues bound in one volume.[34]

Between 1937 and 1950, issues contained biographical sketches of famous and not so famous blacks and whites who were sympathetic to the cause; simple book reviews; challenging lists of questions for the readers; plenty of photographs reminiscent of those found in Du Bois's *Crisis*; discussions of periods and important events in black history; updates about current events mainly pertaining to black schools, Negro History Week, branches, and clubs; art work by leading black artists; a "Book of the Month" section; poetry; information about Africa and the Diaspora; suggestions for Negro History Week; simple plays written by school teachers and lay scholars; and primary sources. Of particular interest were the "Children's Page," the discussions initiated by teachers, and Woodson's polemical columns.

The *Bulletin* sought to instill "the youth of African blood" with pride in their history and culture. In October 1941, a formal "Children's Page" was introduced. The female editorial staff as well as other female readers suggested to Woodson that a section of the magazine be officially designated for children. In November 1940, for instance, Lillian M. Rhoades, the Associate Editor of *Apex News*, told Woodson that she would like for the *Bulletin* "to solicit verse and articles by children." She reasoned that "this column devoted to their contributions will get them interested in their particular page, and familiar with *The Journal of Negro History* as a whole. Then as they grow up," she continued, "they will grow up with the *Journal*, and would not be without it."[35] Increasingly after its debut, the thoughts, prose, and ideas of children were featured in the *Bulletin* as a method of influencing other youngsters to seriously study Black history. In each issue's "Children's Section," readers were challenged to answer questions pertaining to the monthly theme and quizzed about how they could best facilitate a Negro History Week celebration. Under the guidance of Howard University-trained artist Lois Mailou Jones, young readers during the early 1940s were also provided a picture to color or paint, a mask to cut out and wear, or a sculpture to cut out of a bar of soap. While Jones gave her readers very clear instructions, the children were challenged to think creatively.[36]

The *Bulletin* also served as a discussion forum for teachers. They discussed how best to incorporate Black history into their individual classrooms and their schools' curriculums, exchanged teaching methods, joined contemporary political debates, and gave each other advice about how best to celebrate Negro History Week. The February 1939 issue featured articles by school teachers discussing how Negro History Week could best be celebrated in elementary and secondary schools and in colleges and universities. In a sense, the pages of the *Bulletin* belonged to black schoolteachers, serving as their autonomous discursive space. Woodson encouraged this ownership and dialogue by assuring them that the magazine belonged to them and by publishing their ideas just as he published the scholarship of intellectuals in the *Journal*. Woodson also solicited their suggestions and published them from time to time. The *Bulletin* was unique in that it was one of the few journals open to black female teachers. He included photographs of them in the midst of other movers and shakers in the struggle.

Woodson's image and voice, however, resonated above his schoolteacher counterparts. In every issue of the *Bulletin*, Woodson wrote at least one column in which he did a range of things such as addressing problems faced by black Americans, defining his philosophy of history, critiquing black leadership, attacking U.S. racial policies (especially during World War II), or providing his readers with potential solutions.

During Woodson's lifetime, the *Bulletin* underwent various changes and developments. The first major change, in October 1939, was the increase in size from eight to sixteen pages. Woodson resolved that black school teachers were in need of more information to adequately incorporate black history into their curriculums. In order to maintain his audience, Woodson did not raise the price. At the same time, by the magazine's third volume, the articles were becoming more in-depth, thematically organized, and more scholarly in tone. In the February 1940 issue, Lorenzo Johnston Greene featured his statistical research on black labor. Other of Woodson's protégés contributed to the *Bulletin* increasingly during the 1940s. By October 1940, the style of the magazine changed. While the first three volumes resembled a small newspaper, the volumes after 1940 looked more like a journal or magazine, resembling issues of *Crisis*. From October 1937 until April 1950, Woodson's columns in the *Bulletin* became increasingly more political. The gradual radicalization and increased scholarly flavor of the magazine is best explained by Woodson's strong conviction that the magazine was not a vehicle of popular matters or propaganda. He stressed that it was a space where intellectuals with varying interests of history could enlighten and engage each other. Woodson, therefore, tended to couch his polemical diatribes in historical articles, or guard them with some sense of anonymity.

According to Woodson, the *Bulletin* was a successful venture. In 1943, he declared that "nothing attempted" by the ASNLH since Negro History Week "has met with more public approval" than the *Bulletin*. He felt justified in publishing it at a loss because he believed that it was finding its ways into the minds of black people, making black schoolteachers more well-rounded, inspiring black youth, and even helping to deconstruct race prejudice and foster better relations between blacks and whites. Woodson used the *Bulletin* as he had the *Journal*'s "Notes"—as a comfortable place to articulate his dynamic, iconoclastic world view in a simple language. At the same time, the *Bulletin* was one of Woodson's gifts to black people. John Hope Franklin certainly thought so. "The BULLETIN," Franklin noted, "represented perhaps the most vigorous extension of the work of Dr. Woodson into the lives of persons who were soon to share the responsibility of making their communities better places in which to live."[37]

Keeping Black Intellectuals in Check:
The Mis-Education of the Negro **(1933)**
and Woodson's Views of the Responsibility
of the Black Intellectual

Beyond popularizing Black history, Woodson was also one of the first professionally trained black scholars to publicly critique black intellectuals, scholars, and professionals as well as the historically black colleges and universities that produced them. A self-proclaimed supporter of Booker T. Washington, Woodson openly indicted his black professional, scholar counterparts for not contributing as much as they could to the black struggle. During the 1950s and 1960s, his message was re-invoked by E. Franklin Frazier in *Black Bourgeoisie* (1957), Nathan Hare in *Black Anglo-Saxons* (1965), and Harold Cruse in his classic *The Crisis of the Negro Intellectual* (1967). The most recent contribution to this school of thought was Adolph Reed, Jr.'s "What Are the Drums Saying, Booker?: The Current Crisis of the Black Intellectual" published in *The Village Voice* in 1995.

It seems that since the aftermath of the Black Power era such critiques have become unpopular. This perhaps helps explain why Reed's indictments were not embraced and elaborated upon by many black intellectuals. These debates, like battles in hip-hop culture, are necessary to challenge black scholars and spokespersons to re-evaluate their approaches and programs. During the first half of the twentieth-century, most black intellectual leaders did not challenge Du Bois's theory that "exceptional men," "distinguished Negroes," and "college-bred Negroes" were the best-equipped group to save the race, to "guide the Mass away from contamination and death of the Worst" bringing them "in contact with modern civilization" and "broad culture."[38] In outlining the need for a "Talented Tenth" in 1903, Du Bois argued that educated blacks had a social responsibility to uplift the masses of their people, but he did not extensively critique the black intelligentsia of his day or earlier. He indicted only those who were "half-trained demagogues," "vociferous busy bodies," "money makers," and of course Booker T. Washington. He praised his antebellum predecessors for challenging the institution of slavery and he complimented his educated post-Reconstruction counterparts for their unselfish work as teachers, preachers, and professionals.

Nearly three decades later, Du Bois continued to praise the "Negro Bourgeoisie" at a time when Woodson condemned many of them. "For two generations the social leaders of the American Negro, with very few exceptions...have worked unselfishly for the uplift of the masses of Negro folk," Du Bois wrote in the *Crisis* in 1931:

> There is no group of leaders on earth who have so largely made common cause with their race as educated American Negroes, and it is their foresight and sacrifice and theirs alone that have saved the American freedman from annihilation and degradation.[39]

In fact, Du Bois did not level an overt indictment against the "Talented Tenth" until about a half a century after he initially articulated this strategy. In 1948, Du Bois reformulated his turn-of-the-century ideology in an address before Wilberforce State University's prestigious Sigma Pi Phi Fraternity. He stressed that his archaic program needed to be revised to suit the problems of post-World War II America.[40]

Long before Du Bois publicly re-examined his own theory, Booker T. Washington took on the task of critiquing highly educated blacks in a manner that Woodson would decades later. Beginning in the late 1800s, Washington portrayed black intellectuals who opposed him as being "unfortunate and misguided young men" trained only in "mere book knowledge." "My experience," Washington asserted in *My Larger Education*, "is that people who call themselves 'The Intellectuals' understand theories, but they do not understand things." Such "abstract principles of protest," Washington continued, "did not solve the country's race problem." As Adolph Reed, Jr. argued about one hundred years later, Washington asserted that black intellectuals made money off the sufferings of the black masses. Many black intellectuals, Washington ascertained,

> make a business of keeping the troubles, the wrongs, and the hardships of the Negro race before the public. Having learned that they are able to make a living out of their troubles, they have grown into the settled habit of advertising their wrongs...Some of these people do not want the Negro to lose his grievance, because they do not want to lose their jobs.[41]

Woodson re-invoked certain aspects of Washington's program, namely a frank and cynical dismissal of certain black intellectuals, a quest for autonomy, a strategic way to deal with whites in positions of power, and a devotion to the black masses through practical outreach work. In this sense, Woodson was unique since nearly all prominent black intellectuals after Washington's death have sided with Du Bois. In *The Negro in Our History*, first published in 1922, Woodson sympathized with Washington rather than with Du Bois's camp. According to Woodson, Washington stepped forth with "a new idea...as to move millions." Woodson argued that Washington's educational philosophy laid "a foundation for the future." He agreed that Washington should be criticized for falling prey to "certain entanglements in which he of necessity had to make some blunders." But Woodson concurred with his role model that "mere agitation for political rights" could not solve black America's economic plight. In Woodson's estimation, Washington was "the greatest of all Americans, the only man in the Western Hemisphere who has succeeded in effecting a revolution in education." He especially applauded his ability to make education practical "for the masses of the people who had to toil."[42]

Throughout the rest of his career, Woodson continued to defend Washington. In the March 1947 volume of *The Negro History Bulletin*, Woodson celebrated Washington's contributions to the black struggle. Woodson rejected the popular dichotomy of black leadership and supported Washington. "It is doubtful that he ever convinced the majority of his race that he was on the right track," Woodson noted. "No man had been so generally misunderstood by his own people," he added.[43]

In *The Mis-Education of the Negro*, Woodson challenged black intellectuals to be practical and to help the less fortunate, very much like Washington did in *My Larger Education*. In his now famous 1933 polemic, Woodson was not turning over a new stone, but continuing his evolution as a scholar-activist and iconoclastic thinker. Woodson "doffs the garb of historian and assumes the role of commentator on education and educators, social uplift, religion, the professions and business in general as affecting the colored people of the United States," a writer for the *Memphis Commercial Appeal* accurately observed.[44]

One can trace the evolution of this line of thought by reflecting on Woodson's life before the 1930s. According to Jacqueline Goggin, Woodson inherited a "sense of rebelliousness" from his father and grandfather. Woodson was an outspoken critical thinker. The best indicator of Woodson's early iconoclastic approach is revealed in his book reviews and "Annual Reports" in *The Journal of Negro History*. Between 1916 and 1950, Woodson signed his name to more than two hundred and fifty book reviews in the *Journal*. Almost certainly he wrote many unsigned book reviews as well. In these articles, Woodson consistently challenged white and black authors, boldly attacking all those with whom he did not agree.[45]

Woodson's ideas articulated in *The Mis-Education of the Negro* had been brewing in his mind for more than a decade. In a 1931 *Journal* review of the fifth year of Negro History Week, Woodson challenged "successful Negroes" educated at the "best colleges" to help uplift the masses. "Statistics show that the large majority of the Negroes who have put on the finishing touches of our best colleges are all but worthless in the uplift of their people." Woodson continued:

> If after leaving school they have the opportunity to give out to Negroes what traducers of the race would like to have it learn, such persons may earn a living,

but they never become a contributing force in the elevation of those far down.

Woodson denounced the educational system that misled "advanced Negro students" to despise "their own people" and to study things that "have no bearing on the tasks which they confront in life." As a solution, Woodson called for a revolutionary change in the educational training of black intellectuals. He asked black scholars to study their African heritage and to apply their learning to uplifting people of African blood. He called upon teachers of "ripe scholarship" to teach the children. In the 1931 "Annual Report of the Director," Woodson prepared his readership for his forthcoming book on the plight of the black intellectual and professional.[46]

In 1933, during the midst of the Great Depression, Woodson published *The Mis-Education of the Negro*. At the outset, he told his readers that he had decided to present this volume to the public because many people "were deeply interested" in his ideas. Despite the confrontational tone of Woodson's essays, he claimed that he did not intend for his book to be a "broadside" against specific people, but rather a new set of solutions for how to best create an educated body of black reformers in an age that supported intellectual narcissism. His main focus was first showing how "highly educated Negroes" had misled, exploited, and hampered the livelihood of the black masses, and then how these destructive approaches could be reversed.[47]

Woodson's polemic, laced with traces of history, is delivered in simple and straightforward language. The prevailing argument running throughout the twenty-eight chapters of overlapping subjects is that blacks educated at leading white and black colleges and universities during the early twentieth century failed miserably to help improve the status of black America. Woodson posits many reasons and offers various remedies to address diverse political, social, cultural, economic, and religious needs in the lives of black Americans.

According to Woodson, the "educated Negro" acted irresponsibly because he was not trained to serve black people in practical ways, and in fact had been taught to hate Africans and the black masses. The "American educational system" made black people "Americanized" and "Europeanized white-men." Woodson argued that blacks did not receive adequate training in art, drama, and other more creative fields of thought. He claimed that educated blacks strove to gain acceptance by imitating white America and by downplaying their own cultural individuality. Woodson rooted this mentality in the post-emancipation education of black people. During the antebellum era, he argued, there had been many sincere northerners and southerners who believed in helping blacks to help themselves, but after emancipation, these "unselfish" workers were replaced by exploiters of "the race."[48]

In Woodson's view, the educational system established by white philanthropists during Reconstruction did little to help blacks deal with their unique situation. Their scholarship lacked the "spirit of their predecessors." Woodson found fault in both industrial education and classical education. The former all too often turned out unprepared workers for the industrial market and the latter proved impractical. "We do not have in the life of the Negro today a large number of persons who have benefited by either of the systems about which we have quarreled so long," Woodson concluded. Such systems continued to blossom, in Woodson's estimation, because black teachers had not stepped forth, instigating or demanding change. On the contrary, they had been trained "to do what they are told" and were too afraid to challenge the system. Woodson declared that only "few mis-educated Negroes" posed challenges. In his view, most educated blacks bought into the "diploma-mill produce" system. Blacks went to college, he argued, to get a "darkter's 'gree" in order to get a job, make money, and buy happiness.[49]

Woodson argued that receiving a doctorate only contributed to blacks' laziness and lack of scholarly activism. He argued that black doctorates "not only lose touch with the common people, but they do not do as much creative work as those of less formal education." He accused black scholars of resting "their oars" once they received their passes into the "ivory towers" of academia. Black Ph.D. degree holders were too often produced as "Doctors of Philosophy made to order." Woodson accused the Columbia, Yale, Harvard, and Chicago graduates of dismissing black businesses and embracing brands of socialism and communism that did not originate from within the black experience. He indicted them for failing to do the groundwork for blacks in business. He also attacked the educated business owners themselves for being too individualistic and materialistic.[50]

According to Woodson, one of the most detrimental consequences of being mis-educated at black and white colleges and universities was turning one's back on the black masses. Woodson believed strongly that the gap between the masses and the "Talented Tenth" was widening greatly. He noticed that this problem was especially sensed in the religious life. He indicted black leaders for adopting the religion of "the enslaver and segregationist." In comparing black leaders of the late nineteenth century with those of the 1930s, he concluded that while nineteenth century black reformers "went off to school to prepare themselves for the uplift of a downtrodden people," his contemporaries went to school "to memorize certain facts to pass examinations." A lot of black professionals, in Woodson's estimation, viewed their jobs solely as a way to make money. "Too many Negroes go into medicine and dentistry merely for selfish purposes, hoping thereby to increase their income and spend it on joyous living." Woodson's most blatant attack was launched against those blacks who considered themselves leaders of their people. He asserted that all too often leadership had been conferred on a few without popular consent.[51]

Woodson offered a host of solutions to the problems he saw facing all blacks, the masses as well as the middle-class professionals. He called upon his people to be independent pioneers. In simplest terms, he wanted all black people to abandon "slavish imitation" and learn how to think on their own, thus making themselves indispensable to enterprises. In order to achieve this goal, Woodson called for the development of "common sense schools" with dedicated teachers, not those "roll-top desk theorists who have never touched the life of the Negro." Woodson believed that the educated black could solve the problems of black people if he "would forget most of the untried theories taught him in school, if he could see through the propaganda which has been instilled into his mind under the pretext of education," and "if he would fall in love with his own people and begin to sacrifice for their uplift." Woodson claimed that he even preferred grassroots leaders and reformers as teachers over professors from Columbia, Harvard, or the University of Chicago. Woodson called upon highly educated leaders and teachers to be servants of the people guided by unselfishness.

> The servant of the people, unlike the leader, is not on a high horse elevated above the people and trying to carry them to some designated point to which he would like to go for his own advantage. The servant of the people is down among them, living as they live, doing what they do and enjoying what they enjoy.

Woodson added:

> He may be a little better informed than some other members of the group; it may be that he has had some experience that they have not had, but in spite of this advantage he should have more humility than those whom he serves, for we are told that 'Whosoever is greatest among you, let him be your servant.'[52]

Woodson also challenged black leaders and educators to transform the educational system in which they were trained and to take steps to incorporate the African and black experience.

Woodson instructed blacks to become more radical in their politics. He wanted blacks to use politics only to better secure their goals when practical and to create a brand of politics from within. Woodson observed that the political tradition in America that had oppressed his people for so long was not designed to empower black people. Woodson advocated a straightforward, bourgeoisie economic nationalist platform. He believed that blacks should patronize black businesses. Yet he warned his readers that such an alternative would work only if the black businesses had the community's wellbeing at heart. Ideally, he would have liked to have seen black businesses flourish. On the more practical side, he advised blacks not to become enslaved by the vices of materialism. He counseled blacks not to waste money on unnecessary items. While he valued hard, manual labor, he discouraged blacks from leading a life in traditional industrial education. By the 1930s, in his mind such an approach was becoming impractical.[53]

The Mis-Education of the Negro has been praised by scholars and leaders in both the Black Power era and the succeeding Afrocentric movement. However, these generations did not adequately criticize the shortcomings in Woodson's vision. For example, while Woodson elaborated upon the failure of the "highly educated Negro" to deal with the masses on a one-on-one level, Woodson himself exhibited some of this same class prejudice. He believed that the masses needed to be rescued from their state of "backwardness." "Sometimes you find as many as two or three store-front churches in a single block where Negroes indulge in heathen-like practices which could hardly be equaled in the jungle," Woodson commented in his description of blacks in Washington, D.C., "The Negroes in Africa have not descended to such depths." What Woodson labeled "heathen-like" comprised characteristics that made black American religion and culture distinct.[54] Like his "Talented Tenth" predecessors, Woodson believed, at one level at least, that the black masses were "underdeveloped" and needed civilization as offered by a reformed, educated black constituency.

Woodson also drew shallow and even erroneous conclusions from history. In one case, Woodson argued that blacks refused to work under each other and to take orders from each other because "slaveholders taught their bondsmen that they were as good or better than any others and, therefore, should not be subjected to any member of their race."[55] Woodson assumed, without proof, that enslaved blacks internalized what their owners placed before them. Throughout the book Woodson oversimplified the historical record in order to hammer home his conviction that the black middle class was failing to maintain "the race" during the Great Depression. Woodson also did not consider that there were many black scholars who did not fit his convenient prototype. As is the case with most radical polemics, *The Mis-Education of the Negro* contains broad generalizations that are not grounded in rigorous, documented study, but instead are the products of the day-to-day observations and experiences of its author.

In more than a dozen newspapers in the winter and spring of 1933, the majority of reviewers welcomed Woodson's book as a needed criticism of the American educational system. Black scholars of the 1930s certainly could not simply ignore the relevancy of his assessment, but very openly acknowledged that Woodson's book represented a break away from his previous scholarship as well as an attack on the black elite. Most did not take him on in a public forum. Even those whom Woodson indicted seemed to have welcomed his polemic. In *The Survey*, for instance, Alain Leroy Locke applauded Woodson's "articulate and reasoned" statement to a "very great dilemma."[56] While leading intellectuals such as Locke may have agreed with Woodson's belief in re-orienting "the advance-guard" to the needs of the masses, few attempted this enthusiastically in educational terms. *The Mis-Education of the Negro* represents one of the first major publicized assaults leveled against the black bourgeoisie and the black intellectual by a professionally trained black scholar. After Woodson's polemic, only a handful of other black intellectuals re-invoked his message in monograph-length polemics. Among them are E. Franklin Frazier, Nathan Hare, and Harold Cruse.

Several presses, namely African World Press and Jawanza Kunjufu's African American Images, have reissued *The Mis-Education of the Negro*. During the Black Power era and the more recent resurgence of black cultural consciousness in the late 1980s and early 1990s, Woodson's book gained popularity. As an undergraduate student during the early 1990s, I remember my peers talking about Woodson's book, saying things such as: "Brother, have you read Woodson's *The Mis-Education*? Man, you got to read it!" It was one of those many books, such as Akbar's *Chains and Images of Psychological Slavery*; Frances Cress Welsing's *The Isis Papers*; Ayi Kwei Armah's *Two Thousand Seasons*; *The Autobiography of Malcolm X*; Cheikh Anta Diop's *Civilization or Barbarism*; Walter Rodney's *How Europe Underdeveloped Africa*; Malauna Karanga's *Selections from the Husia*; and many more that my generation owned and decorated our book shelves with but often never really read or studied in detail.

Woodson's observations are still very relevant today and can serve as some sort of wake-up call for today's young blacks pursuing degrees in higher education. All too often black Ph.D. candidates are not challenged to make their studies practical by directly linking their scholarship and careers to uplifting the black community. We all have the right to study whatever we want to study in whatever manner we please. Hip-hop generation historians and scholars in the making have the potential to make monumental changes. At minimum, Woodson challenges us to re-evaluate our purpose in life, something very much needed in times of black collective crisis. As Woodson and many black leaders before him argued, those blacks who have greater opportunities and access to power need to make sacrifices in order to help those in need.

Woodson and Black Women

Another aspect of Woodson's program that warrants further discussion is his treatment of black women.[57] As pointed out earlier in this study, black women faced many obstacles in the mainstream academy and within black academic circles during Woodson's lifetime. The first group of black women to earn doctorates in history did so in the 1940s. They were Marion Thompson Wright, Lulu M. Johnson, Susie Owen Lee, Elsie Lewis, Helen G. Edmonds, and Margaret Rowley. While Woodson did not work closely with any of these women, he did promote and publish Wright's scholarly works in *The Journal of Negro History*. Woodson did not highlight the roles of black women, but in the 1930s he did publish several key articles on black women. In a 1930 article, "The Negro Washerwoman," he proclaimed that black women who took in laundry from the antebellum era through the "nadir" helped save the race. Several years later in the *Pittsburgh Courier*, Woodson declared that "our women are so much better than our men...Certainly the women are more faithful to our people and they do more for the elevation of the unfortunate element than our men."[58] During the era of Jim Crow segregation, such thoughts by black men were extremely rare.

After Woodson founded Negro History Week in 1926, black female teachers, club women, librarians, and social activists played essential roles in popularizing the study of Black history. Without the practical work of women, Woodson's efforts at popularizing Black history would not have been nearly as successful. Black women set up activities in schools, such as book displays and pageants; they worked hard to advertise Negro History Week celebrations; and they established branches, clubs, and study groups throughout the country. Together with well-known spokeswomen, grassroots black women were key organizers and participants in the Association's annual meetings throughout the country. Women's clubs often helped sponsor events, hosted dinners, and organized entertainment for the visiting members. Black women were always present at the Association meetings and contributed to the lively discussions. They joined the intellectual ranks of panelists and presenters at a later time.

By the early 1920s, black women were active in the ASNLH conference, Mary McLeod Bethune becoming the first black female to present a major paper at an Association Annual Meeting in 1923. By the mid-1930s, several significant changes took place in the Association. In 1935, Lucy Harth Smith and Mary McLeod Bethune became the first black women elected to the Executive Council. Then, at the Annual Meeting in Petersburg, Virginia in 1936, Bethune was elected President of the ASNLH "to fill the vacancy" opened by John Hope's death in February 1936. Bethune, founder of Daytona Educational and Industrial Institute, served as the President of the ASNLH from 1936 though 1952. Though her presidency has been called "largely ceremonial," Bethune definitely left her mark as Association President. The author of the Associated Publishers' *Women Builders* went as far as asserting that "no connection of Mrs. Bethune's was more important than her election to the presidency, succeeding John Hope, of the Association of the Study of Negro Life and History." One of her biographers added that she brought "prestige and money" to the Association.[59]

When Bethune was elected President of the ASNLH, she was one of the most well-known and respected black public figures. From 1936 until 1945 she was, in one scholar's estimation, "the pre-eminent race leader at large."[60] While Bethune's various responsibilities may have determined the amount of time she could devote to the Association, she did contribute significantly to the intellectual climate of the annual meetings; serve as a well-known representative, fund-raiser, and publicist for the Association; and support Woodson in his quest to democratize and popularize Black history. As President of the Association, Bethune regularly attended the annual meetings, presiding over annual and executive council meetings. From 1935 to 1951, she delivered many addresses, five of which were published in *The Journal of Negro History*. Historian Bettye Collier-Thomas is correct in crediting Bethune with "disseminating the study of Black history through her speeches and writings." In her speeches as Association President, Bethune articulated her vision of the function of history and the role of the black intellectual, reiterating Woodson's goals for the Association of searching for "truth" and stressing that black scholars concentrate their efforts on popularizing Black history. Bethune's philosophy of Black history was essentially pragmatic. The "social usefulness of scholarship and its findings depends on its translation into the common tongue," Bethune asserted in the mid-1930s. Like Woodson, she believed that black historians needed to arm black children with the knowledge of their "glorious" past of "marvelous achievement." Young school children' perceptions of African American history were very important to her. She believed that black children could be encouraged to overcome great obstacles, to "make new history," if they were exposed to what their foreparents accomplished. It was for this reason that under Bethune's reign as President the popular *Negro History Bulletin* prospered, Bethune being one of its most important fund-raisers. Like Woodson, she also optimistically maintained that "world peace and brotherhood" would result from the introduction of Black history into white American culture.[61]

Bethune's faith in the significance of Black history went beyond her presidency in the Association. During her retirement at seventy-eight years of age, she published "My Last Will and Testament" in *Ebony*. In the tradition of Association workers, she sought to pass on to future generations of African Americans her legacy "in hope that an old woman's philosophy may give them inspiration." She reminded her younger readership that "our ancestors endured the degradation of slavery" with dignity so that the future generations could benefit. She believed that this past should never be forgotten or taken for granted. In the tradition of Woodson and the Association, she proclaimed:

> Our greatest Negro figures have been imbued with faith. Our forefathers struggled for liberty in conditions far more onerous than those we now face but never lost the faith. Their perseverance paid rich dividends. We must never forget their sufferings and their sacrifices, for they were the foundations of the progress of our people.

She also called upon the younger generation of black leaders to emulate the selfless works of famous historical figures.

> We have had other great men and women in the past:
> Frederick Douglass, Booker T. Washington, Harriet
> Tubman, Sojourner Truth. We must produce more
> qualified people like them who will work not for them-
> selves, but for others.[62]

Bethune's pragmatic vision of history, like that of Woodson,
sought to inspire younger generations of African Americans to
persevere and promote racial pride.

When viewed within his proper historical context, Woodson
was ahead of his times in relationship with black women. During
the Civil Rights and Black Power eras, black male historians
routinely ignored black women's contributions to the struggle
and history. As Deborah Gray White pointed out in *Ar'n't I A
Woman?* (1985), John W. Blassingame's *The Slave Community:
Plantation Life in the Antebellum South* (1972) "is a classic but
much of it deals with male status," ignoring the dynamics of life
for enslaved black women.[63] Black women were also relegated
to behind-the-scenes positions during the classic Civil Rights
Movement, as epitomized by the Montgomery Bus Boycott.
Martin Luther King, Jr. was the recognized leader of this major
mass movement, despite the fact that women such as Jo Ann
Gibson Robinson and the Women's Political Council were the
movement's driving force.

Likewise, the Black Panther Party and other younger male
Black Power era activists were often openly sexist. Stokely Carmichael's and Eldridge Cleaver's anti-female sentiments were
not uncommon. This carried over to scholarship. During the
Black Power era, male Black Studies proponents and black male
historians who dominated their respective discourses ignored
black female experiences, in turn influencing black women to
create their own sub-fields of study to explore black females'
historical realities. Today, a small school of black male historians and scholars incorporate black women or sophisticated gen-
dered analyses into their scholarship. Black Women's history
and studies have been dominated by black women. Today, black
male-female relationships have approached a low point, as ex-

emplified in low marriage rates, out-of-wedlock births, young black males' strip-club sub-culture, and hip-hop music and videos that often denigrate black women. Woodson was not perfect in his treatment of and relationship with black women. He was certainly molded by the restrictive gender conventions of his times and, after all, he never married and therefore probably had a very limited amount of knowledge concerning black womanhood at one level. Nevertheless, Woodson's ability to acknowledge black women's historical experiences and willingness to work productively with black women can be something useful to male hip-hop-generation college students and historians.

After Woodson: Woodson's Legacy

Woodson's legacy and influence can be measured at many levels. His most obvious legacy is Black History Month. Despite the flaws in current Black History Month celebrations, they represent the culmination of Woodson's work and vision. Today one can readily purchase a copy of Woodson's *The Mis-Education of the Negro* at most Afrocentric bookstores. *Essence* routinely recommends this book to its readers. Many black-owned presses have re-issued Woodson's classic. Jawanza Kunjufu has even published a version of the book with some questions at the end of the text. It is hard to determine how many people are actually reading the book—such books often remain unread and simply occupy spaces on folks' bookshelves as surface-level symbols of consciousness. Those who have genuinely read this study have been challenged to re-think the meaning of education to African Americans as well as the responsibilities of professionally trained black scholars.

Woodson's legacy can be measured in other matters as well. Black historians who came of age from the early 1950s until the Black Power era were directly inspired and influenced by Woodson. Among other things, they certainly had to rely on *The Journal of Negro History* as well as some of his other publications as starting points for much of their research. Woodson also directly mentored many younger black historians and scholars, professionally trained and laypersons alike, who in turn went on to influence others. This is one of his most important contributions to the evolution of the black historical enterprise.

In 1945, Rayford W. Logan criticized Woodson for his so-called "failure to attach himself to a young scholar." More recently, historians have also underappreciated Woodson's role as a mentor and promoter of intellectual talent. Woodson was the principal mentor and promoter of the early Black history movement. He did for this movement what Alain Locke, Charles Johnson, and James Weldon Johnson did for the Harlem Renaissance.[64] He facilitated productive cross-generational dialogues and relationships, something that we need to revisit in these times more than ever. "The majority of serious students of the Negro in American history have become indebted to Dr. Woodson for inspiration, encouragement, and, in some cases, more tangible assistance," Alrutheus A. Taylor testified in 1950, "Indeed, several competent students of other phases of Negro life have become similarly, to a degree at least, obligated to him."[65]

Throughout his career, Woodson maintained a tight circle of seven younger black historians who apprenticed themselves to him for varying periods of time. Included in this group were Alrutheus A. Taylor, Charles H. Wesley, Luther Porter Jackson, Lorenzo Johnston Greene, Rayford W. Logan, William Sherman Savage, and James Hugo Johnston.[66] These scholars, born mainly during the 1890s, often possessed ideals that differed from their mentor, but they usually put these differences aside in order to work with Woodson in establishing the foundations for Black history as a legitimate field of study and source of pride for African Americans. Besides their common affiliation with Woodson, these seven historians were similar in other significant ways as well. Woodson's "Boys"—as they referred to themselves as late as the 1980s—were educated at some of the most prestigious graduate history departments in the country, and their Ph.D. dissertations concerned race relations, Black history and, in the case of Logan, Africans in the Diaspora. They all, especially Greene, Logan, and Jackson, became involved in some form(s) of social and/or political activism and published important monographs. Combined, they published more than twenty major books and countless articles. While they were not as prolific as Woodson, their scholarship was in certain aspects more meticulous and "scientific" than Woodson's and they seem to have been less concerned with writing popular history. Though they had their problems with Woodson, they were wholeheartedly dedicated to the early Black history movement. Most of them promoted Negro History Week celebrations and remained committed to the ASNLH. These scholars would go on to influence countless other scholars.

John Hope Franklin, at one level "The Second Father of Black History," admitted upon several occasions that Woodson paved the way for him. He first met him in 1936. Black nationalist historians such as Sterling Stuckey, Vincent Harding, Lerone Bennett, Jr., and Tony Martin were all inspired by Woodson and paid homage to him. Darlene Clark Hine has paid tribute to the sacrifices made by Woodson. The ASALH has continued to promote many of the ideals of its founder. It has also defended Woodson from certain unwarranted criticisms as evidenced in V.P. Franklin's and the Association's Executive Council's open letter to self-proclaimed Du Bois disciple Henry Louis Gates, Jr.

I am attempting to spark a warranted interest in Woodson's vision among hip-hop generation historians, the African American historical profession, and those interested in Black history. It cannot be denied that Woodson laid an important part of the foundations for the current advanced state of African American history and historiography. Without his efforts, who knows where the black historical profession or our knowledge of African American history would be. No, he should not be worshipped as a flawless saint. "Great Man" history is passé, breeds uncritical thought, and no longer has a place in the struggle. But, yes, Woodson's life, work, and philosophies should be revisited, constructively critiqued, and adjusted to help hip-hop generation historians and scholars leave their mark on the evolving black historical profession and contribute to the enduring struggle for black liberation.

Notes

Chapter 5

Carter G. Woodson (1875–1950): "The Father of Black History"

[1] Sister Anthony Scally, *Carter G. Woodson: A Bio-Bibliography* (Connecticut: Greenwood, 1985), 3–5; Jacqueline Goggin, *Carter G. Woodson: A Life in Black History* (Baton Rouge: Louisiana State University Press, 1993), 3.

[2] Carter G. Woodson, "My Recollections of Veterans of the Civil War," *NHB* 7 (February 1944): 116.

[3] Carter G. Woodson, "Early Education in West Virginia," *JNH* 7 (January 1922): 27.

[4] Sister Anthony Scally, "The Philippines Challenge," *NHB* 44 (1981): 16–18.

[5] Goggin, *Carter G. Woodson*, 18–31.

[6] Lorenzo Johnston Greene, "Dr. Carter G. Woodson: The Man As I Knew Him," unpublished papers, no date, circa 1965–1980s.

[7] Meier and Rudwick, *Black History and the Historical Profession, 1915–1980*, 4. Among the outright racist historians of the Progressive era in Meier and Rudwick's analysis are H.B. Adams, John W. Burgess, Frederick J. Turner, and U.B. Philips. On the other hand, they contend that Hart, J. Franklin Jameson, Clarence Alvord, and W.B. Munro supported African American history and historians.

[8] For an overall discussion of academic racism that addresses the Progressive era, see Michael R. Winston, "Through the Back Door: Academic Racism and the Negro Scholar in Historical Perspective," *Daedalus*, 100 (Summer 1971): 678–719; I.A. Newby, ed., *The Development of Segregationist Thought* (Illinois: Dorsey, 1968).

[9] Albert Bushnell Hart, *The Southern South* (New York: Appleton, 1910), 105. At other points in this work Hart also made claims such as "the theory that the Negro mind ceases to develop after adolescence perhaps has something to it" and that "the average of the Negro race is much below that of the white race." *The Southern South* is an interesting text because if it is not read closely, one may come to the conclu-

sion that Hart was totally sympathetic towards African Americans. Hart, like many liberal white scholars of his time, believed in African American exceptionalism. He praised the success of educated, black leaders, yet argued that the masses of African Americans were inferior to whites. At the same time, Hart's analysis in *The Southern South* is very much clouded by class prejudice. He viewed poor whites as being culturally backward as well, though not as backward and inferior as African Americans.

[10] Earl Lewis, "To Turn as on a Pivot: Writing African Americans into a History of Overlapping Diasporas," *The American Historical Review* 100 (June 1995): 765–787.

[11] Ellen Fitzpatrick, *History's Memory: Writing America's Past, 1880–1980* (Cambridge: Harvard University Press, 2002), 91.

[12] Peter Novick, *That Noble Dream: The "Objectivity Question" and the American Historical Profession* (Cambridge: Cambridge University Press, 1988), 74–84.

[13] Ernst A. Breisach, *American Progressive History: An Experiment in Modernization* (Chicago: University of Chicago Press, 1993), 79–80.

[14] For a discussion of the "corrective" principle of African American Studies, see Marable, "Black Studies and the Black Intellectual Tradition," 3. For Phillips's ideas, see Ulrich Bonnell Phillips, *American Negro Slavery: A Survey of the Supply, Employment and Control of Negro Labor as Determined by the Plantation Regime* (Baton Rouge: Louisiana State University Press, 1966); John David Smith and John C. Inscoe, eds., *Ulrich Bonnell Phillips: A Southern Historian and His Critics* (New York: Greenwood Press, 1990), 2. For Du Bois and Woodson's responses to Phillips, see W.E.B. Du Bois, "Book Review of *American Negro Slavery*," *American Political Science Review* 12 (November 1918): 722–726; Carter G. Woodson, "Book Review of *American Negro Slavery*," *Mississippi Valley Historical Review* 5 (March 1919): 480–482. According to Meier and Rudwick, the first systematic scholarly critique of Phillips came in 1944 with Richard Hofstadter's essay, "U.B. Phillips and the Plantation Legend," published in *The Journal of Negro History*. See Meier and Rudwick, *Black History and the Historical Profession, 1915–1980*, 241.

[15] For a discussion of the AHA and amateur historians, see David D. Van Tassel, "From Learned Society to Professional Organization: The American Historical Association, 1884–1900," *The American Historical Review* 89 (October 1984): 929–956. According to Novick, before 1907 all AHA presidents were amateurs. See Novick, *That Noble Dream*, 49.

[16] Rebecca Conrad, *Benjamin Shambaugh and the Intellectual Foundations of Public History* (Iowa City: University of Iowa Press, 2002).

[17] Carter G. Woodson, *The Education of the Negro Prior to 1861* (New York, no date), 152–153; Thorpe, *Black Historians*, 118.

[18] Carter G. Woodson, "Ten Years of Collecting and Publishing the Records of the Negro," *JNH* 10 (October 1925): 598.

[19] Romero, "Carter G. Woodson: A Biography," 121.

[20] Carter G. Woodson, "The Report of the Director," *JNH* 4 (October 1919): 479.

[21] Carter G. Woodson, *A Century of Negro Migration* (Washington, D.C.: Associated Publishers, 1918), v, 165.

[22] "Notes," *JNH* 4 (April 1919): 237.

[23] "Notes," *JNH* 4 (October 1919): 474; "Notes," *JNH* 5 (January 1920): 135.

[24] Meier and Rudwick, *Black History and the Historical Profession, 1915–1980*, 71.

[25] "Notes," *JNH* 7 (October 1922): 454.

[26] Sterling A. Brown, "The Negro Author and His Publisher," *The Quarterly Review of Higher Education Among Negroes* 9 (1941): 145–146.

[27] Lorenzo J. Greene, *Selling Black History for Carter G. Woodson: A Diary, 1930–1933* (Arvarh Strickland, ed.) (Columbia: University of Missouri Press, 1996).

[28] L.D. Reddick, "As I Remember Woodson," *NHB* 17 (November 1953): 36.

[29] "Notes," *JNH* 9 (April 1924): 239.

[30] Carter G. Woodson, *Home Study Department of the Extension Division of the ASNLH, Inc.: Bulletin of General Information* (ASNLH:

Washington, D.C., no date). For a discussion of Tuskegee's Movable School, Jesup Agricultural Wagon, see Virginia Lantz Denton, *Booker T. Washington and the Adult Education Movement* (Gainesville: University Press of Florida, 1993).

[31] Carter G. Woodson, *Home Study Department of the Extension Division of the ASNLH, Inc.*

[32] "Annual Report of the Director," *JNH* 15 (October 1930): 396.

[33] W.H. Crogman to Carter G. Woodson, April 4, 1927, *The Papers of Carter G. Woodson*, Reel 3, Containers 5-6.

[34] See, *NHB* 1 (October 1937); *NHB* 13 (May 1950), 170.

[35] Lillian M. Rhoades to Carter G. Woodson, November 14, 1940, *Papers of Carter G. Woodson and the Association for the Study of Negro Life and History*, Reel 1.

[36] See "The Saturday Morning Art Class," *NHB* 5 (April 1942): 158; Romare Bearden and Harry Henderson, *A History of African-American Artists* (New York: Pantheon, 1993), 381-388.

[37] John Hope Franklin, "The Place of Carter G. Woodson in American Historiography," *NHB* 13 (May 1950): 176.

[38] W.E.B. Du Bois, "The Talented Tenth," in *The Negro Problem: A Series of Articles by Representative American Negroes of To-Day* (New York: James Pott, 1903), 33.

[39] W.E.B. Du Bois, "The Negro Bourgeoisie," in *W.E.B. Du Bois: A Reader*, ed. Weinberg, 56.

[40] W.E.B. Du Bois, "Talented Tenth: Memorial Address," in *Writings by Du Bois in Periodicals Edited by Others*, ed. Herbert Aptheker (New York: Kraus Thompson, 1982), 78–88.

[41] Booker T. Washington, *My Larger Education: Being Chapters from My Experience* (New York: Doubleday, Page, 1911), 114, 118, 120.

[42] Carter G. Woodson, *The Negro in Our History* (Washington, D.C.: The Associated Publishers, 1922), 274–279.

[43] Carter G. Woodson, "Honor to Booker T. Washington," *NHB* 10 (March 1947): 126-128.

[44] "Notes," *JNH* 18 (July 1933): 341.

[45] Goggin, *Carter G. Woodson*, 3. In his monographs published before 1933, one can see traces of Woodson's iconoclastic character breaking through. For instance, in the final chapter of *A Century of Negro Migration* he makes many observations about how blacks have been victimized in America. In the last pages of The History of the Negro Church, he also offers a solution to blacks' dilemma. For Lorenzo Johnston Greene's discussion of Woodson, see Greene, "Dr. Carter G. Woodson: The Man as I Knew Him."

[46] "Annual Report of the Director," *JNH* 16 (October 1931): 349–358.

[47] Carter G. Woodson, *The Mis-Education of the Negro* (New Jersey: Africa World Press, 1990).

[48] Ibid., 9–37.

[49] Ibid., 26, 15, 23, 34.

[50] Ibid., 35.

[51] Ibid., 56, 65, 176.

[52] Ibid., 44, 131.

[53] Ibid., 144–172.

[54] Ibid., 56.

[55] Ibid., 122.

[56] Alain Locke, "Black Zionism," *The Survey* 69 (October 1933): 363–364.

[57] For a detailed discussion of Woodson's treatment of black women and the role of black women in the ASNLH, see Pero G. Dagbovie, "Black Women, Carter G. Woodson, and the Association for the Study of Negro Life and History, 1915–1950," *The Journal of African American History* 88 (Winter 2003): 21–41.

[58] Carter G. Woodson, "The Negro Washerwoman, A Vanishing Figure," *JNH* 15 (July 1930): 269–277; Carter G. Woodson, "Women Should Have More Voice in Our Affairs," *Pittsburgh Courier*, 17 December 1932, sec. 2, p. 2.

[59] Audrey Thomas McCluskey, "In Pursuit of Unalienable Rights: Mary McLeod Bethune in Historical Perspective (1875–1955)" in *Mary McLeod Bethune: Building a Better World,* ed. McCluskey and Elaine M. Smith (Bloomington: Indiana University Press, 1999), 6; Sadie Iola

Daniel, *Women Builders* (Washington, DC: Associated Press, 1970), 109; Rackham Holt, *Mary McLeod Bethune: A Biography* (New York: Doubleday, 1964), 266.

[60] Elaine M. Smith, "Bethune, Mary McLeod," in *Black Women in America: An Historical Encyclopedia, Volume I: A–L,* ed. Darlene Clark Hine, Elsa Barkley-Brown, and Rosalyn Terborg-Penn (Bloomington: Indiana University Press, 1993), 121. In 1924, she was elected President of the National Association of Colored Women. In 1935, she was elected President of the National Council of Negro Women, an overarching organization that encompassed all black women's organizations. And, from 1935 until 1943, Bethune was Director of the National Youth Administration's Division of Negro Affairs. Bethune was linked to many organizations in the black community, such as the NAACP and the National Urban League. She had a particularly close relationship with Eleanor Roosevelt. It has been said that Bethune had "carte blanche" to the office of the First Lady, who influenced her husband's potential decisions.

[61] McCluskey, "In Pursuit of Unalienable Rights: Mary McLeod Bethune in Historical Perspective (1875–1955)", in *Mary McLeod Bethune: Building a Better World,* ed. McCluskey and Smith, 13; Mary McLeod Bethune, "The Association for the Study of Negro Life and History: Its Contributions to Our Modern Life," *JNH* 20 (October 1935): 409; Bethune, "Clarifying Our Vision with Facts," *JNH* 23 (January 1938): 10–15; Emma Gelders Sterne, *Mary McLeod Bethune* (New York, 1957), 234; Bethune, "The Adaptation of the history of the Negro to the Capacity of the Child," *JNH* 24 (January 1939): 9–13.

[62] Mary McLeod Bethune, "My Last Will and Testament," in *Mary McLeod Bethune: Building a Better World,* ed. McCluskey and Smith, 58–59.

[63] White, *Ar'n't I A Woman?*, 21.

[64] For a discussion of these scholars' roles as Harlem Renaissance promoters, see Cary D. Wintz, *Black Culture and the Harlem Renaissance* (Houston: Rice University Press, 1988), 102–129.

[65] Rayford W. Logan, "Phylon Profile: Carter G. Woodson," *Phylon* 6 (1945), 321; Alrutheus A. Taylor, "Dr. Carter G. Woodson: Inspirer and Benefactor of Young Scholars," *NHB* 13 (May 1950): 186. Taylor (1893–1954), who received his doctorate in history from Har-

vard in 1936, began working with Woodson in the early 1920s. He worked for Woodson full time from about 1923 until 1926, conducting research on blacks during the Reconstruction era. See Meier and Rudwick, *Black History and the Historical Profession*, 75–77.

[66] See Meier and Rudwick, *Black History and the Historical Profession*, 75–95.

CONCLUSION

At the 2001 National Urban League Annual Conference, Franklin D. Raines, the chairman and CEO of Fannie Mae and a trustee of the Urban League, admitted that the "transition of black Americans from a formerly enslaved people to full and participating members of this society is far from complete." He noted that "one hundred and thirty-six years is too long. We have work to do. We have a lot of work to do."[1] Raines's observations are not sophisticated, profound, or analytical. But they are accurate and should be acknowledged. Today, as we enter the 21st century, the majority of black people in the United States still face many serious, life-threatening problems and obstacles that are directly related to their unequal status in the United States since the days of slavery. The most serious issues that confront black communities throughout the nation are: health issues (especially AIDS/HIV); fatherlessness; male incarceration rates; poor college and university retention rates; poverty; lack of representation in academia, media, and other sectors of U.S. society; negative images in popular culture; political disenfranchisement and lack of representation; police brutality; and the state of mainstream hip-hop music and culture. A brief review of some specific facts helps better explain the contemporary status of African Americans.

Blacks make up about 12%–13% of the U.S. population, yet blacks account for roughly

> 37.7 percent of the accumulated AIDS cases, and more than 50 percent of the new AIDS cases. In 2000, Black men made up 40 percent of the new AIDS cases among males; Black women represent 62 percent of reported

> AIDS cases among females; and 6.2 of every 10 chil-
> dren reported with AIDS in the US were Black.[2]

Through the early 1990s, the HIV infection rate for black men
was about three times that of white men, while black women
were infected with HIV nine times more than white women.
Other comparisons between blacks and whites when dealing with
health issues are startling. As W. Michael Byrd and Linda A.
Clayton highlight in their exhaustive two-volume *An American
Health Dilemma*, "A new 'hostile and unequal' racial climate
profoundly affects African American health and health care."[3]

The black family is also being challenged at many levels.
One issue that is particularly frightening is fatherlessness. According to Jawanza Kunjufu, the "lack of men in the home has
reached epidemic proportions. It has become a state of emergency." Kunjufu continues:

> In 1920, 90 percent of our youth had fathers at home.
> In 1960, 80 percent of our youth had their fathers at
> home, but in 2001, only 30 percent of our youth have
> their fathers at home...What happened between 1960
> and 2000, a brief 40 years that could have had such a
> detrimental effect on the African American family?[4]

Kunjufu's question is provocative. Black male-female relationships are clearly in danger as well. In 2001, about seven of every
ten black babies were born out of wedlock. Black children are
handicapped by this trend. In a recent volume of *The Crisis*, senior editor Lottie L. Joiner noted that 53% of black children lived
in single-parent homes, overwhelmingly with their mothers,
about 12% of black children were being raised by a grandparent,
and 30% of black children lived in poverty.[5]

Many hip-hop generation young black men seem to act as if
they have a great lack of respect for black women. Misogyny has
entered a new stage in the black community. Many hip-hop and
R & B artists have contributed to the dehumanization of black
women. The R. Kelly incidents epitomize this lack of respect for

black womanhood. Even after his apparent confession to Ed Gordon and *Vibe* magazine, young black Americans have for the most part embraced the self-proclaimed "pied piper." At the same time, it must be noted that the sexism prevalent within black America's youth culture is very much a byproduct of a sexism that has deep roots in American culture as a whole.

The black prison population, especially the black male prison population, is reaching unfathomable levels. In the fall of 1998, Angela Davis noted that of the two million prisoners in the United States, roughly half were blacks and that the fastest growing group of prisoners was black women. Things are not getting better. Jawanza Kunjufu and others have claimed that currently about one of three black men is in some way affiliated with a penal institution. Since the early 1990s, it has been stated on many occasions that the number of young black men in prison outnumbered those in colleges and universities. As Farai Chideya argued, these statistics are misleading because sometimes they are simply inaccurate and tend to compare "black male prisoners of all ages to the overwhelmingly young college population."[6]

Chideya's critiques of how the American media misrepresents African Americans in her information-packed *Don't Believe the Hype* are provocative and challenge her readers to rethink what they believe they know about the status of black people. Still, it cannot be denied that the black male prison population is disproportionately high. Blacks make up at most about 12%–13% of the U.S. population, yet black men account for much more than 50% of the total prison population in many states. According to the U.S. Department of Justice, at the end of 2002 "2,033,331 prisoners were held in federal or state prisons or in local jails" and "there were 3,437 sentenced black male prisoners per 100,000 black males in the United States, compared to 1,176 sentenced Hispanic inmates per 100,000 Hispanic males and 450 white males per 100,000 white males."[7] For every "successful" black man getting paid, as they are depicted in the media or popular culture, many more are in unproductive and much more humble positions.

This is evidenced by the plight facing young and middle-aged black women seeking to find black mates who match them in terms of educational level, earning power, and socioeconomic status. Popular African American magazines such as *Jet*, *Ebony*, and *Essence* have recently discussed the dilemmas encountered by young black women in search of black mates. *Newsweek* even jumped on the bandwagon and, unlike the black media, openly dissed black men in the process of perhaps over-exaggerating the recent success of black women. The cover story for *Newsweek* (March 3, 2003) declared that "black women are advancing faster than black men." In the feature article, "The Gender Gap," Ellis Cose interviewed a range of young black women, all of whom testified to the problems they faced in establishing relationships with black men. Citing Michael Eric Dyson, Cose concluded that black men are threatened by successful black women and underappreciate what their female counterparts bring to the table. The statistics that Cose shares are significant. It is worth noting that "twenty-five percent of young black males go to college" while "35 percent of women do" and that according to the 2000 Census, "47 percent of black women in the 30-to-34 age range have never married, compared to 10 percent of white women." However, instead of delving into the deeper, historically rooted issues impacting the so-called "gender gap" and crisis among black males, Cose oversimplifies the situation and in the process further contributes to the prevailing negative images of African American manhood.[8]

Even those blacks who make it to colleges and universities are in danger. Educational inequalities between blacks and whites, rich and poor, are obvious in the United States. Jonathan Kozol's *Savage Inequalities* revealed for many Americans the persisting problems in U.S. elementary and secondary education. Affirmative action as implemented in colleges and universities would not be an issue—and in fact could be abolished—*if* the K-12 public schools in the urban and southern rural areas, where most blacks live, enjoyed the same funds and resources as suburban public schools. Black students in institutions of higher education are also experiencing great troubles. Contrary to popular belief, the recent affirmative action case at The University of Michigan does not represent a victory for African American college and university students. The Supreme Court justices made it clear that affirmative action should be phased out within the next several decades. If this is done and major structural and institutional changes are not made, black college students will certainly suffer.

After about six years of education, significantly less than 50 percent of blacks at many colleges and universities graduate. The situation of black students at major universities in Michigan represents some of these challenges. According to a fairly recent investigation by *The Detroit News*, of black students from seven large Michigan universities who were freshmen in 1994, just

> 40 percent got their diplomas after six years, compared to 61 percent of white students and 74 percent of Asians nationwide, the college graduation rate for white students in Division I schools is 50 percent higher than for blacks.

African American students at Oakland University were in the worst situation. Though for ten years they made up about 11 percent of the student population, their graduation rate was about 22 percent.[9]

I could go on and on, but I am sure that the reader has discerned the point that I am trying to convey. As we enter a new millennium, black America faces a wide array of serious problems. These problems, it cannot be forgotten, can be traced back to African Americans' historical experiences since the days of slavery. It is clear that a concrete history of anti-black behaviors, actions, policies, and beliefs has greatly impacted African Americans' present "state of emergency." All of the major problems that black Americans face today can be best understood when one looks closely at the progression of Black history from the emergence of slavery in colonial America in the 1660s or the post-revolutionary American society. The vast majority of African Americans' current dilemmas can be directly and indirectly traced back to the days of slavery and the days of overt anti-black behavior. When one analyzes the present debilitating conditions of African Americans, one cannot ignore the fact that in the United States most African Americans were not accorded basic, fundamental civil and human rights until after the classic Civil Rights era. Malcolm X used to routinely argue that white Americans, Europeans, and "brainwashed" African Americans all too often bought into the myth that the Supreme Court's 1954 Brown decision ended segregation. U.S. slavery (1789–1865); the failures of Reconstruction (1865–1877); the "nadir" (1877–1901 or 1923); the era of World War I; the racial violence from 1919 through the early 1920s; the failure of the New Deal to address African Americans' most basic needs; the long period of Jim Crow segregation in the United States, formally from Plessy v. Ferguson (1896) until Brown v. Board of Education, Topeka, Kansas (1954); and many other detrimental realities and factors have all impacted the present conditions facing African Americans. In contrast, black achievements during these various periods have also helped African Americans achieve what they have up to now. The advantages and gains that many blacks currently enjoy are the products of centuries of compounded struggles.

We need to revisit Black history—blacks' collective experiences in the United States—in order to move on into the future. In his controversial classic, *Chains and Images of Psychological Slavery*, clinical psychologist Na'im Akbar has eloquently addressed the danger, yet necessity, of recognizing how African Americans' collective historical experiences in the United States have impacted our present status:

> There is a certain hesitation about dwelling on events of the past. On the one hand, it creates an atmosphere of determinism which removes the volitional possibilities of people to alter their condition. It tends to excuse the perpetuation of past events which could be altered

simply by initiative. It preoccupies people unnecessarily and purposelessly with old hurts, tending old wounds. It is an emotional tirade that ultimately provides no constructive solutions for the present. But, those who deny the lessons of the past are doomed to repeat it. Those who fail to recognize that the past is a shaper of the present, and the hand of yesterday continues to write on the slate of today, leave themselves vulnerable by not realizing the impact of influences which do serve to shape their lives...

In order to fully grasp the magnitude of our current problems, we must reopen the books on the events of slavery. Our objective should not be to cry stale tears for the past, nor to rekindle old hatreds of past injustices. Instead, we should seek to enlighten our path of today by better understanding where and how the lights were turned out yesterday...It is hoped that by shining the light of awareness on these dark recesses of our past, we can begin to conquer the ghosts which continue to haunt our personal and social lives. We can begin to move beyond the shackles of restricted human growth that have bound us since that kidnapping of "not so long ago."[10]

More recently, scholars have updated Akbar's argument, stressing how black America's current problems are the manifestation of historical problems. Among other key studies in this tradition are Randall Robinson's *The Debt: What America Owes to Blacks* (2000), W. Michael Byrd and Linda A. Clayton's two-volume *An American Health Dilemma* (2000, 2002), Philip F. Rubio's *A History of Affirmative Action, 1619–2000* (2001), and editor Raymond A. Winbush's *Should America Pay? Slavery and the Raging Debate in Reparations* (2003). Byrd and Clayton's argument about African Americans' present health status is particularly enlightening. They asserted:

> The fact that African Americans today live substantially shorter lives than Whites; die more frequently from cancer, heart disease, stroke, and diabetes; and see their infants die at nearly twice the rate of Whites is in part a result of their unique and tragic historical experience in America.

These medical experts wrote their exhaustive studies because they wanted to stress that African Americans' current horrific health conditions were shaped by clear "historical antecedents." While African Americans tend to realize at some level that they have been impacted by the rocky race relations in the United States, recent "surveys show that the majority of White Americans believe that race discrimination, past and present, is not a major reason for the social and economic problems African Americans face today."[11]

In his interesting study, *Afraid of the Dark: What Whites and Blacks Need to Know About Each Other* (2000), former chief writer of the *USA Today* series "Race and Sports" Jim Myers shares Byrd and Clayton's underlying beliefs, highlighting some of the basic, general ways in which blacks' and whites' worldviews differ. Myers suggests:

> Where most whites and blacks seem to divide most fundamentally is on the basic details of black American experience. Is there equal justice for all? Blacks and whites give a contradictory account of the American experience. Most whites describe a country that gives everyone an equal chance, while most blacks believe race still intrudes. And this disagreement reflects another racial divide—over the very existence of the racial divide. Black Americans are more likely to see America as two worlds, one white and one black. White Americans are more likely to believe that this is one nation indivisible.[12]

Joseph L. White and James H. Cones III expanded upon Myers's ideas in their exhaustive study on black men. They argued:

> A discernable difference between Blacks and Whites with respect to how race and race-related events are perceived and assessed interferes with the search for biracial solutions to the social and economic roadblocks Black American males encounter.

These different ideas are the result of blacks' and whites' divergent "experimental/psychological worlds."[13] Black history can perhaps help bridge the great and continuing divide. As it did during Woodson's times, Black history can still help blacks develop their identities and help whites better understand black culture.

Hip-hop generation historians can play a leading role in using Black history in this way. They should expose their students, audiences, and readers to how the past has distinctly impacted the present. One of the easiest ways to stimulate interest about the past among today's youth is by making it relevant to the present. In *Lies My Teacher Told Me: Everything Your American History Textbook Got Wrong* (1995), James W. Loewen passionately contended that many high school students disliked history because of the boring textbooks and the stale, uncritical methodologies employed by many high school history teachers. Loewen criticized conventional history textbook authors for not using the present to "illuminate the past" or the past to "illuminate the present."[14] Hip-hop generation historians must address such concerns. In dealing with Black history, the task that Loewen raises is quite simple to deal with since African Americans' current status is so inextricably bound with their past status.

Hip-hop generation historians could benefit from critically revisiting how the pioneering black historians from the Woodson era through the Black Power movement actively transformed history into a social force and reforming agent. Since the demise of the Black Power movement in the mid-1970s, the pragmatic Woodsonian vision of Black history has been commercialized, watered down, and in some regards abandoned at a rate that warrants concern. Woodson's vision of truly integrating the study of African American history into the curricula of elementary and secondary schools as well as into university settings and mainstream academic culture needs to be vigorously pursued. Woodson and the "Old School" black historians of this study strove to convert Black history into a regenerative social force. Prior to the classic Civil Rights Movement, black historians, as well as other intellectuals and scholars who focused their studies and research on the black experience, participated in scholarly discourses that were unpopular, disrespected, and largely ignored by power-wielding, mainstream academic circles. Though possible, it was extremely difficult for black historians and scholars during the era of segregation to secure funding for research, earn recognition in the mainstream academy, publish their scholarship, and basically enjoy the fundamental rights ensured by American citizenship and the privileges of being a Ph.D.-holder. In *Race and History*, John Hope Franklin poignantly described the trials and tribulations of conducting research during the era of Jim Crow segregation.

Black historians and scholars who came of age after the Black Power era have benefited greatly from the sacrifices of their foreparents. Those of us black historians and scholars who came of age in the 1990s have been especially fortunate when one places our situation within the broader historical context of the struggles for black historians and intellectuals. Hip-hop generation historians who reaped the benefits of race-based fellowships and scholarships should pay back the sacrifices of our foreparents by also contributing to the struggle. Hip-hop generation historians cannot simply imitate, mimic, and uncritically praise Woodson and his disciples' visions and efforts. We must practically and directly address the grave problems that our people face. At the same time, the upcoming generations of African American historians need to re-visit Woodson's and his understudies' approach to taking history out of its "other worldly" realm, bringing it back into a "this worldly" context.

Applying Woodson's enduring ideologies to the realities of the early 1980s, historian Vincent Harding eloquently articulated the responsibilities of the black scholar to the community:

> What are the responsibilities of the black scholar to the community? Perhaps the first responsibility is to recognize that there is a responsibility. Indeed, debt may be a better word; scholars have a debt to that community, and they must always be thinking about how it will be repaid. It can never be repaid sufficiently, for individuals are never complete in themselves, and the community, when it is allowed to, is constantly making its members and remaking them as they enter the dance with it, as they seek to make and remake it. Black scholars must remember their sources...They are products of their source—the great pained community of Afro-Americans of this land. And they can forget the source only at great peril to their spirit, their work, and their souls...The responsibility of the black scholar is constantly to be alive to the movement of history and to recognize that we ourselves are constantly being remade and revisioned...Wherever and however possible, they must direct as much of their writing, their speaking, their teaching, and their singing to—directly to—the life and heart and growth of the community of pain and hope.[15]

Harding's views as well as the specific historical context that molded him seem to be foreign to the majority of African Americans born between about 1965 and 1984. How do we then re-introduce some of the fundamental ideals of sacrifice, responsibility, and historical pragmatism embodied by Woodson, his co-workers, his predecessors, and disciples in a unique era which promotes individualism and in which human alienation has reached incredible levels? This is an issue that hip-hop generation historians must address.

While social and moral reform certainly is still necessary in African American communities throughout the nation, the civilizationist stance of Woodson and his disciples in the first half of the twentieth century is understandable within its context, but of course no longer operative. Similarly, the hyperobjectivity of George Washington Williams, and much later John Hope Franklin and Benjamin Quarles, was once necessary in order to help justify Black history as a field of study in mainstream academic circles, but it is no longer required. Of course, serious research and meticulousness is still a prerequisite, but in order for Black history to reach a broader audience and move out of the other exclusive domains of academia, we need to embrace, modify, and speak to the hip-hop generation whose culture is at the present time defining and directing youth culture movements across the globe.

The recent movement to publish easy-to-read, straightforward textbooks, biographies, thematic studies, and juvenile literature is a necessary step in the right direction of making Black history popular and relevant. Textbooks such as *Black History for Beginners*, *The African American Odyssey*, *1001 Things Everyone Should Know About African American History*, and others are excellent. Spike Lee, HBO, California Newsreel, and PBS, among others, have produced many insightful films and documentaries on the African American experience. There are many informative Black history internet websites. Such efforts need to be continued.

Woodson and "Old School" black historians would certainly critique various detrimental aspects of the hip-hop generation as they critiqued elements of popular black folk culture during their times. However, as they demonstrated during an era characterized by systematic black disenfranchisement, racial discrimination and hatred, and overt anti-black violence, the study of Black history could be beneficially injected into various sectors of black communities nationwide, especially among the working class and impressionable youth.

Without many options, Woodson and "Old School" black historians achieved the ends of popularizing black history in the most practical ways possible during their times, employing easy-to-read publications, Negro History Week celebrations, lectures, the "grape-vine," and other forms of academic outreach. Today, these same methods could be used, but of course would need to be modified to incorporate the present, vital technological tools and developments. As President of the Organization of American Historians, Gerda Lerner, the first woman to assume this position, delivered a timely address in 1982 in which she addressed the necessity of her colleagues to actively work towards "a 'healing' of contemporary social pathology" by teaching in new and innovative ways. She declared that professional historians could best help reform American society as teachers, and she claimed most of her male colleagues appreciated teaching least. She argued that as teachers, U.S. history professors needed to make history relevant to their students even if they needed to "fall back on being performers, seeking to catch the reluctant attention of an audience more accustomed to the frenetic entertainment style of the mass media."[16] Lerner's observations from two decades ago are relevant to the current potential "state of emergency" facing black historians and their relationship with black youth and students.

In an assessment of African American Studies decades after the first program was established at San Francisco State College in 1968, James B. Stewart made an important observation, noting that "the erosion of black student support for black studies in part indicated the failure of the first wave of black studies advocates to achieve one of their principal goals."[17] Stewart's comments are still relevant today. Why is there not a greater interest among black undergraduates in Black history and African American Studies? More important, how can the interest in Black history that black students possessed during the emotional Black Power era be reintroduced in the current era during which the youth all too often choose "individual gain" over "communal cultural integrity," and "a withering sense of values and social responsibility" seems to have taken root?[18] Black historians, especially those of the hip-hop generation, need to create effective, innovative, and appealing mediums with which to popularize and transmit Black history among black communities, especially among the hip-hop generation.

Hip-Hop culture, especially rap music, could serve as one of the most effective and practical transmitters of Black history. Tricia Rose poignantly defined the role of the rapper in the black community in a way that is relevant to the role of the black historian:

> Rap music is a black cultural expression that prioritizes black voices from the margins of urban America. Rap music is a form of rhymed storytelling accompanied by highly rhythmic, electronically based music. From the outset, rap music has articulated the pleasures and problems of black urban life in contemporary America...Rappers speak with the voice of personal experience, taking on the identity of the observer or narrator...Rappers tell long, involved, and sometimes abstract stories with catchy and memorable phrases and beats that lend themselves to black sound bite packaging, storing critical fragments in faced-paced electrified rhythms. Rap tales are told in elaborate and ever-changing black slang and refer to black cultural figures and rituals, mainstream film, video and television characters, and little-known black heroes.[19]

Currently the most popular form of music worldwide, rap could very easily return to its golden years, the early 1980s through the early 1990s, when many rappers transmitted African and African American history to their faithful listeners in ingenious ways. Since the mid-1990s, a small vanguard of hip-hop artists have incorporated discussions of Black history into their music, including Tupac, Lauryn Hill, dead prez, Common, Nas, Mos Def, The Coup, and Talib Kweli, just to name a few. Hip-hop generation historians need to establish ties with such artists and more "commercial" ones, collaborate with them, and provide blueprints for Black history-conscious lyrics and albums.[20] Imagine if Jay-Z, 50 Cent, P. Diddy, DMX, Eve, Lil John, Outkast, Nelly, Ja Rule, T.I. or any other mainstream hip-hop artist produced a CD with a dozen cuts recounting Black history from the shores of Africa to the present. Millions of black and white youths alike would be able to recite Black history, feel the black past, and perhaps even internalize dimensions of the enduring struggle for black liberation.

Given the present "state of emergency" facing black America, such creative means are needed. Black history, as it did during the days of Woodson, still has the potential to play a major role in rejuvenating African American culture and psychologically empowering the black community while helping reform American society. While hip-hop generation historians need to perform the essential function of all historians—rigorously grappling with the meaning of Black history and carefully revising historical phenomena from their own distinct contexts and vantage points—we also need to learn from our elders. They can help us acquire the important skills of being rigorous historians, inspire us with their personal experiences of overcoming obstacles similar to ours, share with us strategies that they employed during their formative years, and push us to contribute in significant ways to the evolution of the profession. Hip-hop generation historians must expand upon the ideas of their elders, assuring them that the foundations they laid will be built upon and not fade away in vain. In the end, during this hard-to-characterize phase of the African American experience it will be hip-hop generation historians who will ultimately be responsible for carrying on a tradition first waged by our earliest historians. Let us hope that we can step up to assume this responsibility.

Many of the hip-hop generation often seem to forget that one of the most important reasons why some of us have been able to succeed in corporate post-Civil Rights America and mainstream American society is because of the countless sacrifices of generations of our foreparents and ancestors. If the times today were replaced by those of the Civil Rights era, the Black Power era, and earlier times, most members of the hip-hop generation would be acting differently. Historical conditions dictate peoples' behavior patterns.

Upon several occasions, Malcolm X sarcastically suggested and joked that he wished that segregation was not declared unconstitutional by the Supreme Court in 1954.[21] He reasoned that segregation forced blacks to unite across rigid class lines and heightened his people's awareness of their struggle. Malcolm intimated that integration allowed members of the black middle-class to flee from the black community and lose touch with the struggles of the black masses. In his controversial *The Truly Disadvantaged: The Inner City, the Underclass, and Public Policy* (1987), William Julius Wilson validated Malcolm's claim with his "out-migration" theory, the idea that as a result of integration, however limited, many upwardly mobile, "nonpoor" blacks moved out of all-black communities, thus creating communities—ghettos—of highly concentrated numbers of poor blacks.[22] Unlike Wilson, Malcolm also believed that the immediate false sense of integration gained by the Civil Rights movement allowed middle-class blacks to gain some headway. Malcolm wanted them to be treated poorly so that they would be forced to unite with, and work on the behalf of, their poor counterparts. In other words, segregation encouraged racial solidarity and when we exist in overtly harsh conditions, we tend to develop more serious approaches to life.

Black intellectuals of the hip-hop generation are existing in a time when it is far too easy to ignore, overlook, forget, and avoid the harsh realities that African Americans face. It is surprising how many young blacks have never heard of the lynching of James Byrd, the murder of Amadou Diallo, the shooting of Timothy Thomas in Cincinnati and riots that followed, and the brutal attacks on Abner Louima or Donovan Jackson. Many hip-hop generationers are also politically aloof, disinterested in vital debates concerning affirmative action and reparations, ignorant of Africa's contemporary status and how it relates to Africans throughout the Diaspora, uninformed about the deeper issues in Black history, and generally unaware of where they fit in the broader picture of the African American experience. This is largely a result of black popular culture's failure to address such issues as has more often been done in the recent past. Today's young blacks are distracted by a multitude of media-generated images and stimuli that no previous generation of young blacks had to confront. At the same time, the hip-hop generation has much to offer to the black struggle. Today's black youth need to be more critical in their thinking than ever before. Hip-hop generation historians have the potential to play a leading role in making and re-inventing Black history.

Notes

Conclusion

[1] Franklin D. Raines, "What Equality Would Look Like: Reflections on the Past, Present and Future," in *The State of Black America 2002*, ed. Lee A. Daniels (New York: National Urban League, 2002), 13–28.

[2] Phill Wilson, "In the Fight of Our Lives: Notes on the AIDS Crisis in the Black Community," in *Race and Resistance*, ed. Boyd, 153.

[3] For specific comparisons at many levels, see W. Michael Byrd and Linda A. Clayton, *An American Health Dilemma, Volume One: A Medical History of African Americans and the Problem of Race: Beginnings to 1900* (New York: Routledge, 2000), 29–33.

[4] Jawanza Kunjufu, *State of Emergency: We Must Save African American Males* (Chicago: African American Images, 2001), 149–150.

[5] Lottie L. Joiner, "Growing Up Black," *The Crisis* 110 (November/December 2003): 24–29. Joiner analyzes the state of black children based upon three main factors: education, health, and juvenile justice. Although black children have made significant gains since the 1970s, the overall tone of the article indicates that a lot of progress still needs to be made on behalf of black children.

[6] Farai Chideya, *Don't Believe the Hype: Fighting Cultural Misinformation about African-Americans* (New York: Plume, 1995), 197.

[7] The United States Department of Justice, "Prison Statistics," <http://www.ojp.usdoj.gov/bjs/prisons.htm>

[8] Ellis Cose, "The Black Gender Gap," *Newsweek*, 3 March 2003, 46–51. This issue of *Newsweek* also features an article by Allison Samuels, "A Round Table of Black Women on Success, Beauty, Love and Loneliness." Unsurprisingly, the opinions in the article do not reveal the beliefs of the masses of black women. Samuels bases her ideas upon the thoughts of rapper Foxy Brown, publisher Terri Woods, co-host of "The View" Star Jones, ABC News correspondent Deborah Roberts, singer and actress Beyonce Knowles, company president Mellody Hobson, and the president and CEO of a bank, Deborah Wright. It would be interesting to compare and contrast the perspectives of these women with those of the masses of black women. Class, among other

components, would certainly be an important factor influencing black women's ideas about black men.

[9] Janet Vandenabeele and Jodi Upton, "Colleges' Retention of Blacks Dismal," *The Detroit News*, 15 July 2001. November 2001. <http://detnews.com/2001/schools/0107/15/a01-247739.htm>

[10] Akbar, *Chains and Images of Psychological Slavery*, 1, 8, 34–35.

[11] Byrd and Clayton, *An American Health Dilemma, Volume One*, xvi.

[12] Jim Myers, *Afraid of the Dark: What Whites and Blacks Need to Know About Each Other* (Chicago: Lawrence Hill, 2000), 133.

[13] White and Cones, *Black Man Emerging*, 8–9.

[14] James W. Loewen, *Lies My Teacher Told Me: Everything Your American History Textbook Got Wrong* (New York: Touchstone, 1995), 13.

[15] Vincent Harding, "Responsibilities of the Black Scholar to the Community," in *The State of Afro-American History*, ed. Hine, 279–281.

[16] Gerda Lemer, "The Necessity of History and the Professional Historian," in Lerner, *Why History Matters: Life and Thought* (New York: Oxford University Press, 1997), 113–128.

[17] James Stewart, "The Field and Function of Black Studies," in *The African American Studies Reader*, ed. Norment, 45.

[18] Kitwana, *The Hip-Hop Generation*, 8, 22.

[19] Rose, *Black Noise*, 2–3.

[20] For an interesting discussion of "commercial" and "conscious" rap, refer to Bynoe, "How Ya' Like Me Now? Rap and Hip Hop Come of Age."

[21] There are many different sources available on Malcolm X. I have purchased many audio and video tapes from African American vendors over the years. He made these statements on some of these recordings. Check out, for instance, "The Speeches of Malcolm X," 41 minutes, MPI Home Video, 1997.

[22] William Julius Wilson, *The Truly Disadvantaged: The Inner City, the Underclass, and Public Policy* (Chicago: The University of Chicago Press, 1987), 49–62.